Jukebox America

Jukebox America

Down Back Streets and Blue Highways

in Search of the Country's

Greatest Jukebox

William Bunch

St. Martin's Press New York

Design by Judith A. Stagnitto

Library of Congress Cataloging-in-Publication Data

Bunch, William.
    Jukebox America / William Bunch.
       p. cm.
    ISBN 0-312-11013-8
    1. Popular music—United States.   2. Popular culture—United
States. 3. Jukeboxes.
    ML3477.B86   1994
    781.64'0973—dc20   94-3879
                                                 CIP
                                              MN

First Edition: August 1994

10 9 8 7 6 5 4 3 2 1

For Kathy—
My #A1 selection, forever

Acknowledgments

It would be impossible, unfortunately, to thank every single person who made a suggestion or otherwise aided the search for America's greatest jukebox, but some people deserve a special mention.

There are two books—both out of print but findable in libraries, nostalgia stores, and elsewhere—that I'd recommend to anyone seeking to learn more about the history of the record machine and its great manufacturers. They are *Juke Box Saturday Night*, by J. Krivine (The Bucklebury Press, 1977), and *Jukebox, The Golden Age, 1937 Through 1948*, by Vincent Lynch and Bill Henkin (Lancaster-Miller Publishers, 1981). Other source books that grounded me in jukebox and music lore included *American Popular Music and its Business* by Russell Sanjek (Oxford University Press, 1988), and the *Virgin Directory of World Music*, by Philip Sweeney (Henry Holt and Co., 1991). Quite frankly, I would have been lost in Hoboken without Kitty Kelley's *His Way: The Unauthorized Biography of Frank Sinatra* (Bantam Books, 1986). And *The Jazz and Blues Lover's Guide to the U.S.*, by Christiane Bird (Addison-Wesley Publishing, 1991), was an especially valuable resource, especially for the Mississippi Delta.

Thanks to the following jukebox tipsters: Fred Newton of the

Amusement and Music Operators Association, Jim Hans and John DePalma of the Hoboken Historical Society, John Marotta, Neil Steinberg of the *Chicago Sun-Times*, Ralph Galliard of the *Chicago Tribune*, Fern Adams of the Patsy Cline Memorial Committee, Charles Zuckerman, Barry-Jean Ancilet of Southwestern Louisiana University, Jim O'Neal of the Stackhouse/Delta Record Mart in Clarksdale, Mississippi, Sid Graves and John Ruskey of the Mississippi Delta Blues Museum, Sue Anne Pressley of the *Washington Post*, Deb Finley of the *Metro Times*, Jordy Wilson of the *Seattle Times*, Patrick McDonald of Seattle's Park Avenue Records, Charles Cross of *The Rocket*, and Dave Blandford of Seattle Visitor's Bureau.

A special thank you to Bill Thomas, who played a critical role in the early shaping of what started out as a pretty raw idea, and most special thanks to my agent, David Black, whose faith in my abilities often exceeded my own, and to my editor, Cal Morgan, who straightened out quite a few rough edges with considerable skill, while at the same time offering an advanced-placement course on the King of Rock 'n' Roll.

Jukebox America

Chapter 1: An Introduction

These Boots Are Made for Walkin'

Thirty-seven days after my thirty-second birthday, I moved to a township with no jukebox. I had been living on a fold-up couch in a studio apartment on Manhattan's Upper West Side, 88th Street between Amsterdam and Columbus. West 88th is a block that normally moves to a steady, sledgehammer beat, like a Four Tops 45 from 1965. The house rhythm section is a macho band of street-corner, slap-boxing Latinos; their banter is often cut by the car alarm from some architect's BMW, like a wailing guitar solo.

Yet when Moving Day finally arrived—February 27, 1991—West 88th Street was blanketed by about five inches of white muffler, a freshly fallen silent shroud of snow. The sounds of silence, already, and I hadn't even left Manhattan.

It figured. By then, the move to a township with no jukebox had become nothing less than the long-awaited Harbinger of My Own Mortality, the first and most lethal step down a forty-year airport corridor of property tax assessments, with a one-way ticket to visit Elvis waiting for me at the gate.

Here are the highlights: I was moving all the way past the suburbs to the exurbs, to a condo-crazed nether land called Lower Makefield, Pennsylvania. Then I was getting married.

Then I was buying a townhouse with an automatic garage-door opener and a green-marble fireplace. All within the dizzying space of ninety-three days.

That much I thought I could handle. But a township with no jukebox seemed to symbolize the end of the world as I knew it. For a moment I toyed with the notion of becoming a Jukebox Survivalist, building the equivalent of a nuclear fallout shelter in the automatic-door safety of my garage, and stocking it with a forty-year supply of Rolling Rock longnecks, a videocassette of *The TAMI Show*, and a foot-high stack of Patsy Cline 45s.

By February 1991, I had been through four of the five predictable stages of moving to a township with no jukebox—anger, denial, bargaining, and depression—and I was trying to move onto the fifth, acceptance. I would focus on all the good aspects of moving from New York to Lower Makefield, a list of dozens of items from the very sexy (my wife-to-be Kathy, a sassy sweetheart with glimmering sea-green eyes) to the very mundane (the federal deductibility of local property taxes). Even so, I was still annoyed by that giant item that blared out from the top of the debit column: NO JUKEBOX.

Why was I moving to Lower Makefield? It was a matter of necessity, a geographical compromise between me—I'd continue to work as a newspaper reporter in New York City—and Kathy, a reporter for the *Philadelphia Inquirer* 100 miles to the southwest. The condo-quilted township symbolized everything in the middle: The nether lands between New York and Philadelphia, the shopping mall culture of Middle America, and a life-style that somehow seemed appropriate for middle age.

Lower Makefield scared the heck out of me.

I could only think of one thing to do on my last night in New York City. I took the advice of Patsy Cline, the greatest jukebox singer of all time: To go out walkin', after midnight.

There were only two items on my post–12 A.M. agenda: to walk the five blocks to a dimly lit dive called the Raccoon Lodge, and to play the jukebox there. I couldn't really say why I was going. I had no plans to meet anyone there. I didn't even know which songs I wanted to play on its record machine, a classic, hopelessly outdated Seeburg that still spins 45s. I just had the idea that if I stayed in a barroom until the very last call, if I could scrape together a dollar to play five more songs on the jukebox, I'd get over the feeling that I was missing something.

The only way I can describe this feeling is that it's like a constant buzzing, a steady hum like the kind you'd hear under the blue neon light of some Air-Cooled ten-room motel on a distant and deserted U.S. highway, miles from the fresh asphalt of the new interstate, where the sign always read VACANCY. It's a problem typical of my generation, the Rear Guard Baby Boomers—the kids who were born too late to dodge the Vietnam draft and too early to enlist in Operation Desert Storm. These nocturnal pangs of restlessness strike us in the 1990s with the same intensity with which our older siblings were struck by the yuppie flu in the 1980s. I think it's an urge programmed during the years of our births, the late 1950s and early 1960s—which, not so coincidentally, were the golden age of jukeboxes.

After all, during the nine months I was kicking around in my mother's womb, Elvis got drafted and Chuck Berry was sent away for violating some law called the Mann Act, which apparently stated that that a black man with a knowing smirk could not become successful in Eisenhower America. January 21, 1959, the day I was born, came during the winter in which rebellion clashed with conformity all over the world. Among other catastrophes, the weight of that struggle eventually forced down a small airplane over Clear Lake, Iowa, shattering bone and metal across virgin snow. Richard Valens, né Valenzuala, Charles Hardin "Buddy" Holly, and J. P. Richardson, a/k/a The Big Bopper, were pronounced dead at the scene. On February 3, 1959, The Day the Music Died, I was only thirteen days old.

We, the Rear Guard Baby Boomers, became the generation that stayed home watching *The Mod Squad* with a baby-sitter while our older brothers and sisters were out researching the theory of better living through chemicals while listening to Iron Butterfly. I turned old enough to perform the two essential functions of democracy—voting and entering a cocktail lounge—on January 21, 1977, the day after Jimmy Carter inaugurated the era of malaise. We were always too late, always missing something. We never even got a nickname, like the Pepsi Generation or Generation X. We are still a question mark—Generation Y.

That's why the Raccoon Lodge is perfect for us. A woody corner bar at 84th Street and Amsterdam Avenue, it's named for the fraternal order that boasted Ralph Kramden and Ed Norton as members. *The Honeymooners*, the 1950s, the Golden Age of Television. We missed that one, too, and so now we tune to Channel 11 each weeknight at 11 A.M. for fuzzy Kinescope reruns, right before we hit the jukebox at the Raccoon Lodge and play the fuzzy, well-worn singles by Albert King and the Left Banke, while reveling in the unpredictibility of somebody else's favorite song.

It was almost midnight when I stepped onto the slush of West 88th Street. I walked briskly, hoping to avoid the neighborhood crack dealers, and found myself slogging past an animated conversation between two men, one black, the other a Native American—unfortunately, not the kind of people I'd likely encounter once I moved to exurban Pennsylvania. I heard only a snippet spoken by the Native American: "A snowstorm like this means that the Great Spirit is sending down his blessing."

I reached the Raccoon Lodge in about five minutes. There's almost always a motorcycle parked outside, just in case the walk down Crack Alley on Amsterdam Avenue doesn't give you enough of a sense of danger. The motif is strictly American hunting lodge, from the log-cabin exterior to the fireplace 'round back to the roughly fifty wooden mallards that offer a surprisingly New York–ish stare of studied indifference from behind the bar.

Some of the patrons—Rear Guard Baby Boomers—are no wiser than the decoys, too, particularly at the pool table, where clean-cropped redheads in Dartmouth green are invariably hustled by Harlem sharks, who speak only a brusk "Good game!" with a roll of two pupils, shielded by the visor of an L.A. Raiders cap. This Raccoon Lodge is a little Ralph Lauren—and still a lot Ralph Kramden.

When I opened the thick wooden door, the bar was

strangely silent, the false calm of the decoy. About two strides in, the needle arm of the Seeburg was cocked. Then a burst of notes, a descending and slightly discordant bass line, both familiar and faintly archaic.

I recognized the riff immediately: the opening of Nancy Sinatra's three-minute pop opera, "These Boots Are Made for Walkin'."

It was a personal message from the Spirit in the Sky, spoken though a strange female muse. This was my sign.

Now I faced the same dilemma that Martin Luther, Brigham Young, the Five Man Electrical Band, and everyone else who'd ever received a sign had encountered: Just what on God's Earth did my sign mean?

Nancy was still pulling herself up by the boot straps as I ordered a beer and pulled up a bar stool. My life was reaching the two-minute warning for the first half. Clearly, my impending marriage and impending mortgage had not cured me of the desire to walk after midnight. But now I was headed for Lower Makefield, Pennsylvania, township where a frozen-yogurt shoppe was situated where the Raccoon Lodge should be. A walk to the nearest jukebox would require a tent, a Coleman lantern, and several days of K rations. But I wasn't becoming a shut-in just yet. I still had the freedom to travel—by Amtrak, the Friendly Skies, or my beat-up Honda CRX.

To me, there was only one possible meaning to the cryptic message I had just received: My mission was to find the greatest jukebox in America.

That was Nancy's command: that I embark on a metaphorical walk across America. It would be something like the stroll I had just taken down Amsterdam Avenue, except that it would be something far more spectacular: a series of midnight rambles across the country, from the blues-belting South Side of Chicago to the tin-roofed roadhouses of the Mississippi Delta, to spots famous and hidden from East to West.

Now, I had seen in my travels a lot of great jukeboxes already, in haunts from a ramshackle sailors' dive in Key West, Florida, to a spanking new brew pub in San Francisco's trendy

SoMa neighborhood. But in my mind there was always a more mystical jukebox out there—call it the Juke of the Covenant—that I hadn't yet played. Once I had combed the juke joints of America and proved, once and for all, that I had found the nation's greatest music machine, I could finally flip on that "No" next to my soul's blue neon vacancy.

The road trip would have to be carried out under the terms of Generation Y, the generation born somewhere between rebellion and practicality. For the reckless Front Line Baby Boomers of the 1960s, it was nothing to drop out of society for weeks or even years, climbing about a psychedelic bus and lumbering across the country, conducting electric Kool-Aid acid tests along the way. But I was getting a mortgage and a marriage license. I would instead use Lower Makefield as a base camp for short trips—weekend or week-long jaunts, pinpoint strikes on America's best jukeboxes.

It seemed the perfect solution to my dilemma, a way to combine the warmth of my romance and my new home with the unpredictability of jukeboxes. I had always loathed the popular TV beer ad during the fiscally booming late 1980s that asked, "Who says you can't have it all? / Who says you can't have pinstripes and rock 'n' roll?" but now, in 1991, an era of recession and rap music, I saw myself bringing those words to life. I could blend in, wearing a tie and reading the *New York Times* on Amtrak's 8:30 A.M. express, and then sneak out after midnight, under the cover of darkness, to carry out my true guerilla mission.

This would be the ultimate road trip for a Rear Guard Baby Boomer. I quickly drank the rest of my beer, slogged back home through swirling snowflakes, and finished my packing. I soon found that my new life-style, with two hours stuck on a train, left me a lot of time to map out strategy.

Now all I had to do was figure out where the best jukeboxes in America were located.

There wasn't an easy way to narrow them down. Calling on my skills as a newspaper reporter, I dialed the flack for the Chicago-based Amusement and Music Operators Association, the trade association for jukebox peddlers, hoping he would steer me toward the Mississippi Delta. Instead, he started telling me about some spanking new café in St. Louis that sounded like a Houlihan's with jukeboxes where the ferns are usually planted. I stored the notes on a computer and never called them up again.

At lunch hour I started hanging out at the New York Public Library in an attempt to ground myself in jukebox history. What I learned was discouraging: There are precious few books about jukeboxes. None are currently in print. And of the books you can find on dusty library shelves, all deal with the same old glittery surface: the long red, green, and blue tubes of neon, the bubbles of glass, the gleaming chrome, the classic nameplates—Wurlitzer, Seeburg, Rock-Ola.

This research wasn't fulfilling; it was like indulging an obsession with baseball by touring the Louisville Slugger Factory instead of taking in a game at Wrigley Field. I do love the way jukeboxes look, but much, much more, I love the way that jukeboxes *sound*—not just the scratchiness of an old 45, but the music itself, Patsy Cline, "Tears of a Clown," "Radio Free Europe."

How would I recognize the greatest jukebox in the land? It'd be easy to echo what that Supreme Court justice said about pornography: "I know it when I see it." But I had a clear notion about what the best record machine would be—and wouldn't be. It wouldn't simply be the most pristine archetype of some classic coin-op phonograph, like the 1946 Wurlitzer "Bubbler"—that would be a body with no soul. The key would be the records—the ghost in the machine. The best jukebox is one in perfect sync with its time and place, which somehow knows when to belt out Frank Sinatra when you're on top of the heap and to spin B. B. King when you've been dumped. I knew that some of the jukebox contenders would strike a theme—capturing Patsy Cline and her sense of loss, or compiling all the great Louisiana records in one box. Yet I wanted to find other jukeboxes that would be both maddeningly and joyously diverse, that would somehow seamlessly segue from Merle Haggard to the Ramones. There would be many false prophets on the road ahead, but I was confident that one and only one would reveal itself to me as the true Juke of the Covenant.

Meanwhile I learned something that confirmed my worst fears, a revelation that brought a greater sense of urgency to my search for America's best jukebox. The jukebox, especially the kind that we grew up with, the kind that plays 45 RPM records, is slowly but inevitably disappearing from American life. It seemed there were three general phases in the history of the record machine.

Phase 1: The novelty years. No less a figure than Thomas Edison is credited as the inventor of the jukebox, since the phonograph he developed in 1877 was for several decades largely a coin-operated device. An event of equal importance—putting a jukebox in a bar—took place in 1889 in San Francisco. But the music machine remained an arcade novelty for the next thirty-five years for one simple reason: The amplifier had not yet been invented, and so only three or four people—holding tentacle-like tubes to their ears—could listen.

Phase 2: The glory years. The electric amplifier was invented at exactly the right time, in 1927, just as the speakeasies of Prohibition were looking for a cheap form of entertainment. Within a decade, there were at least 500,000 jukeboxes across America—so many that there has never been a precise count. A disproportionate share of these were in rural outposts like the Mississippi Delta, where local tastes and the low cost of producing a 78-RPM single helped to break out so-called race and hillbilly records—the twin forerunners of rock 'n' roll.

Phase 3: The peak-and-descent years. The population of the jukebox stayed on something of a plateau from 1948—the year that Wurlitzer introduced the 100-song jukebox—until about 1976, a year when many of those 100 selections were lame 45s by people like the Captain and Tenille or Rick "Disco Duck" Dees. Since then, the jukebox has been in a free fall, thanks to a wide conspiracy that includes the replacement of corner bars and malt shops with chains like Houlihan's and McDonald's, the rise of MTV, and the technology-driven suicide of the 45.

From 500,000 U.S. jukeboxes in the 1930s, an estimate that held until 1976, the numbers fell to 230,000 jukeboxes in the mid-1980s. There are still roughly 230,000 across the country today, but this statistic is slightly misleading. Some 50,000 of these—and the numbers are swelling daily—are compact-disc, or CD, jukeboxes. The industry has hailed the CD jukebox as its salvation because it can increase the number of song selections as much as tenfold, but the image of "choice" that they present is actually a sham.

The jukeboxes of the 1930s and 1940s, with their 78s of Louis Jordan or Bob Wills and the Texas Playboys, were subversive affairs, playing regional songs that the Toscanini-crazed record executives in New York wanted to ignore. Today, CD jukeboxes are geared toward record-label megastars like Tom Petty, Michael Bolton, or Guns 'n' Roses, while indie-label CDs are squeezed out of the mix. If there had been CD jukeboxes in 1954, who would have ever heard Elvis Presley singing "That's All Right, Mama"?

The great jukeboxes of America might disappear before I could find them. Once again, this Rear Guard Baby Boomer was running behind, missing something. Far be it from me to interpret the divine motivation of the Spirit in the Sky, but I couldn't help but think that this was *why* He had sent me the sign through His female muse, Nancy Sinatra. I had been chosen to find the great jukeboxes before the plug was pulled once and for all.

But time was passing quickly—the snows of February had given way to the summer wind. That summer, I came into contact with an editor from a major publishing house in lower Manhattan, a man who shared a passion for one of the most unlikely bars in America: A dive called Joe's on a crack-infested street in New York's Alphabet City, where the jukebox was overloaded with Marty Robbins, Hank Williams, and George Jones. We met at an odd location to talk about jukeboxes, a white-tableclothed turn-of-the-century joint called Harvey's Chelsea where the only noise was the sound of starched waiters carrying your lunch across a creaky hardwood floor.

It was there, with some trepidation, that I broached the

subject of my cross-country search for great jukeboxes. Needless to say, I was careful to omit the part about the Spirit in the Sky and his chosen prophet, Nancy Sinatra.

This editor provided my first lead, which proved to be the only one I came across for sometime. He told me he lived across the Hudson in Hoboken, New Jersey, once famed as the birthplace of Frank Sinatra and now known locally as an emergent home for young publishers, investment bankers, and other up-and-comers. In Hoboken, he said, there was a woody joint, off the well-worn Wall Street path, that had the world's greatest Frank Sinatra jukebox.

Something about Frank Sinatra clicked, because the key to finding the great jukeboxes was not in the steel hardware but somehow hidden in the 45 RPM records—sung by people like Sinatra—that had made the music machine sound so great.

I thought of three recording artists as a set of Jukebox Magi, three wise singers whose offerings from the 1950s and 1960s represented the best America had to offer: Frank Sinatra, Elvis Presley, and Patsy Cline.

As generally useless as the Amusement and Music Operators Association had been, they had sent me something that helped to confirm this notion: Their landmark 1989 survey of the greatest jukebox songs of all time, which placed Elvis's "Hound Dog/Don't Be Cruel" in the no. 1 slot, and Patsy at no. 2 with "Crazy." (Victimized by a rock 'n' roll bias, Frank didn't place until no. 14, with his most recent hit, 1980's "New York, New York.")

Something telling struck me from the start about these three jukebox heroes. None of them came from a glass-and-chrome vacuum. Each was born in a real place that symbolized America at its most raw: Sinatra from the rotting docks and cheese-laden delis of industrial Hoboken, Cline from the rolling apple orchards of northern Virginia, Presley from the red-clay dirt roads of backwater Mississippi.

Jukeboxes, too, had flourished in towns like Hoboken and Tupelo, Mississippi, at mid-century—when there was still a sense of neighborhood or community, when the bartender at the corner bars knew whether to grab a Rheingold or a Schmidt's when you walked in the door. This America—like the jukeboxes it nourished—was disappearing. And it was being replaced by places like my new home, Lower Makefield, a township nestled between the factory homes of U.S. Steel's Fairless Works and the asparagus farms of the Delaware Valley. Now the steel plant was closing, the farmland was sprouting condos, and the entire township had developed and matured without a jukebox.

I don't plan on describing Lower Makefield and its 25,000 residents in any great detail. It is no different from dozens of similar townships—horizonless sprawl of newly built townhouses and "executive homes," only occasionally interrupted by a video-rental center. More important, it's not a town.

Towns have a main street, barber shops with red-and-white striped poles, malt shops, monuments to the veterans of the Spanish-American War. Even the smallest town has a corner tavern, with one of those sawdusty shuffleboard bowling games, a Miller High Life sign, and a jukebox with at least one Patsy Cline 45.

Many a Rear Guard Baby Boomer had seen the tail end of the era of towns, too. I grew up—my age increased from seven to eighteen, anyway—in a town, an old Hudson River burg called Ossining, New York, that retained some turn-of-the-century charm even after it was engulfed by the posh bedroom communities of suburban Westchester County. The main street (called Main Street) forms a giant Y where it meets U.S. 9, and there is a church in the center. When I was an adolescent, there was an Army-Navy store on Main Street where you could buy cheap T-shirts, and the shopping center in Ossining had one movie screen, the Arcadian, that showed *The Poseidon Adventure* for about six months in 1973.

On Friday nights, my parents would take me, my sister Sally, and my brother Jim for pizza at a place called Riglioni's that was paneled in dark wood, interrupted by one of those Miller High Life signs with cresting and falling red and blue streaks of light. From the tiny bar next to the dining room you could hear the jukebox playing the latest Sinatra hits—music to eat pizza by.

Ossining was a town. Even New York City, my more recent haunt, seemed like a town: The Big Town.

A Township is very different. The main drag there is likely to be Route Something, like our Route 332. The barber shop has become a unisex salon called "Innovations," the malt shop a frozen yogurt shoppe (there are no shops in exurban townships, just shoppes). And the corner tavern has become the local chain-outpost-and-fern-garden, a Bennigan's or a Fuddrucker's.

I wanted to get back to towns. I came to think of these places, towns like Ossining and Hoboken, as Jukebox America, the land where I'd find America's Greatest Jukebox, if I wasn't too late.

And so, with Frank, Elvis, and Patsy as my guides, I began to draw the rough outlines of an itinerary, my roadmap of my quest.

I mapped out a very sketchy itinerary. I placed X's on Hoboken and on Winchester, Virginia. While Patsy Cline was no doubt in Heaven and Sinatra was in the even more rarefied air of Rancho Mirage, California, I thought it was still possible to capture the feel of their music—and locate their kind of jukebox—by visiting the towns of their birth. Then there was the Elvis Trip—a mystery-train ride into the heart of America. But where? Should I visit Tupelo, Mississippi, where the King was born, or Memphis, where he reigned, or Kalamazoo, where he was most recently sighted buying a Whopper and fries? I left a question mark.

And beyond that? On our honeymoon, Kathy and I explored the wide open spaces of the American West—and decided that for jukebox purposes they were a little too wide open. I figured that I would probably set my watch on PST at least once more, but the more fertile ground would be the South and the Midwest. In particular, I knew the Mississippi Delta to be the primordial valley where jukeboxes got their name—and many of their best records. The raw, seminal music of Louisiana's Cajun country was just a few hours away. In those early days, I determined also to visit a jukebox factory, to learn more about my beloved machine and its history—a visit that would most likely take me to the American industrial heartland and, I hoped, to the windswept streets of Chicago and Detroit. A Middle American swing would also allow me to carry out a personal mission—to revisit a dark country roadhouse called the 924 Club, the first place I had thrown quarters into a jukebox. But that was as much detail as I'd commit to early on: one thing that makes jukeboxes great is their spontaneity—will the next song be Pearl Jam, or Minnie Pearl?—and I wanted my odyssey to have a similar sense of chance about it.

While I plotted this junket, events that I had dreaded that snowy night in upper Manhattan had come to pass, including the summer day when we got our first property-tax assessment in the mail. I was even closer to meeting Elvis.

And so, despite the delight of my new marriage and comfort of my new home, there were many nights when I still yearned for that other America, America on the Edge, Jukebox America. I found myself imagining the uneven, asymmetrical lands somewhere beyond our green marble fireplace, past the rows of identical rooftops.

Nevertheless, six long months passed after that night in the Raccoon Lodge, and I had done disarmingly little to fulfill my end of the deal with the Spirit in the Sky.

Then came a Saturday afternoon in September, and a wicker-shopping trip that took Kathy and me into a Pier One store at a gigantic mall in Northeast Philadelphia called Franklin Mills. The chain was apparently seeking to lure a Baby Boomer clientele by playing a tape of 1960s soft-rock hits.

It was there, in a shopping mall of all places, that my distant muse, Nancy Sinatra, returned to remind me of my calling. In the days that followed, Nancy's closing words—which I heard for the second time in 1991 somewhere in the aisle between 3' × 5' patterned rugs and marble ashtrays—still buzzed in my ear, a buzz that finally pushed me onto the road.

"Are you ready, boots? Start walkin'."

Chapter 2

....

Summer Wind

As I emerged from the darkened womb of New York's transit system, my first steps into Jukebox America were like the halting, sporadic steps of a child.

To be more specific, they carried me up the grime-encrusted exit from the Hoboken Subway station and into a purplish twilight on the very first day of October 1991; it had been a balmy fall during which the summer wind had refused to die. I landed to find suspender-harnessed investment bankers slurping margaritas at the oddly named Santa Fe Yacht Club, while a high-kicking caffeine-crazed aerobics class looked down from a second-story window across the street.

This nocturnal refuge for Wall Streeters seemed like the last place on earth to look for the one of the greatest jukeboxes in America, the all-Sinatra jukebox. I toyed with the idea of returning to the safe familiarity of mass transit, tunneling back under Hoboken, which is what I did every day on my commute to Lower Makefield.

But faith and a stubborn optimism caused me to keep walking, turning away from Washington Avenue, the yuppified main drag where bursts of underground steam waft in front of neon night spots, just like those beer commercials they run on Boomer shows like "Saturday Night Live." And when I turned left on Second, I was heading west, head-on into the heart of Jukebox America, even if it was an actual advance of only four city blocks.

Within two minutes my pace picked up, lured by the aroma of freshly baked bread from Marie's Bakery and its fading Italian red, white, and green. By then, I was passing below a thicket of crisscrossing overhead wires that bound together the three-story brownstones that comprise old Hoboken.

This was Frank Sinatra's Hoboken, the blue-collar immigrant part of town into which America's greatest saloon singer was born in 1915. It was right here in this pocket-sized city, sandwiched between the Holland and Lincoln tunnels and crisscrossed by the train tracks of a far-off era, that Sinatra went to school (well, until he turned sixteen), dressed in sissy clothes, and most important, muscled his way into a singing trio that became the Hoboken Four.

But Hoboken is truly an incredible American city even without Sinatra. It's the place that gave us our greatest beverage (the first American brewery was located here in 1641), our greatest sport (baseball; the first organized game was played on Elysian Field in 1846), and, arguably, our greatest movie, *On the Waterfront*, filmed on the docks here and released in 1954.

In 1991, there are only echoes: the Mets play two tunnels away; the kegs roll in from St. Louis and Golden, Colorado; and the docks once ruled by the fearsome, if fictional, Johnny Friendly are sitting idle, waiting for voters to decide on a condominium plan. And Sinatra makes his home 3,000 miles away from the waterfront, in arid Rancho Mirage, California, with the former Mrs. Zeppo Marx, dropping by Hoboken every five years or so for an honorary degree.

My destination in town was, I thought, one of the last monuments to the old Hoboken of legend that still stands, a five-story brownstone ringed by white Christmas-style lights. It was Leo's Grandevous restaurant, nestled in what truly seemed a fitting and proper location for the world's greatest Frank Sinatra jukebox.

Still, I was a nervous wreck as I pulled on the thick oaken

door. It had been seven months since the Raccoon Lodge and my decision to search for America's best jukebox, and the tip from my Hoboken publishing-world friend was still my only hard lead. And there were so many things that could go wrong: Leo's could be deserted, or a hangout for bourbon-breathed refugees from the nearest OTB parlor; Leo might be a moonlighting PR man for MTV, or I might enter to the sound of Color Me Badd singing "I Want to Sex You Up."

On the ride over on the PATH subway, I had clamped the music of a newly purchased cassette, *Sinatra Reprise: The Very Good Years*, over my ears and thought long and hard about the irony that Frank Sinatra—once my archenemy on jukeboxes and on AM radio—was now the object of my first pilgrimage.

No question, Frank Sinatra was a crucial figure in the history of the jukebox. He didn't invent the record machine, and he wasn't even the first great artist, but his singles, tales of romance and regret rendered in smokey, barroom tunes, came to symbolize the Jukebox Empire in the glory days of the 1940s, '50s, and '60s, when there was a box in every two-bit malt shop and gin joint in America. In the same way that America was the political powerhouse that blew away Nazi Germany, Sinatra was the musical powerhouse that gunned down Bing Crosby and the soggy crooners of the 1930s with a voice packed with muscle—the same kind of muscle flaunted by high-rolling gangsters like Chicago's Sam Giancana that put jukeboxes on all those corners.

Since I wasn't born until 1959, I saw only the tail end of Sinatra's very good years. In fact, until maybe a decade or so ago, I would have thought the best jukebox in America was the one that had the fewest Frank Sinatra records.

Sinatra was the guy my parents had on the radio, WNEW-AM, eleven-three-oh in New York, when I came downstairs in the morning for a bowl of Kaboom cereal in the morning. My prepubescent analysis was that Sinatra's voice carried the gravity of far-off mortality, a man with close-cropped, graying hair who was always grousing into his Chivas Regal about how "When I was 21, it was a very good year."

So what happened? My conversion wasn't an overnight

process, but there was one turning point—a Budweiser-soaked night in Birmingham, Alabama, the only decent-sized city in America that would take a chance on this fledgling newspaper reporter back in 1982.

In Birmingham, all the reporters hung out in a decrepit corner bar on the city's south side, a cramped semicircle of fading brick plastered from floor to ceiling with redneck bumper stickers and assorted barroom flotsam and jetsam dating back to the days when local hero Bear Bryant was still a cub. There was a jukebox that blasted pick-'em-truck music like "The Night They Drove Ol' Dixie Down" and "Polk Salad Annie" until 3 A.M. On a small sign over the doorway hung the name of the bar, upside-down: "Plaza."

One Saturday night about two months after I had moved to Alabama, I began to feel queasy: it was a mix of the thrill of living in the heart of blues-and-barbecue land with homesickness for Shea Stadium and bagels, amplified by five or six Bud long-necks. Then I heard it—a horn riff that knocked me over like an icy gust of winter wind off the Hudson River.

It was Sinatra, of course, singing "New York, New York." Yet now, this man whom just ten years earlier I had dismissed as a middle-aged whiner suddenly sounded brash and arrogant, the goddam-right king of the hill, and he didn't seem to care who knew it. It was a stomp-on-a-few-toes and takin'-care-of-business approach to life not to be found in the mush-mouthed South.

About twenty-six seconds into the song, I found myself right in the center of the Budweiser-puddled floor of the Plaza, surrounded by a crimson tide of bodies, the natives from Besse-mer and Hueytown, all kicking like the chorus line at Radio City Music Hall. I was singing lead, my off-key voice stabilized by the longnecked bottle. By the song's snarling, high-ankled finale, my shirt was about two-thirds unbuttoned and some friends had to pull me away before I finished the strip tease and found myself in violation of Alabama's blue laws.

From that night on, I vowed to keep an open mind about Frank Sinatra and the music of my parents' generation. Later, when I met Kathy, Sinatra's 1950s hep-cat coolness seemed the perfect backdrop for our courtship, over candlelight dinners and lazy winter nights in our favorite neighborhood joint, Philadelphia's 16th Street Bar and Grill. We giggled at the screwball romanticism of rhymes like "Use your mentality / Wake up to reality" and "When you arouse that need in me / My heart says, 'Yes, indeed' in me." By then, I was in my thirties—a decade I had never really planned on—and I was a Frank Sinatra fan.

Hey, when I was twenty-one, it _was_ a very good year, dammit.

Now I was thirty-two, and hearing Sinatra on my beloved jukeboxes seemed like a bridge between the rebellion of youth and the sloppy sentimentality of pre–middle-age. I wasn't sure if the all-Sinatra jukebox was the absolute best that America had to offer, but—after my near-religious conversion that night in Birmingham—it seemed like a good place to start.

I pushed open the heavy door. The first thing that hit me was the mirror behind the bar, which is positioned in such a way that Ol' Blue Eyes—about fifty, or twenty-five pairs, of them—stare at you from every which way, the reflection of dozens of photos and publicity shots. Here is Sinatra, cutting a rug with Gene Kelly in a movie poster; Sinatra, airy breadstick of a 1940s icon, oversized fedora cocked sideways and coat slung over his shoulder; middle-aged Sinatra, fattened by decades of veal and adulation, hair cropped evenly like a Roman emperor, or even a classical god.

Even though I'd never been to Leo's before, I was overcome for a moment with a vague sense of déjà vu. For one thing, the warm-and-dark wood paneling and neon beer signs reminded me a lot of Riglioni's, the former pizza parlor in my hometown of Ossining, where I had tried to play Creedence in between Sinatra songs in the early 1970s.

But there was something else, more recent and more mystical. I was reminded of something I'd seen just a few months earlier, when Kathy and I were out West on our honeymoon. We visited an extraordinary religious site in a dusty hill town just outside of Santa Fe. It was a small, twin-spired adobe-and-wood church with a dirt floor, called El Santuario de Chimayo, in a tiny hamlet called Chimayo. There, according to legend, a shining crucifix was discovered around 1810. Almost two centuries later, the chapel is awash in images of Our Saviour—statuettes in primary splashes of blue-and-red, and two-dimensional folk paintings—inspiration to generations of the humble who have left behind their crutches and ink-smeared appeals for divine intervention for everything from polio to the Persian Gulf war.

Well, the wall of Leo's looked a lot to me like El Santuario de Chimayo—that is, if you shaved off the Saviour's beard, dressed him in a tuxedo and gave him a Roman haircut. Then, as if on cue, a churchly organ swirl emerged from a jukebox in the far corner of the bar. It was the keyboard intro to the Chairman's greatest jukebox song of all, "Summer Wind," from 1966. Services at Leo's had begun.

Before I did anything else, I approached the neon altar to pay my respects, perhaps to make a $1 offering of my own. But I was hit with a staggering blow: The jukebox at Leo's Grandevous was no 45 RPM Arc of the Covenant: It was more like the short-circuiting control room where the meek Wizard manipulated the good people of Oz.

This was not the world's greatest Frank Sinatra jukebox, even though the report of the Chairman was blaring from the speakers. It was, in fact, a brand new compact-disc model, circa 1991, and as I flipped through the selections I found mostly the money-changers of the 1990s—Madonna, Paula Abdul, Billy Joel. Only near the very end of the seventy-six listings did I find the Sinatra selections: Two greatest-hits packages, two out of seventy-six.

I looked around to get my bearings, to find who was playing the Frank Morgan role in what was fast becoming a jukebox tragedy. My eyes came to rest on a meek figure behind the bar, a slightly stooped man dispensing white wine from a glass jug. He was a sharply angled figure—square-jawed, with a level haircut and rectangular, wire-rimmed glasses—and he spoke with the gruff tone of a frontline chaplain offering communion.

It was, indeed, Leo DiTerlizzi, the seventy-six-year-old owner of Leo's Grandevous.

Determined to make something of my trip to Hoboken, I decided in that split second of recognition that this stooped neighborhood barkeep was as good a story as his new CD jukebox was not. Leo would tell me the whole saga of how his jukebox went south, symbolizing the decline of Jukebox America, and hopefully give me an interesting story about his Hoboken contemporary, Frank Sinatra.

I established contact with Leo, awkwardly babbling my idea of searching for jukeboxes, searching for Sinatra.

"You want to know about Sinatra?" Leo asked, his eyes igniting behind the wire-rimmed glasses. Sure, said Leo, Sinatra, he used to come here, back in the first couple of months after the Grandevous opened in 1939, when he was still hanging around in Hoboken. In fact, he recalled, there was this one night that Frankie came over to his table at the Rustic Cabin, a long-gone nightspot in nearby Englewood Cliff, New Jersey, the place where Sinatra was discovered that same year . . .

I strained to hear Leo's soft voice over the orchestra still surging from the jukebox (I had played three of the few Sinatra tracks for $1 in an effort to cheer myself up). Leo DiTerlizzi was starting to tell me a story about his old friend. I started to pull a notebook from my back pocket, then glanced at the clock. I had stalled for too long, and it was a long trip—via the bowels of Newark, no less—back to Lower Makefield.

"It's dead tonight," Leo said. "Come back on Friday, and you'll get a good story."

I didn't get a chance to ask my real question—what had happened to the jukebox? All I knew was that, on the trail of Jukebox America, I had found my first guide.

The three days until Friday passed quickly. The second time I opened the thick door and entered Leo DiTerlizzi's shrine, the twenty-five pairs of Ol' Blue Eyes were outmatched by a Happy Hour crowd that was half Wall Street and half Mulberry Street:

Clean-cut guys in newly loosened ties, booze-bellied old-timers chain-smoking and grinding the ashes into half-eaten plates of provolone.

"Hi, remember me? The jukebox guy." I proudly proclaimed.

Leo gave me a glare of recognition speckled with disgust.

"It's really busy now," said Leo, overlooking the fact that I had arrived at precisely the hour and day he had advised. "Maybe you should come back on a weeknight."

My whole plan was shot. I had thought I would interview Leo, then meet a New York friend for dinner, but now I just sat at the bar, throwing an occasional question at DiTerlizzi as he ambled up and down the long curve of the bar.

Even the story about the Rustic Cabin—the hook that brought me back to Hoboken for a second try—had vanished. I had brought one of those minicassette recorders along to capture Leo's oral history of the Chairman of the Board, and somewhere I still have the tape. To listen to that garbled recording today is to hear a muted "The Lady Is a Tramp" in the background and Leo's seventy-six-year-old voice fading in and out, uttering bland or unintelligible comments about Sinatra.

"You know, he's coming to the Garden next month," is about the only complete sentence on that tape recording I can make out today.

The frustrating part was that Leo was so likable, a grandfatherly if occasionally grumpy figure who was clearly beloved by his many customers and who had a witty and glib remark for almost everything and everybody. Everybody except Sinatra.

At first, I blamed myself.

I figured I just wasn't asking the right question, the key that would unlock the trove of stories about Sinatra and that fabled jukebox. After a while, I even began to fantasize about what that story might have sounded like. ("I'll never forget this night back in '60. I can still hear "Witchcraft" playing on the jukebox. Suddenly, the door pushed open, and in walks Frankie, with Sam Giancana, a bunch of other mugs, and that dame, Judy Exner . . . ")

But it never happened. I tried all night that Friday, and then twice more. Once was an unplanned ambush when I spotted Leo running errands outside a Hoboken bank after he stood me up for a scheduled meeting; the other was yet another slow Tuesday night back at the bar. Eventually, it became a matter of pride; I was a journalist who had covered bent-nosed politicians and trash haulers in New York for years, but I couldn't even get the keeper of a Frank Sinatra jukebox to tell me his story. I fired questions at Leo DiTerlizzi, but after a while he adopted that deer-in-the-headlights expression that by 1991 was universally known as "the Dan Quayle look."

If Leo wasn't such a sweet old man, I might have blamed the problem on *omerta*, the legendary Sicilian code of silence, but Leo DiTerlizzi was no friend to the Sam Giancana crowd; he wasn't even Sicilian.

The last time I went to Leo's, I sat at a bar stool talking to the old man and his twenty-six-year-old grandson, Nick DePalma.

I was reduced to begging.

"Just tell me one good story about Sinatra, and I promise I'll never come back again."

Nick interjected. "That was a long time ago. That was almost fifty years ago."

Now my humiliation was complete. I had utterly failed to find the first jukebox on my itinerary, and now I was badgering and hounding a stooped seventy-six-year-old man for scraps of weathered memory. I had hit rock bottom.

But as I spent those hours at the bar, watching Leo fluidly chat up everyone but me, I realized—oddly enough—that on all matters non-Sinatra he had an impeccable memory. And so, as he ambled up and down the thirty-foot curve of the bar, and as I made small talk with Nick DePalma or with Leo's devoted customers, I learned quite a bit about the man. I learned that he was born in 1915—yes, the same year as you-know-who—in a small Italian fishing town on the Adriatic Sea called Molfetta, a place that sent so many of its residents to Hoboken-on-the-Hudson that decades later there's still a local paper published for the Molfettan-Americans. Leo came to New Jersey when he was fifteen but never lost sight of his two main loves in life.

Sinatra and jukeboxes? Hardly. Rather, they were soccer and a woman named Teresa Monsiello. One day during the Depression, Leo was playing wing in a big game and he spotted Teresa on the sidelines; a few minutes later Leo got Teresa's attention with a powerful but errant kick, which struck her in the head. Fifty years later, they're still arguing at Leo's bar whether the kick was an accident or the result of skill, but it got something going; Teresa Monsiello became Teresa DiTerlizzi. That's a fact that's inescapable to any customer of Leo's, because—with all the Sinatra relics and sacraments—it is Teresa's picture, holding hands with Leo at their fiftieth anniversary party, that is the largest artifact, and it holds down the most prominent spot over the bar.

It was a touching love story, and as I listened to it, it seemed like Sinatra was always scatting in the background, blasting off for the moon and exchanging glances with unfamiliar dames. The songs from the jukebox served to remind me why I was hanging out in Leo's—the all-Sinatra jukebox that didn't exist.

I hadn't missed it by much—only by a couple of months, as it turned out. The paramount Frank Sinatra jukebox, it seems, had become a victim of old age, the same entropy process that was eating away at all of Jukebox America as surely as Scotch was eating away at Sinatra's pipes.

The Sinatra-jukebox phenomenon at Leo's had been no master plan but a slow evolution throughout the jukebox glory years of the 1950s and 1960s; the local jukebox distributor gave Leo's a healthy share of Sinatra 45s—this was Frankie's old neighborhood, after all—and the customers responded, so much so that when the thrill of their old Sinatra 45s had faded, they'd donated them to Leo.

Soon more than half the songs on the jukebox were Sinatra cuts, then well over 100 of the 144 selections. It was never an all-Frank Sinatra jukebox; Leo's grandson, Nick DePalma, told me that when he was kid in the early seventies his favorite selection had been "Billy Don't Be a Hero" by Bo Donaldson and the Heywoods.

But no one will dispute that it was the greatest Frank Sinatra jukebox of all time—until the summer of 1991. Like Sinatra himself in 1991, the jukebox's nightly performances here hit or miss, prone to unscripted breakdowns. But while Sinatra's problems didn't stop him from charging $50 a seat at the Garden, the jukebox distributor came to Leo's one day and pulled the plug on the Chairman's jukebox.

The old thing was a relic, anyway: all the bars in Hoboken—and there are still about 200 of them in a mere square mile—were dumping the 45 players for new CD models that carried hundreds of selections. Leo could have his Sinatra, but also the stuff that the young kids want to hear—dance music, Madonna, Paula Abdul. Don't worry about Sinatra, said the jukebox distributor, he would supply two entire discs.

Two out of seventy-six CDs; that comes to less than 3 percent, down from a peak of 70 percent. Young Nick DePalma, a graduate of Holy Cross, wasn't against technology, but he tried to set the jukebox distributor straight: the 3-percent Sinatra jukebox would not do for Leo's Grandevous.

"We had a problem with the jukebox guy," recalled DePalma. "We had asked him for a lot of Sinatra. He really didn't understand our clientele."

Nick DePalma didn't take as pessimistic a view of the jukebox situation as I did; he noted there were still twenty-four blank slots on the jukebox, and there was talk of amassing some other Sinatra CDs. But my view of the Chairman of the Board was driven by the bottom line: The world's greatest Frank Sinatra jukebox was gone. And the keeper of the jukebox, Leo DiTerlizzi, wasn't talking.

I had taken my first steps into Jukebox America, and I was stumbling.

I called up in my mind the Frank Sinatra songbook, and sought inspiration. After all, this was the man of "High Hopes," of unbridled post–World War II can-do America, who taught me and all the the other Rear Guard Baby Boomers the story of the ant and the rubber tree plant.

So on a drizzly fall Saturday afternoon, I launched a sneak attack on Hoboken from the rear, approaching by car from Lower Makefield. My theory was this: Hoboken was a prime example of the turf that I called Jukebox America, and buried in its 200 corner bars were surely other jukeboxes, other tales of Sinatra and his scratchy 45s.

In my early ramblings through this city—which packs just over 40,000 souls into little more than a square mile—I couldn't escape the sense that this was something even more than a much-ballyhooed American melting pot, that Hoboken was more like a stock pot that was constantly enriched with new ingredients, German potatoes, Italian plum tomatoes, the fishy taste of inside traders from Wall Street.

To stroll up the wide, low-rise expanse of the main drag, Washington Avenue, where aging Italian men in windbreakers and sweats still trade opinions about who sells the best mozzarell' (no *a*, please!) or whether Simms or Hostetler should get the football on Sunday, is to see this. Behind this cluster, invariably, is some trendy restaurant like East L.A., where the Morgan Stanley crowd down fajitas and argue about cheap rents (if you call $750 a month for a third-floor walk-up cheap) and subway commutes.

Hoboken was just the place I was looking for; a relic of a city that was only about sixty miles from Lower Makefield and its frozen-yogurt shoppes, yet seemed to be light years removed. Hoboken had broken free from the example of a host of similar cities that began the slow limp into old age and near death in the 1950s, like Camden, New Jersey; East St. Louis, Illinois; or Gary, Indiana. These cities all served a similar function throughout the Industrial Revolution in America. If we think of the big cities— New York, Philadelphia, Chicago—as the grand living rooms of mid-twentieth century America, decorated with splashes of Art Deco, partying to a jazz beat, thriving with the electricity of commerce and wealth, then we must think of Hoboken or Camden as the utility closet off the hallway that feeds those urban living rooms. They are crammed with all the unsightly wires and works—the seedy docks, oil refineries, garbage-truck parking lots and railroad yards—that keep things out front presentable.

Even Frank Sinatra didn't understand the importance of Hoboken. After a disastrous nightclub gig during his career nadir, in 1952, when a hometown crowd booed him from the stage, Sinatra has not only largely avoided Hoboken for four decades, but has gone so far as calling this landmark American city "a sewer." A gritty and sometimes grimy city like Hoboken might be mistaken for a drainpipe, but Frank should have realized it was actually the fuse box for the Paramount Theater—where he swooned his way to superstardom in 1943—and the liquor cabinet that kept things flowing for the singer and his pals at Toots Shor's in midtown.

By 1991, that utility closet was losing its place in the scheme of things. The largest factory in town and its most famous landmark—the sprawling riverside Maxwell House coffee plant with its massive electric dripping coffee sign—was due to close in six months. The sign was always a beacon to office-tower Manhattanites, a foreshadowing of the industrial American heartland that started on the left bank of the Hudson River and stretched to the Golden Gate Bridge. In its heyday, the plant produced the equivalent of 30,000 cups of coffee every minute, but American coffee consumption is down 24 percent since 1963—too much caffeine. And so Maxwell House was cutting back, killing 600 jobs and consolidating its operations on the sunny Houlihan's-lined boulevards of low-wage Jacksonville, Florida, far from Hoboken's jukeboxes.

Now the last drop was splattering against the filter.

This was October, the glorious month of *both* Octoberfest *and* the World Series, and it would have been easy and most proper in this birthplace of American beer and baseball to pull up a bar stool, suck on a Sam Adams, cheer in vain for the Atlanta Braves, and toast Hoboken goodbye. Instead, I walked on, after midnight and before, searching for jukeboxes and searching for Sinatra.

The most popular bars in town were no help. Elysian

Fields, the high-ceilinged turn-of-the-century hangout where reporters were going to interview the soon-to-be-laid-off Maxwell
House workers, was empty: Devoid of coffee grinders and jukeboxes both. A block to the north is Hoboken's great bar of the
1980s and 1990s, Maxwell's, the launching pad for great alternative rock bands like The Feelies and home of what I must say
in all fairness is a *killer* jukebox, featuring everything from Bob
Seger's "Ramblin' Gamblin' Man" to the Inspiral Carpets and
Jesus Jones. Maxwell's deserves high praise for keeping Hobok-
en's musical traditions alive with a twist of "slacker" rebellion,
but its art-school, flannel-shirted clientele brought me no closer
to Frank Sinatra than had my first sighting of Paula Abdul on
Leo's jukebox.

Next, I walked westward across Hoboken into the heart of
the Italian district, looking for the home at 415 Monroe Street
where Frank Sinatra was born.

But there was no plaque, no skinny, elephant-eared bronze
statue of Sinatra, not even a building to gaze at—just a balding
man in a white shirt, sitting in front of a two-story brick townhouse next door, idling on his tiny front porch in a folding picnic
chair with two large dogs sitting lazily at his feet.

"It's a garage—he parks cars there," said the old man,
pointing to what was in reality a vacant lot next door. There was
a green rusty pickup truck parked outside, and a heavy brick wall
that looked about as inpenetrable as one of Sinatra's bodyguards.
The owner of the birthplace-turned-parking lot had constructed
a brick arch over the entryway, an arch that—inexplicably—is
said to be a tribute to the singer.

A few blocks away, I hoped to find the remnants of Marty
O'Brien's, the bar that Dolly Sinatra owned, where son Frank
met the singing trio that he would later join to form the Hoboken
Four.

I didn't find that bar. Across the street was a private club
("Members Only") called the Monroe Buddies Bar, where the
buddies were a few grumpy old men watching a college football
game, while slabs of watermelon sat mysteriously stacked on a
nearby table. It had no jukebox—and I had no membership card.

I searched out the Union Club, the historic restaurant and nightclub where Sinatra got some of his early breaks, singing at weddings and christenings, and where he suffered that big setback in 1952, when he dodged pieces of fruit from a hostile crowd.

What I found was merely the latest condo conversion on the riverfront side of town: The Union Club had closed its doors for good, and was being transformed from a sacramental ballroom to a condominium complex full of $200,000 bedrooms with newly stuccoed walls and brass sconces on either side of the doorway.

A young man in shorts was down in the moat surrounding the basement of the Union Club, installing a new storm window and shouting up at me: "No one lives here—it's all tied up in the courts."

And so after two weeks of unsuccessfully trying to move the rubber tree plant that Hoboken, Frank Sinatra, and jukeboxes had become for this ant, I retreated to the thick-windowed security of my office on Park Avenue in midtown Manhattan, and tried yet a new approach.

I let my fingers do the walking.

I dialed "201" repeatedly, made contacts gleaned from all corners: fleeting references in Kitty Kelley's maligned but excellent biography of Sinatra, *His Way;* the Hoboken Historical Society and in faded newspaper clippings. I tried without success to reach Jimmy Roselli, the poor man's Sinatra.

It didn't take long before I struck paydirt. For still manning his post on a low-rise block right there on Washington Avenue, halfway between the ponytails of Maxwell's and the greasy kid stuff of Leo's, was an 82-year-old man—friend and contemporary of Sinatra—who I came to think of as The Source: Don "Mike" Milo.

Mike Milo didn't have one jukebox, but he had been an uncle to many. Milo was Hoboken's music man, giving Ol' Blue Eyes his start in the music business and then, from his cramped storefront record shop, selling many of the Sinatra 45s that had made up Leo's Sinatra selection for the last, ironically, forty-five years.

Milo told me to come by his store when he opened up, 9 A.M. on a Wednesday morning. I arrived about forty-five minutes late—thanks to my new friends at New Jersey Transit and PATH—but stared into a darkened and closed record store. In the darkness, I made out a lifesized and menacing stare. Frank Sinatra? Sam Giancana? No, it was the snarl of Axl Rose of Guns 'n' Roses, staring down at me from a promotional poster—a snarl that carried the myth of perpetual youth about fifty decibels higher than Sinatra's 1943 display for the bobby-soxers at the Paramount.

About fifteen minutes later, Milo shuffled in; despite his age he walked in adagio time. Little more than five feet tall, Milo wore a gray windbreaker and gray pants, white sneakers and white socks. His forehead bore the acne pockmarks of time, but his graying moustache was perfectly trimmed. His expression, too, was a study in contrasts: A mischievous and youthful smile that overcame the heaviness of his eyelids. Milo's left ear, one of the few on earth that had heard The Voice when it was raw and overflowing with postpubescent testosterone, now requires a hearing aid. His voice was scratchy, high-pitched, and a joy to hear, like a dusty Decca 78.

In eight long decades, Mike Milo has seen Hoboken re-made and remodeled over and over again. As a big-band leader in the 1930s and 1940s, he thrived on the factories, playing Guy Lombardo tunes for them at Christmas parties. Since the end of World War II, he's been selling records on Washington Avenue to the kids, Sinatra to the bobby-soxers, Springsteen to their kids, Guns 'n' Roses to the Wall Street yuppies who redesigned the brownstones, installed microwaves and VCRs, and moved in dur-ing the 1980s.

But he didn't have many pauses for reflection that morning. Three teens from the Puerto Rican section of town were roaming the store, flipping through a shoe box of 45 RPM records that were once the lifeblood of his business but were now a curiosity.

One of the teenagers found "Simon Sez," the 1968 hit by the 1910 Fruitgum Co.

"Is that the same thing as the game?" he asked Milo.

"Why don't you take it home and play it. If it isn't, just give it back."

A few seconds later a new customer, a bearded young man in blue jeans and sneakers, stepped forward to buy Springsteen on compact disc.

"Okay, Mr. CD," said Milo, "that will be $12.50 plus tax."

But between the interruptions, Mike Milo took me back to a day more than fifty years ago when you could have stocked an entire Wurlitzer jukebox for less than $12.50, and when Frank Sinatra needed Mike Milo, needed him bad.

It was the early 1930s. The Sinatra family was doing pretty well; mother Dolly was active in the local Democratic Party, while father Marty was making fire captain and opening up that corner bar under his boxing name, Marty O'Brien's. The family purchased a comfortable brownstone on the more prosperous east side of the city, and moved away from the Italian district to 841 Garden Street.

Milo, six years older than the Sinatras' son Frank, was making a life for himself, too. The son of an engineer for the Erie Lackawanna Rail Road, the link between Hoboken and heartland, his family lived almost directly across the street from the Sinatras, at 820 Garden Street.

Not that Milo was spending a lot of time at home. He worked all day across the river in Manhattan as a purchasing agent for Republic Pictures. At night, Milo—who learned to play the saxophone like his idol Freddie Martin—was the leader of a band, playing gigs all over the city and the suburbs, swank joints like the Bay Shore Country Club out on Long Island, where his movie studio boss was a member.

Every now and then, Milo would walk down the stoop of his brownstone and hear a voice—the voice of a young man who quit working the waterfront after just four days, who lasted little more than a week as a copy boy in the sports section at the *Jersey Observer*, who fantasized about attending the prestigious Stevens Institute and becoming an engineer, despite having left school at age sixteen.

The voice was The Voice, but no one knew it, not even

Milo. But Milo began to talk about music, their common interest, with his across-the-street neighbor who'd watched Bing Crosby in a Jersey City movie house and vowed to become a big-time singer. Sinatra's mother had bought him a $65 PA system—big bucks in those days—and orchestrations that other singers couldn't afford. Young Frankie would practice for hour after hour with one of his friends, a guitar player named Golizio, and he started begging Milo to take him out on his jobs.

Even in 1991, with Frank Sinatra considered the top pop singer of the half-century, Milo doesn't waver; he still recalls that Sinatra didn't impress him that much. But many of the halls that booked him wanted a lead vocalist, so once in a while, if no one else was available, Milo asked Sinatra.

The friendship finally paid off—for Sinatra, the protégé, not Milo, the mentor—in 1935.

Milo's daytime employer, Republic Pictures, was filming some movie shorts with the legendary Major Bowes, the host of radio's popular "Amateur Hour" (the forerunner of the show that was hosted in my childhood by Ted Mack), where little-known talent could get exposure on New York City's most popular station, WMCA.

The filming was about to start at the Biograph Studios up in the Bronx, and Bowes needed some musicians. The studio boss remembered Milo's gig at the country club, and asked his employee to perform.

Oh, and could Milo round up a few vocalists, too?

By then, Sinatra had started singing sometimes with three other guys from the neighborhood calling themselves the Three Flashes who hung out at Marty O'Brien's. So when Milo came back to Hoboken that night looking for singers, Sinatra and his mother began pestering the Three Flashes to become a foursome (to which, several members told Kitty Kelley in the early 1980s, they reluctantly agreed)—and the Hoboken Four was born.

Dolly Sinatra arose at 5 A.M. that fateful morning to fry up some breakfast for Milo and the four vocalists, and then they shot across the brand-new, traffic-free George Washington Bridge for their date with history.

They filmed two shorts, "The Night Club" and "The Minstrel," for Bowes' Theatre of the Air. Looking back through the prism of the 1990s, the whole thing seems rather embarrassing: Major Bowes, after the fashion of the era, wanted Milo, his orchestra, and the Hoboken Four to perform in blackface: A surviving picture shows Milo waving a baton in a white top hat and tails, his skin painted the color of charcoal, his lips large and white. The Chairman of the Board was put to work in one scene as an extra, a waiter with a towel draped over his shoulder. Later, one of Milo's bosses with the movie company pointed out Frank Sinatra and, Milo remembers, made this prophetic remark:

"Wait 'til he gets a little older."

The wait wasn't that long. In September 1935, again with some help from Milo, the foursome was invited by Bowes to appear on his radio show. The Hoboken Four, singing a tune called "Shine," stole the show, and Major Bowes signed them up for his traveling show at the princely sum of $50 a week. Frank Sinatra wasn't yet a star, but he was officially on his way—a big enough name to headline at the Rustic Cabin, get carried on WNEW-AM, and get the attention of bandleader Harry James.

By 1943, Frank Sinatra was the most popular male singer in America, a fixture on every jukebox, and, with his legendary show at New York's Paramount Theatre, at the first peak of his career. It was there that packs of teenaged girls, some planted by his publicist, some Frank-happy for real, most looking for an outlet for their World War II angst, began to faint at the feet of the singer dubbed "Swoonatra." Among the Hobokenites in the audience at those Paramount shows were Leo DiTerlizzi and Mike Milo.

While we were talking, Mike showed me a picture of a gig he had played in 1943. The band leader and his orchestra, shrouded in tinsel, played the Christmas Party at a Belleville, New Jersey, factory.

Sinatra was starting to make eyes at Ava Gardner about the same time that Milo settled down, left the film business, and decided the future lay in selling records to the youth of America. His store opened just in time for Hoboken's Frank Sinatra Day in 1947; Milo recalls blaring "Ol' Man River" from a giant speaker as Ol' Blue Eyes paraded past.

Since 1947, Hoboken has awarded Frank Sinatra—the absentee hero, tenth-grade dropout, and occasional hometown-basher—the keys to the city, an honorary high-school diploma, and an honorary degree from the prestigious Stevens Institute of Technology.

If it were up to me, the city would hold a parade for Mike Milo instead.

Ever since that parade day in 1947, it has really been Mike Milo, and not Frank Sinatra, who has been the music man of Hoboken, New Jersey. It was Milo who sold literally tens of thousands of records from his tiny storefront, filling the maritime gin joints along Hudson Street—there were once dozens, all torn down now—with vinyl pleasure.

It was a good enough living for Milo, a widower, to raise two daughters in Hoboken, where he has lived his entire life except for an eight-year stretch in nearby Newark. But now the financial picture is different: in 1991, Milo sells mostly compact discs.

"I don't feel good about it at all," he said. "Kids don't have $15 to pay for a CD every week, they don't have $9 to pay for a cassette. With 45s, we used to sell 200 to 300 every other day, if it was a hit or no hit. 'The Tennessee Waltz' sold 16 million records, and I sold 700 of them in one week."

By the time Patti Page's record was released in 1950, Milo's contacts with Frank Sinatra were mostly through 45s. A few times in the 1950s, he saw Sinatra play live at the Copacabana, and Dolly Sinatra used to tell Milo how to successfully slip backstage.

"I was a little shaky, nervous," recalls Milo of those meetings, even though just two decades earlier he was finding Sinatra work and telling him how to dress.

Not that Mike Milo is totally forgotten by the Sinatra family; he says his name is on a list of Hoboken old-timers that daughter Nancy uses to issue complimentary tickets when her dad sings at local arenas like the New Jersey Meadowlands.

On December 12, 1990, Frank Sinatra sang there to celebrate his seventy-fifth birthday, and Mike Milo tried to visit his old pal during an intermission.

He got no further than a gauntlet of private security guards, wearing badges that bore the word Sinatra.

"I tried many times," Milo said. "If he knew I was out there . . ."

Milo's voice trailed off.

"We were told nobody could come in. If his mother was alive, it would have been different."

After hearing Milo's story about Sinatra, we bantered some more about other celebrities; he showed me a picture of himself outside that Meadowlands concert with Henny Youngman, and he told me about some of his favorite musicians, bandleaders like Woody Herman and Guy Lombardo.

As travelers often do, I found that my original itinerary for Hoboken had proved meaningless. I had come to Hoboken to find a jukebox, and instead I found salvation in a record store. I came hoping to glorify Frank Sinatra, but now it was Mike Milo—the real music man of Hoboken—that I was ready to canonize.

And so it wasn't Milo's memories about Sinatra that stayed with me the most as I walked slowly the six long blocks from his store back to the rail station. It was another remark from this man who still peddled music to Hoboken six days a week at age eighty-two, a patron saint of lost causes.

"I think 45s are coming back," Mike Milo told me. "I have a feeling."

After meeting Mike Milo, I didn't go back to Hoboken for a long time. The World Series ended in defeat for the underdog Atlanta Braves, and the summer wind that had stubbornly hung in that October seemed to die down the moment the last Minnesota Twin crossed home plate. During my nocturnal ramblings and weekend hikes up and down the brownstone streets of Hoboken, chores had been piling up back in Lower Makefield; there was wood to stack for our fireplace, Christmas presents to stockpile for December.

The commuter train from Trenton to New York's Penn Station plodded back and forth every day, giving me more time than I needed to reflect on what I had seen in Hoboken. And there was one image that repeatedly flashed in my mind: the wall of Frank Sinatra pictures that cluttered the wood paneling in Leo's Grandevous—the shrine that in turn reminded me of the dusty chapel in New Mexico.

But I knew there was one big difference between Leo's and El Santuario de Chimayo. The bright-hued images in New Mexico of Jesus Christ depicted a Saviour that was a warm, caring God, backed by soothing swirls of color, heavenly warmth.

The images of Frank Sinatra in Leo's were posed studies in formality: stark outlines of black and white—even the color photos—that conveyed a chilling distance of a stern Old Testament god. One photograph in particular stayed with me: the Chairman, smiling smugly in tuxedo and close-cropped hair, inscribed with dashed-off words: "Leo: All the best—Frank Sinatra '88." A greeting—to a man who had amassed the world's greatest Frank Sinatra jukebox and shrine—with all the warmth of the latest Hallmark card. In the photo, the arms of this far-off, judgmental god are firmly crossed.

Nevertheless, the adobe-walled chapel and the wood-paneled barroom walked much common ground. To the thousands who had visited the New Mexico shrine—nervous Army moms and weary polio victims—the presence of the Saviour in this poor desert town, a place a nonbeliever might describe as godforsaken, was a tangible thing. And Francis Albert Sinatra of Rancho Mirage, California, a man who badmouthed Hoboken and who hadn't dropped in on the neighborhood for a beer in at least four decades, was still a real, daily presence in places like Leo's Grandevous, for one reason: The music, the voice that carried the "coulda been a contendah" echoes of waterfront Hoboken long after Sinatra caught the redeye for the Coast.

The faith of the true believer—even in the overwhelming face of reality—had been everywhere I looked in Hoboken. What better example than Mike Milo, who believed that 45 RPM records were coming back even as his customers lined up for Springsteen CDs, who believed in Frank Sinatra even as the singer's thuglike bodyguards kept Milo cement walls away from his former protégé.

And what about Milo's contemporary, Sinatra's contemporary, seventy-six-year-old Leo DiTerlizzi? It took my encounter with Milo to realize that Leo, too, was a man of faith—faith that paid off in his lifelong love affair with Teresa Monsiello, in his offspring, in his loyal customers. To him, Sinatra was no god—no sane person would mistake him for one—but was something of an icon. And what he inspired was not worship but more a *sacrament*, a daily round of hymns to the romantic power of "Witchcraft," the sustaining memory of "A Very Good Year."

In all my frustrating encounters with Leo, I still remembered the most positive reaction he had ever given me. I had pulled a dollar from my wallet and asked if there was a song I could play for him.

For once, Leo DiTerlizzi didn't hesitate, not for a second. "Play sixty-oh-eight," he said with the reverence of the parish priest, announcing the final hymn of the service. "Fly Me to the Moon."

I answered the call. However, by then, my final visit to Leo's, I had already begun to notice something strange about his CD jukebox, the one I had held in contempt ever since my first inspection.

In Hoboken, the city of faith, within the dark walls of Leo's shrine, there had been a *bona fide* miracle, the jukebox equivalent of the story of the loaves and fishes.

The miracle was this: in all the many hours of sitting at Leo's barstool, I had not once heard any of the Madonna or Paula Abdul songs, the evil, modern-day temptations of the glistening CD jukebox. What I heard was Frank Sinatra, over and over and over: "Summer Wind," "That's Life," "The Lady Is a Tramp."

It's a fact: I even have it on tape, in the hours of aimless conversations I recorded in my search for lost Sinatra lore.

As critical as I am of modern, digital technology, there is one advantage to the computerized record machine. It can compute, and flash in a cold red readout, the ten most popular songs in its selection.

Here are the greatest hits of Leo's Grandevous, for October 1991:

1. 6008 "Fly Me to the Moon." Frank Sinatra
2. 6013 "Summer Wind." Frank Sinatra
3. 5914 "Hey Jealous Lover." Frank Sinatra
4. 6407 "I Left My Heart in San Francisco." Tony Bennett
5. 6403 "Rags to Riches." Tony Bennett
6. 6701 "Devil Went Down to Georgia." Charlie Daniels Band
7. 6011 "I Got You Under My Skin." Frank Sinatra
8. 6012 "Strangers in the Night." Frank Sinatra
9. 2104 "Say Goodbye to Hollywood." Billy Joel
10. 6017 "The Lady Is a Tramp." Frank Sinatra

Frankly, after the time I spent at Leo's, I was a little shocked that four of the top ten songs were not Sinatra's; maybe the pickup trucks of the Charlie Daniels crowd circled Leo's at lunchtime, when I wasn't there.

But the bottom line is this: on a jukebox that offers only 3 percent Frank Sinatra, the record shows that Ol' Blue Eyes has 60 percent of the top selections, and by my own unscientific observation was belting from the jukebox about 85 percent of the time.

No, I hadn't found exactly what I was looking for in Hoboken, a jukebox featuring nothing but the records of Frank Sinatra. But I'd found something even better: a music machine that, overwhelming my initial crisis of faith, had proven itself to be, without question, The World's Greatest Frank Sinatra jukebox.

Oops, there goes another rubber tree plant.

The ungodly Sinatra family had proved a holy trinity. Frank the father had handed down his first commandment in the beer-puddled Plaza in Birmingham: Remember thy very good years, and cherish them always. Then the holy daughter, Nancy, had dispatched me on my pilgrimage with "These Boots Are Made for Walkin'." Now, quite by surprise, I had found Sinatra's holy spirit, spoken in tongues by Mike Milo and Leo DiTerlizzi.

Like Leo, I had a lot to give thanks for: the good love of an Italian woman, the warmth of a home. But as easy as it would have been, Leo did not turn his back on the music—he'd still be playing 6008 until that day that he rolled himself up into a big ball. Indeed, the advanced age of Leo and Mike Milo and the sad thought that such jukebox lore would soon be gone made me feel the press of time more heavily than before. Yet their simple faith seemed stronger than time, stronger than the Maxwell House layoffs and the other cruel winds that were likely to buffet Hoboken. I, too, was infused, for after Hoboken I believed in the wonderful folly of my jukebox search more than ever.

This is the gospel according to Frank. Start spreadin' the news.

Chapter 3

....

The Gambler

Time was not on my side.

The mute and rusty smokestacks of southwest Chicago were in my rearview mirror as I sped down Interstate 55 at 77 MPH, veering every minute or two to dodge the rolling steel pipes, busted tires, and other kinds of industrial decay that blocked the road. It was nearly 1 P.M. on a Friday, August 7, 1992, and I was way behind schedule.

The whole point of my search for America's best jukebox was to catch up. And yet the summer wind that had warmed Hoboken, New Jersey, well into October 1991 had given way to an autumn wind that was more like winter, and then to powerful Arctic gusts like my monthly mortgage bill—daily economic forces that kept me off the road for nearly ten months.

Now, finally, the warm wind was at my back again—I would dedicate the entire month of August to my long-postponed search. And I had short-term catching up to do: I was already an hour behind schedule when Amtrak's Broadway Limited pulled into Union Station in Chicago, and I had to drive like Richard Petty to make today's goal of happy hour in the 924 Club in Banner, Illinois.

I decided I might relax by locating WLS 890 on the AM

dial—the great clear-channel Top 40 station where I had first heard so many summer jukebox selections, from "Crimson and Clover" by Tommy James and the Shondells to "My Sharona" by The Knack. But the only sound on AM 890 was the midday blather of Rush Limbaugh—not the way things ought to be. WLS was now talk radio. I punched the "seek" button ten or eleven times until I found the Rascals' "People Got to Be Free." Then there was a disc jockey.

"It's a Class of '69 Reunion Weekend!"

There it was, my latest cue card from the Spirit in the Sky, for that's what this twenty-four hour, 1,200-mile jaunt was all about—a Class of '69 reunion involving me and my very first juke joint, the 924 Club.

That love affair started on a hot summer's day just like this one, twenty-three years earlier, on my family's yearly trip to Peoria, Illinois, my parents' original hometown. It wasn't your typical jukebox experience. The day began at 5 A.M., with my Dad shaking me from my slumber on a guest bed in a fly-infested room just off Grandpa A. B. Bunch's bacon-splattered kitchen. I was still half-asleep when we stopped at the Southside Worm Ranch for bait, and then the Krispy Creme donut shop, whose nutritious breakfasts went perfectly with a cooler full of Coca-Cola and—for my Dad, Grandpa, and Uncle Dale—Miller High Life. By 7 A.M. or so we reached our destination, a weed-infested cow pond allegedly stocked with fish. I can't really remember catching any; what I do recall is the glare of a July sunrise on the flat Illinois earth—and the eternal rattle of thousands of unseen insects, punctuated every five minutes or so by the popping of a beer can.

Even though I was a little naive, even for a ten-year-old, I came to realize that the predawn maneuvers were really just an excuse for the 9:30 A.M. retreat to the cool darkness of the 924 Club in Banner, Illinois. Not surprisingly, we were the only customers on that sunny July midweek morning. I remember how my grandfather, who was about sixty-four years old at the time, always sprinkled salt into his beer so that the head would foam up; his robust health in those days was fairly amazing, considering his steady diet of beer, salt, bacon, and greasy fried chicken. At the 924, I got to order yet another Coke, and—probably sugar-and-caffeine crazed from all the soda pop—demanded handfuls of quarters from my Dad, quarters to play pinball and, more important, to play the jukebox, to hear Blood, Sweat and Tears do "Spinnin' Wheel" one more time.

It sounds trivial, but I still recall playing the jukebox at the 924 Club as a crucial evolutionary stage. It was a blissful exercise of free choice, something a ten-year-old boy almost never gets to do. I couldn't drive a car or rig a fishing pole without a grownup around, but with a jukebox I could choose to play "Honky Tonk Women" by the Rolling Stones or choose not to play "Love Is Blue" by Paul Mauriat. And everyone in the joint—adults included—would have to listen.

For a ten-year-old, choosing songs on a jukebox was exhilarating—and easy, too. From that point on, I got to make more and more choices—where to go to school, where to work, who to marry—and each seemed fraught with more risk as well as more reward. I think that's why I still love playing jukeboxes as a thirty-three-year-old: it brings back the thrill of being alive—without any of the danger.

I didn't have to wait for college to find out about existentialism from Jean-Paul Sartre. I had already learned it from Tommy James and the Shondells.

Now, I didn't think I could find America's best jukebox without a pilgrimage first to that one extra-special jukebox, my first. Everything in my new stage or life seemed so different. I couldn't have imagined owning a condo-townhouse or commuting daily to work on Amtrak—neither suburban condos nor Amtrak even existed in 1969.

There was something else different, that I couldn't have fully imagined twenty-three years ago: I was becoming a father. This was the other reason for my jukebox tardiness. Kathy and I were having a baby. When I learned the news back in February—just before the first anniversary of my jukebox scheme—I wondered if I should call the whole crazy idea off. But Kathy adopted the role of that long-suffering wife in *Field of Dreams*, encouraging me to follow my vision if it meant losing the family farm.

And so I left for Illinois much closer to my future than to the past I was seeking to recapture, and also quite remote from the key players of yesteryear. My father was 4,000 miles away, on a vacation in England, and my grandfather was buried in a cemetery just outside of Peoria. I couldn't bring back A. B. Bunch, buy him a beer, pass him the salt, and play what later became his all-time favorite song—"The Gambler" by Kenny Rogers—but I could at least summon his spirit by playing that jukebox one more time.

The faster I drove, the farther I fell behind. The route across central Illinois took much longer than I expected, since every podunk town of 5,000 or more now had a new string of traffic lights, thanks to the proliferation of Wal-Marts. By 3:30 P.M. I was passing the flag-draped front porches of Pekin, Illinois, and then a Caterpillar tractor plant with an endless parking lot that in better economic times would have been emptying just as I passed, sending hundreds of cars headed for the closest watering hole. On this day in 1992, there were only fifty or so cars there. The name of its cross street was Terminal Road.

I was just outside Banner, Illinois.

The 924 Club was hard to miss in Banner, a town of just 250 people. There were just four business establishments—the Banner Motel, Jerry's Motel (Lowest Rates for 50 Miles), the Sportsmen's Lounge, and the 924 Club. It was a roadhouse in the truest sense of the word: just a modest ranch-style building with white siding and a red shingle roof. A row of small windows sported signs for Pabst Blue Ribbon, Busch, and Miller Lite. There were just two other cars in the parking lot, and a Honda motorcycle; on one side of the building was an ice machine, on the other a small canopy and a sign advertising Sweet Corn. No person was there, just a golden retriever napping in the shade.

I looked around for a few minutes before I got up the nerve

to approach the white screen door. Above the knob, in grease pencil, was written the following, which is not a typo: TUBN HERE. My heart was pounding. Inside, it was just as dark as I remembered. There was no one behind the bar, but there were three customers, huddled intently around two clanging video games.

The jukebox was in the far corner, where I remembered it; it still glowed pale orange, but was now silent. The three customers—a middle-aged woman, a man in a half-buttoned flowered shirt, and a man in a business suit who looked more out of place than I did—and I warily looked one another up and down. Then I noticed the video game they were playing. It bore the legend AMUSEMENT GAME—MANUFACTURED IN THE USA. The man in the suit pushed a button, and three rows of cherries, oranges, and dollar signs whipped around, just like a slot machine in Las Vegas.

My childhood memory was a gambling den.

Disoriented by the darkness and this activity of questionable legality, I didn't head straight for the jukebox, as I had planned. I wanted to speak to the lady in charge, whom I knew to have the wonderful name of Agatha Upchurch.

"Is Agatha Upchurch here?" I asked the woman.

"Hey, Aggie!" the woman yelled.

From a back room, a woman who appeared to be about sixty-five ambled out slowly. Her cheeks were a healthy shade of pink, and their vitality contrasted with her eyes, which had a far-off gaze that seemed to be looking beyond the barroom, beyond Jerry's Motel, beyond the lazy Caterpillar factory, into a void. Her hair was a somewhat unnatural shade of soft red. A lit cigarette was dangling from her mouth.

I had spoken to Agatha Upchurch once before, about a week ago, on the phone from New York. I asked her if the 924 Club still had a jukebox. "Yes," she said. I asked her if she would be there the following Friday. "Yes," she said. I asked if I could talk with her. She paused for about ten seconds, then said "Okay."

Acting on that conversation, I had bought a round-trip train ticket from Philadelphia to Chicago, rented a car, and traveled nonstop for the last twenty-six hours.

Today, I gave her my full-blown, rambling speech about jukeboxes. As the much-anticipated machine kicked on with the unfamiliar twang of a steel guitar, I asked if she could spare five or ten minutes to tell me about the bar and about Banner.

There was a pause. "I've been here eighteen years." Then she fell silent again.

The interview proceeded clumsily. I learned that she and her late husband, Cotton Upchurch, had leased the bar most of that time, but that Agatha finally bought the place outright in 1991. I learned that she was born in Minneapolis and had lived in nearby Pekin, a town of about 30,000, before coming to Banner. The facts were pretty unspectacular.

"This is the place that used to get hit by trucks," she said.

I wasn't sure how to respond, but it seemed like we were finally onto something. "How many times did that happen?"

"Three times in fourteen months." Then Agatha Upchurch ambled slowly into the back room. I sat at the bar for an entire minute, wondering if that was the end of the interview, the end of my twenty-six-hour pilgrimage. Then she came back, with a book of articles by a local newspaper columnist that told the story of the 924 Club and the never-ending waves of assault by a convoy of trucks.

The 924 Club gets its name from its location at the junction of two main roads, Illinois 9 and U.S. 24, and while most of Illinois is flat as a vinyl record, this intersection is on a steep downgrade toward the Illinois River valley. Therein lies the problem. The tiny white roadhouse is close up against the main intersection, good for drop-in business . . . but it seems that a few eighteen-wheelers took the invitation too seriously.

The big outbreak of truck crashes seemed to take place during the early 1980s, and each had its own odd twist. My favorite was the coal truck that rounded the curve too fast and tilted on its side in the front parking lot, depositing its sooty cargo right up against the white screen door, piling the coal all the way up to the doorknob. A regular customer had to call his wife and explain that he couldn't come home, that he was being held hostage by a pile of coal.

"You lying sonuvabitch, you be home in five minutes!" said the wife, as she hung up the phone.

Another time it was a load of hogs that tipped over, and Cotton, Agatha, and the befuddled customers had to stage a miniroundup in the parking lot.

Incredibly, no one was seriously hurt during any of the truck onslaughts. The worst thing that happened was the time that a man dashed inside to buy a six-pack of beer to go, and left his wife in the car. Sure enough, a speeding lumber truck rounded the curve too fast, and a giant plank came through the rear windshield of the parked car, showering the woman with flying glass. Several times the trucks slammed into Cotton Upchurch's kitchen, which—thankfully—was always empty when the big rigs came flying. Nevertheless, word soon spread far and wide that drinking at the 924 Club was hazardous to your health. Business suffered. The customers who did stop by tended to congregate at the barstools on the far southeast side. Agatha Upchurch wanted her husband to sell the place.

"I'm so stubborn I think I'll stay here and get killed," Cotton Upchurch said back then.

Instead of terminating his lease for the 924 Club, Cotton Upchurch started lobbying every politician and bureaucrat that he knew to get the intersection fixed. One day a man from the Illinois Department of Transportation came down and proposed a giant mound of dirt between the highway and the 924 Club. Cotton Upchurch vetoed the plan.

"Instead of them coming through my kitchen wall, they'll be coming through the damned roof," he said.

By 1986, the state agreed to redesign the crossroads, moving the road away from Cotton Upchurch's front door. But Upchurch—the man who had dodged flying lumber planks and airborne hogs—had cancer by the time the first shovel was dug in the intersection of Routes 9 and 24. In October 1986, at 62, he passed away; he had just collected his first Social Security check. He died with the knowledge that no force was too powerful to take away his little roadhouse—not even gravity.

Meanwhile, I had yet to so much as inspect the jukebox, but the saga of the 924 Club and its demolition derby prompted me to call Kathy back in Pennsylvania, tell her I was safe. The only pay phone in Banner was across the street, on the porch of Jerry's Motel. Before I crossed Routes 9 and 24, I looked both ways for about a minute and a half.

Cotton Upchurch had the good sense to position his prized possession safely in the far southeast corner of the bar, far from all the truck traffic. And, I later learned, the same old jukebox, the one on which I had played Tommy James and Blood, Sweat and Tears, had been sitting there all these years—until just a year ago, when it was replaced with a spanking new Rowe/AMI that was all molded plastic, fairly unadorned except for a string of orange ball lights on the top. So the old jukebox was gone. Once again, the Rear Guard Baby Boomer was running a couple of steps behind. My one relief was that this jukebox, unlike every other new one I had seen, still played 45s—144 of them, and no CDs.

But not only the jukebox itself was different: I was in for one more surprise. As I looked down the rows of 45s, there was no evidence of Tommy James, no sign of a single Shondell. Instead there was Garth Brooks, George Jones, Alan Jackson, Dwight Yoakam, Marty Robbins, Hank Williams, Jr., Hank Williams, Sr.

The jukebox at the 924 Club had gone all-country.

Oh, there were a few pop songs sprinkled on there, soft stuff that wouldn't be too hard on the ears of the forty-somethings and fifty-somethings who kill time at the 924 Club: Eric Clapton's "Tears in Heaven," and, appropriately enough, Cher's "If I Could Turn Back Time." I even spotted one song that might have been a holdover from my old fishing days, Neil Diamond's "Sweet Caroline" from 1970. But I was no more likely to play that song in 1992 than I was back then.

The songs on the 924 Club's jukebox made me realize I couldn't turn back time either. Oddly enough, the first song that caught my eye was "Down at the Twist and Shout" by Mary Chapin-Carpenter, a woman I had attended college with in Rhode Island and who now was a nationally known country singer. The people making the jukebox music were now people I had literally grown up with.

That said, I liked the jukebox at the 924 Club. I'm not a huge country fan, but I enjoy the whiskey-throated traditionalism of George Jones or Dwight Yoakam, and I made sure to play one song by Kitty Wells, Patsy Cline's spiritual ancestor. It was called "Your Wild Life's Gonna Get You Down."

Country music is still more rooted in the individual song than in the "concept album" or CD of rock, and that's why Nashville is still pressing 45s, keeping 45 RPM jukeboxes alive in rural enclaves like Banner. In fact, jukeboxes are still popular enough in country-music bars that many of the songs at the 924 Club refer to them: "Jukebox Charlie" by Johnny Paycheck, "The Jukebox Played Along" by Gene Watson, "Jukebox in My Mind" by Alabama, and something by Travis Tritt called "If Hell Had a Jukebox."

Speaking of jukeboxes from Hell brings up the dreaded Billy Ray Cyrus issue.

In my initial conversation with Agatha Upchurch, I asked her what the most popular song was at the 924 Club. She couldn't remember the title right off.

"Hey, Bonnie," she called over to the one female customer. "What's the name of that 200?" referring to the selection number. "What's the name of that song?"

" 'Worm I Gun Live,' " Bonnie replied. ("Where Am I Gonna Live.")

"No, the other side."

" 'Achy Breaky Heart'?"

"That's it," Aggie said. " 'Achy . . .' "

" 'Breaky Heart,' " I finished, a little heartachey myself. How was I going to explain to Kathy and the other backers of my search for America's best jukebox that I had just traveled

1,200 miles, sleeping upright in the hard seat of an Amtrak train, to check out a record machine where the top song was by Nashville's Vanilla Ice?

The jukebox at the 924 Club clearly was not the Juke of the Covenant, but Kitty Wells was singing and happy hour was commencing. I was damn glad to be here.

Twenty-five years after my first visit, I was old enough now for barroom banter. The first Bannerian I met after Aggie was Donny Engle, who pulled his black-and-tan GMC pickup truck into the parking lot of the 924 Club at about 4:30 or so, as fast as he could get away from the sin and filth of the big city, Peoria, some twenty-five miles to the north. That's where Donny had found construction work, pouring concrete for the expansion of the Peoria Civic Center. It was tough work under a hot sun, and Donny's white T-shirt had patches of brown earth on it.

He was thin, and time and hard work had weathered his pale midwestern countenance somewhat. But the most noticeable thing about Donny Engle was his blue-and-white baseball cap. It read: "WANTED: Good woman who can clean and cook fish, sew, dig worms, and owns boat and motor: SEND PHOTO OF BOAT AND MOTOR." The word "WANTED" was covered with a large brown patch of dirt.

He walked in and plopped his obligatory pack of Camels— I didn't meet a single nonsmoker during five hours in Banner— on the Formica bar top.

His eyes met Aggie Upchurch, who stood behind a half-empty bottle of beer.

"Are you drunk already?" Donny Engle asked.

"I never get drunk," said Aggie.

"Bullshit. Let me have a bottle."

Then something strange happened. Aggie Upchurch placed a bottle of Bud in front of Donny Engle, and then handed him a dice cup. Donny rolled three dice on the table, then gave a quick look of disgust at the outcome and scooped them up. He then pulled out a couple of dollars for the brew and change. I sipped innocently on my Coke, trying to stay in my ten-year-old-boy cocoon. Things were going on at the 924 Club that I didn't want to know anything about. Over at the "amusement game," the man in the suit and tie was plugging away. I later learned that he was a prominent attorney from Peoria. There would be no interview.

I tried to make some small talk with Donny Engle.

"So what do you think of the jukebox here?"

"I like it."

"What's your favorite song?"

"Ricky Van Shelton." He paused. " 'Simple Man.' "

Donny Engle said he had been coming to the 924 Club for about fifteen years, and he said that things have changed. "People aren't as giving," he said. "We had benefits for people. Nobody asked for nothing." Banner may have changed, but Donny Engle's routine had not varied much, it seemed. After downing his cold Bud at the 924 Club, he would be heading to the other bar in town, the Sportsmen's Lounge, to see which buddies were anchored to its bar stools. Only then, once he was satisfied that he had checked out everything in the greater Banner area, could Donny Engle go home to his wife and three kids.

Donny Engle, the sandblasted construction worker from little Banner, Illinois, and I, the writer from Lower Makefield, Pennsylvania, had something in common. We didn't want to miss anything.

Now it was 4:45 P.M., and life in the 924 Club was proceeding, albeit in slow motion. Three new customers strolled in. They wore blue jeans and white T-shirts like Donny, only Donny's shirt was blindingly white compared to theirs. They all wore baseball caps, and two had long blond hair flowing behind.

Donny Engle gave them a look and said mockingly, "I know I'm getting the hell out of here." I had the same brief thought. A few minutes earlier, I had glanced at the bar's cash register, and a note right next to it: "Sheriff: 547-2277."

A few minutes later, though, the two newcomers were busily engaged in a conversation with the criminal attorney, who was finally taking a break from video slot game. Class distinctions didn't matter much in a place like the 924 Club, where everybody gets a roll of the dice, and everybody's entitled to seven songs for a dollar. Several times while I was there, I walked outside to use the phone or to get my camera from the car; invariably a pickup truck would slow down as it passed the 924 Club and the driver would honk his horn, just a way of saying hello.

In all my years of bar-hopping, I have never seen anyone honk their horn to say hello to a Houlihan's.

The only problem at the 924 Club seemed to be that more people were honking their horns than actually pulling into the parking lot. It seemed there were never more than eight or so patrons at the bar at any one time, which is not terrible in a town of only 250, but not so great for Friday Happy Hour, the time when most bars turn a profit.

When I had arrived at the tavern, one of my first questions for Agatha Upchurch had been about business.

"It's not as good as it used to be," she said.

That didn't surprise me in the least. I had always followed Peoria, my ancestral home, in the newspapers, and I knew that in 1992, times were tougher here than just about anyplace else in America. When I was ten years old, Peoria was still making three products that were essential to the day-to-day life and lubrication of the Heartland: Hiram Walker whiskey, Pabst Blue Ribbon beer, and, most important of all, Caterpillar tractors. There were Caterpillar plants everywhere you looked—up the Illinois River toward Chillicothe, fifteen miles out Interstate 74 on the road back toward New York in Morton, and the big one just five miles north of the 924 Club. In 1969, when I was ten, there were more than 20,000 people working for Caterpillar in the Peoria area alone.

Very few lives were untouched by the tentacles of Caterpillar Tractor. It was typical out there to meet people like Penny Foust, another bartender at the 924 Club, whose father had just retired from Caterpillar and who had three brothers on the payroll. My grandfather, A. B. Bunch, worked in the parts department in the East Peoria plant for 30 years. Even my dad, a confirmed egghead, spent a summer on the assembly line; a couple of summers later he was working in the Brooklyn Public Library and writing beatnik poetry, but he still had his UAW card.

In two decades it all went to hell. The Hiram Walker distillery went first, in 1981, putting almost 750 people out of work. Then the Pabst Blue Ribbon brewery in Peoria Heights and its 800 workers fell by the wayside in 1982, around the time that twenty-somethings discovered about Corona and limes. And Caterpillar Tractor and its decent paychecks were not much of a match for the Japanese tractor companies like Komatsu, which paid lower wages. There was a bitter strike by the UAW against Caterpillar in 1982, and when it was all over, months later, the workforce was about half what it had been. Then, in the spring of 1992, there was another strike, but the economy had gotten so bad that management bullied the workers into returning to their jobs with no contract. That meant no raise and an uncertain future, and so the 10,000 who are left at Caterpillar in greater Peoria, the handful of cars that I had seen at the factory outside of Banner, were saving their money. Pabst Blue Ribbon at the 924 Club was no longer in the budget.

If that wasn't enough, there was another reason why business was slow at places like the 924 Club. This is the way that Agatha Upchurch described it to me:

"The laws changed."

The laws changed. Although I didn't realize it yet on that afternoon, I would hear the same phrase again and again, in Chicago corner bars and from jukebox distributors in rural Virginia, as I searched for Jukebox America. The laws changed. They didn't have to say which laws; everyone knew that in the early 1980s, drunk driving went from being a slap-on-the-wrist offense to a real felony that could land you in jail. All bars lost business, but especially those like the 924 Club, the roadhouses, for what is a roadhouse without a road? As Agatha Upchurch described what happened—as others in the bar and jukebox business would—there was never a sense that drunk-driving penalties were good, or that any lives had been saved, even though the lone female customer, Bonnie, had told me a story earlier in the afternoon about a drunken man whom Cotton Upchurch had refused to serve one afternoon and whose trip to another roadhouse—not to mention his life—ended when he drove into a ditch.

There was only a sense that the time before the crackdown on drunken driving was an era of lost glory, of good times that taken away by mean bureaucrats.

For all these reasons and more, a way of life was slowly disappearing in central Illinois. Bonnie told me, and others around the bar all confirmed it, that recently there had been as many as five taverns operating in Banner, maybe even six. That's one bar—better yet, one jukebox—for every fifty people. And here I was living in Lower Makefield, Pennsylvania, a township with 25,000 residents, with no jukebox at all.

There were so many bars in Banner that today people still argue about their names. Of course there were the two that are still left, the 924 Club and the Sportsmen's Lounge, where they still have rock 'n' roll on the jukebox and draw a younger, rowdier crowd. There was a joint called the Banner Inn, and another place that was named the Duck Inn, where the motel now stands. There was a place called Neff's, and, according to one source, some dive called Macavitch's that later become a Phillips 66 station. Of course, not all the customers came from Banner; many were duck hunters who stayed in a row of cabins down near the Illinois River that were recently demolished by the state. Others were early-morning fishermen like my grandfather, A. B. Bunch.

I wanted to know what happened to all the other places in Banner. Bonnie and Penny Faust, a bartender, told me to ask an older couple that had pulled up to the bar, a couple that had once owned their prime competitor, the Sportsmen's Lounge, before selling it a few years back.

"So what happened to all the other bars?" I asked, expecting a long discourse.

"The owners just all died," the woman said. "And nobody bought them."

And that was it. I looked over at Agatha Upchurch. She was taking a deep drag on her cigarette, leaning halfway over the

Formica bar top, staring forlornly into that deep vacuum that was past the jukebox and past the muddy Illinois River.

Death had deprived Banner not only of its tavern owners but also of some of its stalwart customers—among them my grandfather, A. B. Bunch.

If A. B. Bunch were still alive today, I would do nothing but talk with him for hours, so I could hear every story about Missouri farm life in the early twentieth century, about Kansas City and the Roaring Twenties, about the 1930s and the industrialization of America, about all the jukeboxes in central Illinois and what happened to them. But my grandfather suffered a stroke in 1983 and died without warning. I was twenty-four years old, still too young and too stupid to appreciate the treasure that was buried forever in a cemetery on the outskirts of Peoria.

A. B. Bunch was like a fifth-grade American history textbook come to life. He was born in 1906 on the family farm on the plains of western Missouri, about two hours southeast of Kansas City. There was no indoor plumbing on the farm, and back in that summer of 1969 I remember listening with amazement to stories about how my great-grandmother would routinely behead a chicken for dinner when company was coming.

What happened in the 1920s, when A. B. Bunch became a man, was always a little vague, and it wasn't until I was a young adult myself that I learned why. My dad tried to explain it to me once, and he struggled for the right words, until he finally blurted it out: "Well, I guess you could say he was a petty criminal."

My grandfather, who by the end of his life was driving a Lincoln Continental and living on a large spread of land with a heated swimming pool on the side, a petty criminal? Dad laid out the evidence. Throughout the Calvin Coolidge era, my grandfather had roamed America and its cities, Kansas City, Chicago, even New York City (I sometimes conjure up this farmboy in the Big Apple as I stroll past the Empire State Building to work each day), stealing mason jars of beer from illegal speakeasies and hiding from the law underneath the city sidewalks, ice-cold brew snuck under his shirt.

In the early 1950s, after A. B. Bunch had settled down and had a wife and three children, he took them to California for a summer vacation, following the two-lane neon-lit pathway of the old U.S. highways. They were on the outskirts of Dodge City, Kansas, when he turned to my dad and said: "I know this place. I've been here before."

My dad, who was about fifteen, looked around. There was nothing but fields of wheat.

In a confession Dad could hardly have expected, my grandfather said he had been arrested once in Dodge City for loitering. The next day, the sheriff brought him to this wheat field.

"Look over here," the sheriff had told A. B. Bunch. "Dodge City is *this* way. You go *that* way."

There had always been an air of mystery about my grandfather. His Christian name was Alfred Bryan Bunch. Some folks called him Al, and as a child that's what I was told to call him: Grandpa Al. But his wife, my Uncle Dale, and others always called him A. B., and so that's how I think of him today. But I knew other relatives called him Uncle Bryan. And in the 1920s, when he left the farms of western Missouri to roam the speakeasies of America, they called him something else.

They called him "Toughie" Bunch.

It's odd, but I can see some parallels between the story of A. B. "Toughie" Bunch, the beer-thieving high school dropout, and myself, the college boy now searching for America's best jukebox. Like most other folks, rambling Toughie Bunch reached a crossroads a couple of decades into life: He met probably the only woman in America who could tame him, a tough-minded twenty-seven-year-old widow named Arline Hammond who was bent on a college-administration career forty years ahead of her time. He started to take on conventional work, selling shoes in St. Louis—where my father was born in 1936—and then following the economic currents to Peoria, Illinois, where Caterpillar Tractor was hiring.

But A. B. Bunch still felt that neon road-sign buzz. He

"settled down," but he never stopped cruising the flat earth of the Midwest, plumbing every river for hypothetical bass; later in life, when he and Arline became the owners of Midstate College, they continued to criss-cross the prairie, convincing lifelong farmers that their daughters would be safe as students in Peoria— "Sin City."

That was how a ten-year-old boy ended up watching his grandfather unload a salt shaker into a pitcher of beer at 9:30 A.M. in a darkened roadhouse—and how he learned all about jukeboxes. In 1969, at the age of 63, A. B. Bunch, who had ridden the rails to New York, Kansas City, and intermediate points a half-century before, still had the wanderlust. He wanted to trade the latest dirty jokes and fish stories.

It's kind of sad that my most vivid memories of my grandfather are from a decade later, the summer of 1979, when I was twenty and A. B. Bunch was seventy-three. He had long suffered from diabetes, and in the mid-1970s his left leg was amputated just below the knee. I was a college student so desperate for any job with a newspaper that I took a summer job out west in Peoria with a small weekly called the *Penny Press*, where I would be allowed to write one story a week if I pasted ads the rest of the time. That meant living with my Grandpa Al and Grandma Arline for about ten weeks.

But things had changed. With a wooden leg, it wasn't easy for my grandfather to go out fishing at 5 A.M. like he used to do. So he puttered around the big house all day, fixing toasters and cars, whatever was broke at the time. After dinner, he and my grandmother ate cookies with whipped cream (Kathy thinks I'm making this part up, but I'm not), and drank several glasses of Andre champagne. The rest of the time, A. B. Bunch crabbed at me, about how I couldn't fix things, about how I wasn't scoring with the women the way that old Toughie Bunch did when he was twenty, about other things too petty to remember.

And then there was "The Gambler."

A few days after I arrived in Peoria, my grandfather asked me about music.

"Do you like that old 'Gambler'?" He was talking about the popular song by Kenny Rogers.

"Yeah, that's a good song," I said. Relatively speaking, the song *was* better than anything else Kenny Rogers would ever record in the 1970s or upcoming 1980s. Really, I was into the Cars and Talking Heads in 1979, but "Psycho Killer" was just too complicated to explain to a seventy-three-year-old man from west-central Missouri.

The next day, I was out by the swimming pool, and my grandfather's old hi-fi, which dated from sometime during the Eisenhower administration, creaked to life. Kenny Rogers was singing "The Gambler," but it was in slow motion, a 45 RPM disc turning at roughly 41 RPM. "You got to knoooow when to foooold 'em . . . " Kenny Rogers sang, deep and slow. The record clicked off, and I felt a sense of relief, until the automatic replay arm touched down again. And again.

I don't know how many times I heard "The Gambler" that afternoon. It might have been twelve times. It might have been twenty times. It might have been covered by the Bill of Rights proscription on "cruel and unusual punishment."

I thought maybe it was the wooden leg at first, and so after the fifth or sixth time I offered to go in the house and change the record. My grandfather gave me a sour look.

"Don't you like the old 'Gambler'?"

Old Kenny Rogers himself couldn't have heard "The Gambler" as many times as I did in the summer of 1979. It might have been 500 times, maybe 1,000—who knows? I knew when to walk away already, knew when to run. I had no money to speak of, but I finally parted with $4.99 to buy that summer's hottest record, "Get the Knack." On a good day, my grandfather would putter in the garage long enough for me to beat him to the hi-fi.

I can still hear that LP spinning around at 29 RPM. "My-yyyy Sharooooona . . . " Then, as I floated in the deep end of the pool, I'd hear a scratch, and a pause.

"Yooooo gooottt ttooo knoooo . . . " Grandpa invariably

forgot to change the hi-fi knob from 45 to 33⅓, and, even worse, forgot to notice. I've have to dry off and go inside to fix it.

Looking back, I'm sure my grandfather longed for the old days, for some dive like the 924 Club with "The Gambler" on the jukebox, unlimited supplies of beer and salt, and Caterpillar cronies to tell fish tales with. Instead, he was stuck around that chlorinated swimming pool, listening to that one 45, the only contemporary record he owned. That's why "The Gambler," corny as it was, meant so much to this crabby old septuagenarian.

He didn't know when to fold 'em.

In fact, he didn't until a July night in 1983, two days before his fiftieth wedding anniversary. In seeming good health for a seventy-seven-year-old amputee, he went to bed peacefully, and the way he died always reminded me of that song's dopey ending: "Somewhere in the darkness, the gambler he broke even."

But we never got a chance to make up for that 29 RPM summer we spent together, and I never got to ask him all about Route 66 and his Spike Jones 78s and the jukeboxes he'd met in his day. But I felt I was following in his footsteps in my own strange way, casting for jukeboxes instead of small-mouth bass. And now, thirteen years after our lost summer of 1979, I wanted to play "The Gambler" till it wore out. But "The Gambler" had moved on a long time ago, replaced on the jukebox by an "Achy Breaky Heart."

In theory, customers like A. B. Bunch would have been replaced by their sons. But many of them—like my dad—decided there was more to life than the Caterpillar assembly line and moved away.

That meant that the 924 Club had to compete for the few souls who were left behind, and, to my surprise, there was a whole slate of activities to woo the smaller customer base. If I could have stayed until Sunday, Aggie Upchurch was planning a free fish fry, and several customers were planning to come by with their teenaged children. Then there was the matter of the "bonacali."

"You should come by tomorrow night," Aggie Upchurch told me. "We're going to have bonacali."

I gave a blank stare.

"It's an Eye-talian dip," Aggie said, somewhat bewildered that this man from New York, where there were millions of Eye-talians, didn't know the national dip. "You dip your bread in it. Or you can dip vegetables."

I grew up eating Italian food in places like Riglioni's back in New York, and I married a woman whose four grandparents had all been born in Italy before moving to Philadelphia. I had never heard of bonacali, which is apparently some sort of oily dip made largely from crushed anchovies. It didn't sound like the kind of thing that would rope in the pickup trucks now whistling by the lot of the 924 Club. I wondered if they'd ever heard of Buffalo wings in Banner.

But that was tomorrow night. This Friday night, if I stayed at the 924 Club until seven o'clock, I would witness a momentous event in the long history of the tavern. For this night would be the debut of Dale Evans (his real name), the Singing Bartender.

There were signs posted in every corner of the L-shaped bar proclaiming his arrival, each accompanied with a smiling picture of this man with a cowgirl's name—a middle-aged fellow with just a touch of gray in his wavy brown hair, wearing a baggy sweatshirt.

For the past few years, Dale Evans had been building a following in the greater Pekin, Illinois, metropolitan area, singing and bartending, simultaneously, in a string of local bars. Now, Aggie Upchurch had booked him for the 924 Club, and there was an air of excitement. Penny Faust told me that Dale Evans spent half the year in central Illinois and half the year in Texas, and it was her belief that he lived in a Winnebago camper along with the 250 tapes he sang along to each night. I tried to imagine this man's rootless existence, dropping anchor each night in some dive in a place like Banner, and I knew that I had to stay long enough to meet him.

The wait wasn't long. It was about 6:45 P.M. when I heard

a buzzing from the four or five patrons sitting closest to the screen door.

"Hey, Will, he's here!" Penny Faust shouted over to me. For Banner, this was like the Beatles at Idewild Airport.

I ambled out to the parking lot, and saw a man climbing out of a brown Winnebago. He was the man I had seen on the poster behind the bar, but about fifteen years older. His hair was steel gray, and his hard, ruddy face looked like his publicity shot after a long day in the wilting prairie heat. His cowboy shirt was sky blue, with silver tabs depicting a horseshoe on each collar, and he wore a string tie with a turquoise pendant. In one hand was a large-size coffee cup, while the other held the obligatory pack of cigarettes.

Dale Evans, the Singing Bartender, was reporting for work.

The Singing Bartender had no roadies. After lugging in his sound system, his wireless microphone, and his prized possession—a box of 250 cassettes, each with the lead vocals electronically deleted—Dale Evans was happy to pull up a bar stool and chat for a few minutes.

"So, do you really live in the Winnebago?" I asked.

Dale Evans gave me a look that said something like, "Who'd want to do a crazy thing like that?" He explained that he was staying at his aunt's house over in Pekin for a month or two. He had a routine, in fact, two months or so in Pekin, followed by a couple of months in an apartment he rented in Dallas.

Yet Dale had been on the road almost continuously since he joined the Navy in 1952. He spent two decades in the Armed Services; one of the myriad bases where he was stationed was near Schenectady, New York, and now his two sons, close to my age, were in a rock band in upstate New York called Hevansent—a bad pun on the family name.

His turning point came one night in 1978 in a restaurant called the Swiss Chalet in Baldwinsville, New York, an upstate town near Syracuse. Dale had tried managing bowling alleys after leaving the Air Force, but now he was making some money tending bar. One night, he was closing up when the jukebox kicked in with the old Marty Robbins ballad "El Paso." Dale Evans burst into song, at full volume, into an icy glass, "Down in the south Texas town of El Paso, I fell in love with a Mexican girl . . . " There was only one customer left.

"Hey mister," the customer said. "You got a hell of a microphone there."

Thus an idea was born. Dale Evans became the Singing Bartender, pouring Genessee Cream Ale and washing dirty glasses while he belted out along with George Jones and Hank Williams on the jukebox, trying to drown out their vocals. Eventually he worked his way back to a hotel lounge in Wichita Falls, Texas, but in 1987 the hotel went bankrupt. By 1989, he was back in Pekin, the town where he was born, doing his little act at a place called Miller's Arlington. The Pekin newspaper did a profile of him, and soon Dale Evans, the Singing Bartender, was much in demand in the little roadhouses along the Illinois River.

But the once-symbiotic relationship between Dale Evans and a jukebox had changed, thanks to technology. In the early 1980s, somebody told him about a new gadget called a "vocal eliminator." The device allowed Dale Evans to make a cassette recording of a song, with all the steel guitar and strings intact, but with George Jones and Marty Robbins suddenly plunged into silence. Dale Evans didn't need a jukebox anymore. It was a clear case of transubstantiation. He *was* the jukebox.

The main thing I had wanted to ask Dale—now fifty-eight years old, divorced, more than a thousand miles from his adult children—was whether it got lonely being a human jukebox, traveling from roadhouse to roadhouse.

"I enjoy people," he said. "That's why I do neighborhood bars. I like to do it in places that don't have room for a band."

In the 1960s, a record machine with the latest 45s from Nashville and the Brill Building was major-league entertainment in a minor-league town, but that was before the satellite dish (the local distributor was the only thriving business I saw on the ten-mile highway between Pekin and Banner) and The Nashville Network. Now Billy Ray Cyrus was appearing every hour in the TV rooms of Banner, and so people needed more than jukebox enticement to go visit the barely breathing 924 Club. They needed Dale Evans, the human jukebox.

Today, in Banner, Illinois, population 250, our paths were fated to intersect. I had traveled 1,000 miles west, a person in search of a jukebox. Dale Evans had traveled 1,000 miles north, a jukebox in search of people.

At seven o'clock sharp, the jukebox at the 924 Club was shut off for the night. Dale Evans stepped behind the bar, brandishing his footlong wireless microphone, which looks something like a big flashlight. He pressed the play button on his cassette deck, and started singing. "Tiny Bubbles" by Don Ho.

I looked around the smokey twilight of the bar. Bonnie was back in her usual spot, sitting about eighteen inches from the Singing Bartender, puffing away on a cigarette. Further down the bar, two middle-aged woman were intently dissecting a large pizza—where that came from in little Banner was a mystery—and largely ignoring the music. Including myself, owner Agatha Upchurch, bartender Penny Foust, and the Singing Bartender, there were maybe ten people in the 924 Club.

By the second number, Dale Evans filled a glass with ice, but with so few customers and with Penny on duty there wasn't much call for his bartending skills. After the song ended, Bonnie offered to buy him a beer.

"I could use one already," Dale Evans said.

Just like the manufactured jukebox, Dale Evans, the Human Jukebox, didn't have Kenny Rogers's "The Gambler" on his playlist. I couldn't bring back A. B. Bunch that Friday afternoon, and I didn't even get to hear his favorite song. But by revisiting the 924 Club, I had done my best to carry on the Bunch family traditions—making a new friend or two, trading some fish stories, listening to a Kitty Wells song, getting out of the house. I still couldn't fix a car or a toaster, and I would never score with as many women, but on that lazy evening in Banner I thought my grandfather would finally have been proud of me.

I ordered up a beer myself—something I'd never done before in my twenty-three-year history with the 924 Club—and Penny handed me a red, white, and blue Pabst Blue Ribbon and a little six-ounce glass. I grabbed a salt shaker—there was one every twenty inches or so—and sprinkled a little in. The beer foamed up over the top of the tiny glass.

I put down two bucks and got three quarters in change, good for five songs on the jukebox if it hadn't been shut off for the Singing Bartender. I glanced over at the idle record machine, but my view was blocked by a tall man at the end of the bar, the kind of younger customer Agatha Upchurch would need to attract to stay in business. He had a long, stringy beard and deep-set eyes; like the other men I had seen—except the criminal lawyer—he was wearing a baseball cap. His carried a silhouette of a buxom, reclining woman, and it read: "You are cordially invited to join our intercourse club. No fees. No dues."

Now the Singing Bartender was singing "Mr. Bojangles," a song that was probably on the jukebox back when I was there in the early 1970s. I took a sip from the salty glass. It tasted like a margarita that had been sitting out for four or five hours.

Dale Evans was singing: "The dog up and died, the dog up and died—after twenty years he still weeps." I took a longer, bitter swig and tried to imagine what Toughie Bunch would have thought of all of this.

Chapter 4

....

Mannish Boy

At 3:30 P.M. on a hazy August Saturday on North Clark Street in Chicago, I was standing at the front entrance to a club called The Wild Hare & Singing Armadillo Frog Sanctuary. The bar was the size of a small warehouse, a cavernous room with a twenty-foot ceiling, and every square inch was packed with sweaty, sunbaked human flesh. On a tiny stage, about 500 shoehorned bodies away, a band called Grizzard was churning out a pulsating reggae beat. With each pulse, the wave of humanity swayed to the breeze of heavy bass guitar.

My friend Adam from New York City had joined me on my jukebox adventure. We had emerged from the friendly confines of Wrigley Field, a place where we thought we could recapture some of the magic of 1969 by watching our favorite team, the Mets, do battle against the hated Cubs. But this was not 1969—my trip to Banner the day before had proved that—and the Mets' bullpen had blown the game in the 9th. Within moments, 36,000 gloating Cubs fans had staked a claim to every square foot of breathing space in the sports bars and music clubs that line North Clark Street. They had packed the Cubby Bear, which is catercorner from the old ivy-lined ballfield, and about

600 people were bumping biceps as they tried to swill beer to the sound of Meat Loaf. Next door at a joint called Sluggers ("Welcome, Mets Fans"—I feared the sign was some sort of evil trap) there were yet another 600 Budweiser-drenched souls. And then we tried to squeeze our way into this place called The Wild Hare & Singing Armadillo Frog Sanctuary.

I had never seen so much rowdy fun at one time in my life, and certainly never on a cloudy Saturday afternoon. As we shimmied into the front door, a comely blonde woman grabbed my friend Adam—a proud bachelor—by the arm, ostensibly to guide his way. She massaged his arm for about five seconds.

Adam's eyes were on fire, like popping orbs of some cartoon character. "Hey," he exclaimed, brimming with gusto. "Do you want to stay and get a beer?"

I felt like Carry Nation without an ax. "We can't stay here," I said, and I made a sour look to try to emphasize my resolve. "There's no jukebox here."

I don't want to give anyone the impression that I'm a teetotalling, claustrophobic reggae-hater. On 9,999 days out of the last 10,000, I would have ordered up a Bud right there and knocked elbows with such a throng, even this throng of hated Cubs fans. But this was supposed to be Day 10,000, the day I was going to dig through the muck and odor of smelted steel and slaughtered bovines until I found the real Chicago—a place I had been looking for all my life.

From that snowy night the Spirit in the Sky had steered me into the search for America's best jukebox, Chicago had been one of the cornerstones of my itinerary. For many years, the city has been the home of two of the three greatest manufacturers of jukeboxes—Rock-Ola and Seeburg—and so I didn't really see how I could avoid the Second City. But while I had arranged a tour of the Rock-Ola factory—now removed to a suburban zip code—for my last day in Chicago, I also had grandiose plans for a two-day expedition that might uncover the mystical Juke of the Covenant as well. For one thing, the city is a font of music lore:

many of the greatest jukebox howlers, like Muddy Waters, Willie Dixon, Bo Diddley, Chuck Berry, and even Fontanella "Rescue Me" Bass emerged from the corner dives of the South Side onto classic 45s like Waters's "Mannish Boy." Most of them were recorded by Phil and Leonard Chess. But, deep down, I knew the real reason I was headed to Chicago was something so fundamental, so much at the core of my search for America's best jukebox that it took me a long time even to articulate.

For most, Chicago means Michael Jordan and *Bob Newhart* reruns, but to me the city was more like a theme park of smokestack mythology. I didn't fully understand this concept myself until one illuminating night in that jukebox-hunting year of 1992 when it came to me—and this is the honest-to-goodness truth—in a dream.

In the dream I had just been to the Windy City, and was on my way back home to somewhere flat and Ohio-ish, when it dawned on me that I had to turn around and head back to Chicago. Soon, in fabulously abbreviated dream time, I was cutting through the cornfields of Indiana, passing the exit for South Bend, where a large football stadium loomed on my left. Four seconds later, I was in what looked like an industrial Disneyland, with smokestacks replacing the giant castle. It was Gary, Indiana, the city that gave us both Michael Jackson and acid rain, but I still felt lost. On the horizon was the plain 1950s lettering of the Chicago Skyway, the Main Street of American steel-mill rust, but I couldn't find the entrance ramp. I couldn't get to Chicago.

I woke up in a cold sweat.

It was in the early morning haze that I realized I had been trying to get to Chicago for thirty-three years. It was when I was a toddler, just two or three years old, that my mom and dad started lugging me back to Illinois once a year to see our relatives. Superhighways like I-80 and I-74, which today can whisk you between New York and Peoria, were still figments of some Washington bureaucrat's imagination, and so we took the New York Central railroad to Chicago. Then, for a few years, we drove the northern route, filling the coffers of New Jersey, Pennsylvania, Ohio, and Indiana at toll plazas until we reached that infamous Chicago Skyway. To my prekindergarten mind, Gary and the Chicago Skyway were the most incredible places I had ever seen, New York City included. There were so many smokestacks, as infinite as the twinkling of the Milky Way, far off into the flat horizon. The sky was some color that could never be reproduced, a blackish purple, and the windows of our Ford Galaxy 500 were powerless against that odor. And the Chicago Skyway—a road, for ten miles, in the air!

It was a sense of awe I could never quite recapture. When I was ten or eleven, we stayed with my grandparents in the then-swank Palmer House for a night or two, but this was the sterile Miracle Mile, and the haze of the Skyway was a far-off fire. It wasn't enough. Then, for fifteen years, nothing. When I was twenty-six, I wrote newspaper stories about traffic on Long Island, and I conned my editors into sending me to Chicago to do a story on the Minutemen, state workers who keep the roadways clear during rush hour. I had exactly eighteen hours in Chicago, and I frantically ate disappointing ribs at a place called Carson's and saw a blues band on North Halsted, which allowed me two hours of sleep before the morning rush. It wasn't enough. Two years later, I flew to Chicago en route to visiting my grandmother Arline—wife of the earlier-dissected A. B. Bunch—for her eightieth birthday, and made a mad fifty-minute dash out to the South Side for some authentic ribs from a bulletproof-window place called Leon's. It wasn't enough. As bizarre fate would have it, Arline died four days after my return flight touched down in New York. And so I was back in Chicago, killing time, a week later. I drove around for an hour or two, eating Lithuanian food in Boss Richard Daley's old neighborhood of Bridgeport.

It wasn't enough.

This search for America's best jukebox was clearly the answer to another of the long-unsolved riddles in my life—Chicago. The Chicago Skyway was the metaphor—one hundred feet in the air, never touching the surface. Now I was getting off the Skyway, into the shadows of Chicago's neighborhoods, looking for the source of the smoke, the aroma, the place where steel, steaks, and singles were made. It didn't even bother me that—as

I passed through Gary on the Broadway Limited at about 9 A.M. on this August morning in 1992—the sky was clear blue and many of the mills were guarded by tall stands of weeds. That weedy scene was a foreshadowing any amateur movie buff would have understood, but I was blissfully oblivious. I *knew* I was finally going to find what I was missing in Chicago.

But the beer-swilling, Cub-crazed crowd that filled North Clark Street wasn't part of my Chicago plan. I had researched the Windy City for months, compiling a list of about a dozen bars that were reputed to have great jukeboxes—none in the immediate vicinity of Wrigley Field. Furthermore, we were supposed to meet a local guide—a *Chicago Sun-Times* reporter and author named Neil Steinberg, and his lawyer wife, Edie—who would advise us on the city's colorful neighborhoods and seedy bars. He had helped by uncovering a not-too-stale clipping from the *Sun-Times* in which the paper's music critic listed his ten favorite jukeboxes.

After a fifteen-minute cab ride toward Lake Michigan, Adam and I arrived at Neil's place, a grandiose duplex apartment with a spiral staircase that probably would have cost about $10,000 a month in New York. Neil, whom I'd never met before, greeted us at the door wearing shorts, a T-shirt, and a flowery shirt on top—he looked like he was en route to a luau. A few seconds later, Edie descended down the spiral staircase like some 1950s television starlet in a stylish white dress—she looked ready for a night at the El Morocco.

The complete failure to synchronize our wardrobes made me wonder if any of us knew what the hell we were getting into, but then I decided maybe this was the right approach for the jukebox underbelly of Chicago: we were ready for anything.

"You're not going to believe this, but I left my ten-best list on my desk at work," said Neil. We realized we would lose too much time retrieving it, so I pulled out my notes—a magazine clipping, a couple of guidebooks, a few phone tips—and quickly tried to figure out an adhoc itinerary.

For a half hour we paddled upstream against Chicago's one-way streets, virtually entangled in a spider web of freight lines and El tracks that recalled the urban grime I remembered so fondly from my youth. Eventually, we found ourself cruising among rows of two-story brick houses in Wicker Park, a quasi-hip neighborhood where twenty-three-year-old slackers live among hard-working Latinos.

We were looking for the Riptide Lounge, which *Chicago Magazine* had described as "a dim, cozy, neighborhood bar with an authentic period feel . . . " We were finally just a half-block away when Adam spotted a different joint—a well-repaired little shotgun shack on the right side of the street, with no apparent name but a blue neon musical note as an outdoor sign.

"That place looks cool," called Adam from the backseat. "Do you want to check it out? I'll bet it has a jukebox."

I threw Adam a dirtier look than the frown I'd given at the reggae bar—I wanted spontaneity in my jukebox search, but not chaos. I was determined to stick with our short list of jukebox tips.

Thirty seconds later, we pulled up to a weedy corner hard against the Kennedy Expressway, a seedy urban vista framed by a modern Shell station. The Riptide Lounge was in a two-story brownstone across the street from the gas station. There was no sign of human activity in the building except for three—count 'em, three—stark signs that each said Beware of Dog.

The Riptide Lounge was closed, shuttered tight.

"Okay, no problem," I said. "Let's check out Danny's"—another colorful-sounding joint that was just three blocks away.

So we turned around to go the three blocks west on Armitage, but there was still the problem of the shotgun shack with the blue note and the neon Harp and Bass Ale signs that stood in between, like a stray enemy tank.

"We really should check it out," said Adam from the back seat.

"Okay, okay," I said, so the four of us opened the door to this wood-frame structure, and were hit with a stainless-steel-and-Formica vision that looked like every beer commercial's idea of a nightspot. The bar was long and black; the bar stools were black; the small tables were black, illuminated only by wisps of inert, gaseous blue. There was a mural with three nude women—Pop-Art porn—behind the bar.

The bar was named the Blue Note, and it seemed pretty cool.

Too cool, in fact, for customers. There was a young guy, a Latino, in a T-shirt, staring morosely into a draft beer, and an attractive blonde woman—did Adam know something?—behind the bar.

I wandered through the blue blackness to the rear and the pale light of the Blue Note's jukebox—a spanking new CD model, of course. I started punching the button to flip through the selections, and, much to my surprise, the owners of the Blue Note had found a way to make a CD jukebox almost appealing to an anti-technology crank like me, by cramming it full of really offbeat selections. There were Clarence "Gatemouth" Brown, Clarence Carter, "Truckin'" with Albert Collins, Slim Harpo, compilations of contemporary blues from Chicago's Alligator Records.

It might have been fun to stay, but the blackness on a bright August afternoon, and the dearth of customers didn't seem so cool—they were downright numbing. While I was studying the jukebox, Adam was engaging the sole customer in conversation.

"This used to be a place called Jim's," the man said. "It used to be really wild. It used to be real." He put his money down on the black bar and headed for the light.

I should have realized trouble when I saw it, but I pushed on, around the block to Danny's, which had been compared to "a friend's arty hovel." It, too, was closed. The time had come to move on, to check out the South Side of Chicago—the "baddest part of town."

Chicago's South Side has been the spawning ground for three generations of the blues—from Willie Dixon to Li'l Ed and the Blues Imperials—as well as for at least as many generations of urban neglect. We drove under the shadows of the Loop's monolithic skyscrapers onto the Dan Ryan Expressway until we faced a horizon of drab brick apartment houses—it reminded me of a trip to Moscow a decade earlier—that was broken only by the light towers of the new Comiskey Park.

The Dan Ryan Expressway slices though some of the poorest zip codes in America. With an incredibly high crime rate, the South Side is not the kind of area where you'd want to run out of gas—especially if you're a foreign carload of white yuppies in Hawaiian shirts, party dresses, and assorted high-priced gear from Banana Republic. And yet there we were at about South 35th Street or so when Neil's gas light went on. The needle was on empty. From the backseat, there was audible mumbling about Tom Wolfe.

Luckily, there was a gas station at the top of the South 43rd Street offramp. Within seconds, we were descended upon by the burned-out civilians of the Reagan-Bush recession: a woman offered to pump our self-service gas for a small fee, while platoons of twelve-year-old boys roamed the service-station lot, looking to wash windows for spare quarters. It seemed like there were no jobs coming into the South Side, just a few stranded motorists, and now some crazy white guy who was looking for a jukebox.

Gassed up, we headed east toward Lake Michigan on South 43rd Street, now called Muddy Waters Drive: it was a sad tribute of a street, heavily dotted with pawn shops and iron-gated liquor stores. Then our destination, the New Checkerboard Lounge, crept up on the right, with a Budweiser sign extending from a low-rise brick building that looked like an auto garage—on closer inspection, part of it *was* a garage. The Checkerboard used to be run by the legendary bluesman Buddy Guy, and it's still a popular nightspot for black-jacketed Eurotrash to mingle with meat packers from the South Side so they can hear their blues unadultered by the uptown glitz. The publicity chief for Alligator Records had told me it also had the best blues jukebox in Chicago.

Neil found a parking space right in front, just as a man emerged from the adjacent garage.

"Here, why don't you park your car in the garage. It's only $3."

The four of us looked at each other. Why pay to park when we had a free space on the street?

The man proceeded to tell us why. "This is a pretty rough neighborhood," he said. "You wouldn't want someone to break into your car and take your radio?"

There's always a thin line between friendly advice and a protection racket, and the four of us—three cynical reporters and a lawyer—saw the latter. I decided to run inside the New Checkerboard Lounge to see if this jukebox—if any jukebox—was worth such a hassle. I walked briskly inside and straight to the back, past about a dozen customers. At the rear was something I didn't expect: A CD jukebox that was nothing like the relic that the Alligator Records man described. The first choice that caught my eye was Michael Jackson's "Dangerous," and it didn't get much better; while there were some chestnuts from bluesmen like Kenny Neal and Magic Slim, I stopped flipping when I hit Michael Bolton.

The jukebox at the New Checkerboard Lounge was awful. And I was relieved, because that meant Neil could pull away with his car intact. I took a quick look around. In a front-corner nook of the bar, a cloud of thick smoke hung over a table where four or five old-timers were engaged in a high-stakes poker game. I zoomed in for a closer look, and one of the players was wearing a cowboy hat and one of those black eye masks like the Lone Ranger.

For a split second, I wondered what would happen if I tried to join the game ("Not so fast there, Kemosabe," I'd say, as I'd pull the stack of chips toward me) but almost instantly thought better of it and jogged back to the getaway car. The thought ran through my mind that here, as in the 924 Club the day before, bargoing Americans preferred gambling their dollars away to surrendering them to a jukebox.

After the New Checkerboard Lounge, believe it or not, things went downhill.

Army and Lou's was a soul-food restaurant alleged to have a great jukebox—and it was getting to the time when a plate of collard greens would have hit the spot—but what we got was a large sign in the front window saying Closed for Remodeling: Watch for Our Reopening.

After an incongruous dinner at a weinerschnitzel joint called the Berghoff, we hit the trail again. I insisted on returning to the Riptide Lounge, trio of killer dogs be damned. We met another couple there, and walked into a film-noir kind of bar with red lava lamps, a fish tank, a stainless steel jukebox (finally!), another Beware of Dog sign—and no customers.

I plugged in four quarters and started looking for my ten selections. There were classics, Patsy's "Walkin' After Midnight" among them, but a more typical string of selections was "If I Were a Rich Man" by Zero Mostel, followed by "Cherish" by Madonna, followed by "Melody of Love" by Wayne King, followed by "The Twist"—not Chubby Checker's 1960 hit, but his remake with the Fat Boys. After about my seventh selection I started running flat out of songs I wanted to hear—even at the bargain-basement price of ten cents.

The Riptide Lounge, after all this trouble, did not have America's best jukebox. And so we wandered back across the way to the Blue Note and its CD jukebox, where there were two stragglers besides our party of six. Neil was entertaining his small audience with the tale of a now-closed and much-lamented downtown tavern called the 1944 St. Louis Browns Bar, which had a great old jukebox whose most popular song was entitled "I'm Fucking Your Wife."

"We're telling stories about jukeboxes!" I scribbled in my notebook. The exclamation point was one of anger. I was finally getting into the neighborhoods of Chicago after thirty-three years, but as for my jukebox search I could have saved hundreds of dollars just having Neil phone it in. I insisted that we go around the corner to Danny's.

True to my expectations, Danny's was mobbed. The two-story brick house is one of the most unique taverns I've ever seen: The concept was to take a working-class West Side house, and serve lots of beer and play loud Pink Floyd, like a Northwestern U. keg party from the early 1970s. There were old kitchens and dining rooms left intact, as customers leaned against the sink and swilled Stroh's underneath fluorescent graffiti and paintings of male genitalia. There was also '70s music blasting downstairs—from a cassette deck.

"Hey, there is a jukebox—it's upstairs," Adam reported over the first-floor cacophony. So I raced up the narrow stairway, only to be met by a twenty-something woman, holding our her arm in the "stop" position.

"You can't come up here," she said. "It's a private party until 10:30." I glanced at my watch. It was 10:15.

"I don't really want to join your party," I said. "All I want to do is take a look at the jukebox. I'm looking for the best one in America."

The woman became more resolute. To her there was a larger issue than jukeboxes: This balding thirty-something stranger from the East wanted to contaminate her party.

"You can see the jukebox—after 10:30."

The meaning of the expression "crashing a party" hit me for the first time: I was considering several strategies that involved the use of force myself. Instead, we argued for three or four minutes more, until the woman realized I couldn't be more of a nuisance inspecting the jukebox than I was arguing with her on the stairway.

So I trotted up the remaining stairs, but at first I couldn't find this rumored jukebox. I wandered through the maze of upstairs rooms, until I stumbled into a pantry just off the kitchen and saw it—on the pantry wall. It was a CD jukebox, one of those space-saving wall consoles manufactured by NSM, and it was playing the Beatles' "Dear Prudence." I flipped through the list of CDs, which was half twenty-something alternative rock and rap—Sonic Youth and Big Daddy Kane—and half FM-radio rock—the Beatles, the Stones, the Velvet Underground. Other than the fact that it was in a kitchen pantry, the juke was nothing too special, hardly worth the mental strain of the Great Stairway Debate. A few minutes later, Neil and Edie dropped out of our quest. Needless to say, I was embarrassed; the spontaneity of my search for America's best jukebox must surely have seemed to them more like time-wasting folly.

What went wrong? I had begun to realize, now that I was well off course, that my whole methodology for jukebox-hunting in Chicago was totally screwed up. All my informants and tip sheets—that *Sun-Times* list of the city's ten best jukeboxes, *Chicago Magazine*, even the publicity guy at Alligator Records— were charter members of an art-school elite. For them, a great jukebox is just a quick beer and some Patsy Cline at 1 A.M. on a Sunday morning, wedged between the latest Pedro Almodovar flick and a 3 A.M. rave in some old warehouse. These bars weren't true outposts of nitty-gritty Jukebox America, but merely campy after-midnight nostalgia museums for the terminally hip. Now it was a few minutes until midnight, prime jukebox time, but I was bone-tired.

Around the turn of the hour, Adam and I hailed a cab and headed back toward the towering skyline of the Loop. We got out near the corner of Rush and Division streets, on the strip of discotheques touting mud-wrestling that is Chicago's answer to Bourbon Street. Our destination was the Lodge Tavern, described by *Chicago Magazine* as "an unassuming oasis in the midst of the Division Street meat market."

As it turned out, the Lodge Tavern was so unassuming that about fifteen people were lined up just to get in the door. Inside, a fire-code-violation of a crowd was singing along to a brand-new 1940s-style Wurlitzer "Bubbler" jukebox, blaring out the Eagles' "Take It Easy."

"We may lose and we may win / But we will never be here again," the crowd wailed. In less than ten minutes we made it to the front of the line, where we encountered a baby-faced, short-haired 260-pound bouncer.

"Why is this place so packed?" we asked.

"Atmosphere," he answered. Adam and I looked through the front window at the shoehorned crowd; it didn't look like there was oxygen inside, let alone atmosphere. We looked back at the bouncer, raising our eyebrows in disbelief.

"Meat." He shrugged.

Twenty minutes later, we checked into our hotel room for the night.

It felt like only a few minutes had passed when I rolled out of the hotel bed the next day, but grabbing my watch told me it was already noon. In theory, I had an entire day to resume my search for America's best jukebox, but the truth was, I had exhausted all my A-list prospects—save one—on that overcast Saturday. So when Adam finally dragged me out of the room at about 2 P.M., we decided to go with the flow of the hordes of summer tourists on Michigan Avenue.

With little planning, I saw four things that Sunday afternoon that made me rethink some of the ideas about Chicago my subconscious mind had clung to during the three decades since my first ride on the Chicago Skyway.

The first thing was an incredible place called Nike Town, a three-story futuristic store disguised as a contemporary monument to the era of consumption, where I saw at least 100 or so tank-topped people—enough to fill the Riptide Lounge three times over—sit catatonically in front of a massive TV screen, mesmerized by a string of sneaker ads featuring the likes of local hoops star Scotty Pippin. These were the great masses that I hadn't found in Chicago's juke joints the day before.

The second thing was a place that I hadn't heard of until my arrival in Chicago and that proved to have the most popular jukebox in all the town, if not the world. It was the Rock 'n' Roll McDonald's, which was kind of a faux–Hard Rock Café for the five-burgers-for-a-dollar crowd, complete with gold records and posters of the Beatles and Elvis everywhere. The Rock 'n' Roll McDonald's had a jukebox, of course—a classic, stainless steel Seeburg machine from the 1950s with red push buttons. But it was raised about a foot off the ground on a pedestal—as if this were the Smithsonian or something—and it didn't even take quarters, simply playing, at no charge, whatever songs the Big Mac munchers wanted to hear.

The jukebox at the Rock 'n' Roll McDonald's didn't pre-
pare me for my discovery late that afternoon, my third revelation,
in the unlikely setting of the Chicago Library and Cultural Center. Under the gilded ceiling of the library's main exhibition
room there was an exhibit by something called the Polish Arts
Club. The room was set up with table and chairs for a polka
party, except there was pricey impressionistic art on the wall. The
art was so dazzling that it took me a minute or two to realize
what I had bypassed in the near corner—a jukebox, probably the
best jukebox in Chicago, maybe the best one I had seen since my
search began. Except for the very major problem that this jukebox wasn't even plugged in: it was intended instead as a piece of
pop art.

This jukebox was circa 1959 or so, with quasi-psychedelic
green spirals along the base and those red-plastic push buttons.
It was a Rock-Ola model—no doubt manufactured about a mile
away on Chicago's West Side—boasting "200 Selection Stereo-
phonic High Fidelity." Those 200 selections were nearly perfect—they included Sinatra's "That's Life," "Takin' Care of
Business" by the Bachman-Turner Overdrive, "Disco Inferno"
by the Trammps, and Steve Earle's "Guitar Town." It even had
Kenny Rogers's "The Gambler," two days after I had craved to
hear it.

The name of the machine was "The Music Miracle."

I was pondering this spectacle when two older women—a
matronly woman who appeared to be in her fifties and a gray-
haired companion who seemed to be her mother—strolled into
the Polish Arts exhibit.

"Look at the jukebox!" the grandmotherly one declared, as
if she had just seen a Model-T or a back issue of the *Saturday
Evening Post.*

"Remember how big jukeboxes were in the 1950s," said her
daughter. "They were all we knew back then."

"Kids today probably don't even know what they are," said
her mother.

The Emerald City of Jukeboxes that I had inferred from

my trips through the steel mills of Gary and from the Chicago Skyway as a child was a childish idea, the romantic notion of a Mannish Boy. That time and place that was mostly gone, vanished long before Gary's Michael Jackson got his first nose job. Those weeds I had seen from the Broadway Limited, overgrowing the vast cemetery of the American steel industry, should have told me. The gritty blue-collar city that I had imagined now offered only a choice between the too gritty—the New Checkerboard Lounge—or too phony, like the Riptide.

The Chicago I had dreamed of now belonged to history—its jukeboxes were "Music Miracles" on consignment to museums or McDonald's.

Still, I refused to believe that Jukebox America had been totally decimated in the nation's second-largest city. I clung to the hope that there were pockets of resistance.

By 5 P.M., I was back in our hotel room, dialing an obscure blues bar out on West Armitage called Rosa's and its thirty-three-year-old proprietor, Tony Mangiullo—a true freedom fighter for Jukebox America.

I couldn't even find out whether Rosa's had a jukebox without listening to a long sermon from Tony Mangiullo about the blues. He told me that the University of Chicago was trying once again to close down Maxwell Street, a flea market that was home to free Sunday morning blues bands. In fact, that night his little club on the West Side was showcasing a Maxwell Street bluesman named "Iceman" Robinson.

Fine, fine, but what about the jukebox?

"Yeah, we have a jukebox. It has 45s and CDs, but the CD part doesn't work right now," Tony said. "Anyway, I like the old kind."

"Me, too," I said. "There are probably a lot of great blues records that aren't even out on CD."

"I know. I know."

Sounded like Tony Mangiullo was going to save my trip to

Chicago single-handed. He told us to get there by eight o'clock or so, to get a good earful of his jukebox before the live music started.

So Adam and I headed west, into a shadowy cityscape of dry cleaners, gas stations, and run-down dives. When we finally turned onto Armitage, the sign for Rosa's was like a beacon from the 1950s, when Muddy Waters and Tampa Red performed just around the corner at the long-closed Sylvio's. The word "Rosa's" is written in cartoon red, inside a circle along with musical notes, a bubbling martini glass, and "Live Blues/7 Nights." On the bottom, in stark black-and-white, surrounded by more notes, it says: "Dancing."

It's hard to say what is most unlikely about Rosa's: The bar's location, its story, or the simple fact that it has survived for nearly a decade now.

There are two audiences for the blues in Chicago: the mostly older, working-class blacks who still hear the blues at a handful of remaining joints on the South Side, and affluent white college kids from places like Northwestern who've made Lincoln Park, on the more upscale and predominantly white North Side, a 1990s music mecca. Rosa's, in the middle of a lower-middle-class, mostly Hispanic neighborhood on the city's West Side, is worlds away for both groups.

Inside, Rosa's looks pretty much like the kind of working-man's bar you'd see in older, big-city neighborhoods from Bensonhurst to the Embarcadero—there's a pool table out front with a couple of unshaven neighborhood derelicts who've been playing a running grudge match since 1986, and a decor of Early American Beer Distributor Handout, giving a minor neon glow to the light-absorbing wooden bar and tables. There was a Persian rug on one wall, lots of officially sanctioned graffiti on another, and a tiny stage at the far end of the bar, a dark, foreboding place with a unexplainable grainy blowup of a man's face.

And, yes, there was a jukebox.

True to Tony's word, it was against the back wall, a stainless-steel, mostly 45 RPM juke, a mid-1980s Rowe/AMI model, four plays for $1, and it was probably the best blues jukebox that

I had seen so far. There were a lot of classic 45s, such as Albert King's "I'll Play the Blues for You," Johnny Taylor's "Who's Makin' Love," B. B. King's "The Thrill Is Gone," Don Covay's "Mercy Mercy," and Little Milton's "Walkin' the Back Streets and Cryin'." Other songs, however, were clearly just local Chicago bluesmen who asked Tony Mangiullo to put their cheaply recorded 45s on his jukebox—many of these noted by just the singer's last name, like "Your Sweet Man," by Revson. There were also four or five CDs—John Lee Hooker's recent "The Healer," "John Littlejohn's Blues Party," and a compilation called "The Blues at Christmas."

It was the blues jukebox I had dreamed about before coming to Chicago. And—I had come to expect such things, really, after two days here—it wasn't turned on.

The problem was clear as Adam and I walked into Rosa's. The night's featured attraction, Iceman Robinson, a thin man in a white T-shirt and woven cowboy hat, the three members of his band, and their assorted wives, girlfriends, and the like, were sitting rapt in front of a giant projection TV screen.

"Yeah, yeah," about four or five of them shouted in unison, pointing at the screen, where the Iceman himself was wailing on the lead guitar. The crowd was watching a videotape Tony had made of Iceman's combo last fall on a "blues cruise" of Lake Michigan, and now they were totally fixated on the big screen.

To ask to hear the jukebox would have been an invitation to a riot.

Behind the bar was a sixtyish woman with close-cropped gray hair and glasses, the very image of a grandmother—that is, a grandmother with a cigarette dangling constantly from her lips and her hand on a Stroh's tap all night long.

This was Rosa herself—the mother of Tony Mangiullo, imported direct from Milan to set up her son in the bar business.

In a minute or two, an olive-skinned man, early thirtyish, with a well-trimmed beard and a flamboyant white fedora, strolled into the long barroom—Tony Mangiullo—and before we could ask him anything else he had a confession to make:

Hardly anyone ever plays the jukebox at Rosa's.

Mangiullo sees his little nightclub as a showcase for live music, which he presents seven nights a week. And it's not a neighborhood tavern, so the place is only open for an hour or two before the music starts. When Tony is behind the bar, he uses one of those remote-control gadgets to play selections from the five CDs in the jukebox. Just about the only person who ever drops in a quarter to play the 45s on the jukebox, occasionally, is Rosa Mangiullo.

"When it gets used is when we're open and Momma is by herself," said Mangiullo. "Momma doesn't know how to work the remote control—so Momma plays the jukebox."

Tony's jukebox was like a millionaire kid's Christmas present, an expensive toy that never gets played after December 26. And the image seems appropriate, because Tony Mangiullo is basically a big kid at heart. Some kids want to be grow up to be cowboys, some want to grow up to be president; Tony Mangiullo wanted to grow up to be a Chicago bluesman—no small feat when you're the son of a fruit-and-vegetable man in Milan, Italy.

The story of Tony—who at thirty-three was the same age as me—convinced me that the problems of the Rear Guard Baby Boomers were a trans-Atlantic phenomenon. Now, some folks may remember there was a minor blues revival in the United States in the late 1960s—white hippies like Paul Butterfield suddenly became spiritual kin to Muddy Waters—but it wasn't until the 1970s that the word of this trickled down to Italy. Like some of my adolescent peers in America, Tony and his restless teenage friends were listening to some well-worn records—presuccess Fleetwood Mac interpreting the licks of Elmore James in one record he especially remembers—and began trying to re-create the music, with Tony on drums. Like any true Rear Guarder, Tony had *missed* something, missed the 1950s, missed Chicago, missed the blues. But he and his friends were doing what they could to catch up.

"The band was so *raw*," says Tony of his all-Italian blues band, 5,000 miles and light years away from Maxwell Street. "So full of power."

But more than any of his blues-playing pals back in Milan,

Tony Mangiullo was full of piss and vinegar. One night during the mid-seventies, bluesman Junior Wells made Milan one of his stops on a worldwide tour. After the show, it was Tony who had the nerve to walk over to Wells's table.

"I just had more guts," Tony said with a shrug. Junior Wells was more than happy to meet an Italian bluesman, it turned out, and he even scrawled something on a piece of paper.

"This is my home phone number," Junior Wells said to Tony Mangiullo. "If you ever make it to Chicago, just give me a call."

Nine-hundred and ninety-nine out of 1,000 people would have forgotten that chance encounter, or saved the phone number in some kind of scrapbook, but that's not Tony Mangiullo's style. Instead, in August 1978, he boarded a plane for America, and found his way to Chicago. Most white visitors to Chicago are told to avoid the mostly black, crime-plagued South Side at all costs, but Tony—a stranger to American cities who spoke little English—received no such warnings. So, as soon as he arrived, he headed for Theresa's, a world-famous South Side blues bar—now, sadly and predictably, closed—to hear real Chicago blues. Tony was virtually the only white face in the club, but he says the African American musicians treated this strange foreigner—no one knew exactly who he was, even—like family. Incredibly, within a year, Tony was the drummer in a blues band, Jimmy Rose's Southside All-Stars.

A year passed, then another, and then it became clear that Tony Mangiullo wasn't coming home. Half a world away, Rosa Mangiullo worried about her son. Her husband, Tony's father, had died, leaving the family with enough money to live on. Finally, one day in 1985, she couldn't take it anymore: she flew to Chicago to talk some sense into her crazy son. It only took a few weeks for her to realize that Tony was a lost cause. But if he insisted on being a Chicago bluesman, Rosa insisted that she buy him a nightclub of his own—get him a real job, in other words. She would even help him run the joint.

So it was Rosa who handled the business deal. When she went to see a real-estate agent, she had no idea about location, that any entrepreneur who wanted to make money off the blues was heading toward Lincoln Park, where air-guitar-playing Future Inside Traders of America would plunk down $10 to see a real-life bluesman in the Wonder-Bread safety of the North Side. What the real-estate agent offered was this rundown dive in Wicker Park, the No Man's Land of the blues.

There was something else besides the real-estate market that Rosa Mangiullo said she didn't know when she came to Chicago: That Italians are supposed to scorn black people.

"Momma came here, and she liked the music, liked the people," Tony said. "Then she finds out that Italians are prejudiced against blacks. . . . We didn't know." Today, Tony still walks freely through the South Side, even though police cruisers frequently pull over to ask him if he is lost.

It appears that racism is one lesson neither Tony nor Rosa will have to learn, as long as they remain on Chicago's forgotten West Side. Tony Mangiullo struggled to bring attention and record deals to some obscure South Side musicians like Sugar Blue and Melvin Taylor, but he and Rosa have discovered that often means serving less as a musician's manager and more as his surrogate parents, shielding him from friends and family who will squander his talent on drugs or alcohol. In the case of Taylor, he's lived in Tony's little apartment—which is upstairs from his barroom—for months at a time.

It cost time and money—two things that are in short supply for Tony—to keep Melvin Taylor going, when most club owners would have left him on the mean streets of the South Side. But Tony Mangiullo never does things the easy way. Ironically, with Tony's impeccable blues credentials and his contacts, he could have cashed in on the yuppie-blues phenomenon of the 1980s. A wealthy uncle back in Italy wooed Tony for months to come back to his homeland and open a 600-seat nightclub at a Mediterranean beach resort near Venice, presenting the Chicago blues to free-spending European vacationers starved for American pop culture.

The offer was tempting, but Tony Mangiullo couldn't bring himself to leave the dumpy confines of Wicker Park. He wouldn't even move a few miles to the lucrative confines of the North Side, where Adam and I had witnessed the thousands of beer-swilling, free-spending Cubs fans just twenty-nine short hours ago.

Instead, he was determined to be the Jefferson Smith of the Chicago blues scene, hanging on to the faith that "a lost cause is the only cause worth fighting for." And so he spent all day and all night promoting the blues, organizing a series of lectures, promoting the annual "blues cruise," presenting live music in his out-of-the-way tavern seven nights a week. He printed thousands of fliers he designed on his own home computer, billing Rosa's as "blues with an Italian accent." Now he was leading the campaign to save Maxwell Street from the university's wrecking ball.

"For me, to support the blues, that would be the greatest result," Tony said. "My father was stubborn—I'm the same way."

My theory is that it was sheer stubbornness that led Tony Mangiullo to create the best jukebox in Chicago, knowing full well that it would only be turned on for a few minutes every day by his mother. For him, the all-blues jukebox was merely another symbol of his battle to promote his blues music every second of the day. The struggle for Tony Mangiullo was not to record Sugar Blue and Melvin Taylor at 45 RPM, but quite simply to keep their music—and, more important, them—alive.

What I was fast learning in my travels was that Jukebox America was more than a collection of Wurlitzers, Rock-Olas, and Seeburgs. It was a case of transubstantiation: people—Hoboken's Mike Milo, still waiting for the comeback of 45s; Dale Evans, the Human Jukebox; and now, Tony Mangiullo and his improbable blues bar—had become the vessels of jukebox spirit, even as the machines themselves rusted away.

In that same mode, I couldn't help but think that Iceman Robinson—the live entertainment that night at Rosa's—was a man who would have been on jukeboxes everywhere from Muddy Waters Boulevard to Wrigley Field if he had been born just twenty years sooner.

In 1956—right around the time that Bo Diddley recorded

"I'm a Man" for Phil and Leonard Chess—a twenty-three-year-old Iceman Robinson left his hometown of Marks, Mississippi (a tiny outpost of clay-red dirt roads and wood-frame shacks that I passed through a month later on one of my jukebox expeditions), and headed north on the Illinois Central.

He went back for his mother's burial a decade ago, and maybe a couple other times, but Iceman has declared, "I left that state. And when I leave, I'm gone."

Instead, he's spent that last thirty-six years working hard, toiling by day for a succession of meat-packing companies on the South Side. On Sundays, he's out at Maxwell Street by 7 A.M. to make sure that his band gets the best possible spot. He plays Thursday nights at an unknown blues dive called Diamond Don's on South Kedzie, but the rest of the week he's too bone-tired from working in a meat cooler to rehearse.

Hard work is all that Iceman Robinson has ever known. "I had to go to bed with bread and water and get up at the same time," he said. "I've worked from sun to sun. That gives you the blues, man."

On this day Iceman Robinson was fifty-nine years old, yet his bulging biceps—the direct result of lugging around cow carcasses for more than a decade—still looked ready to burst through his white V-neck T-shirt. The rest of his appearance—a tan cowboy hat, a faint goatee and broad sideburns—was about as untrendy as the music he plays. There was a time when his life story—migration from the Deep South, blue-collar jobs, and blues guitar—was entrenched in the mainstream of the African American experience, but those days have gone the way of Silvio's and Muddy Waters. They call him Iceman because when he picks on the lead guitar on stage, his expression is downright glacial.

"I think white people are going to pick it up," the Iceman said of the blues. "Black people went to disco and rap . . ." He paused for a moment. "And drugs—don't forget that."

I might be overromanticizing, but I like to believe that thirty years ago Phil and Leonard Chess would have brought Iceman into the studio and cut a 45, giving him at least a shot at quitting his day job. Instead, he's had to settle for performing on Maxwell Street for a string of admirers like former Chicago Bears quarterback Jim McMahon and some people from "out-of-state," places like Venezuela and England, which he pronounces "Ang-Land."

"Man, I am willing to go anywhere to make some money," Iceman said. "But I got to hold my day job. I had offers to go to London, *Ang-Land*, and a few other places."

But this is as far as he gets—Wicker Park, that familiar vista of dry cleaners and gas stations. As time goes by, Iceman's finding it harder and harder to keep a rhythm guitarist ("The rhythm boys—they think they should play over *you*"). Steve, a grungy, white twenty-something who joined the band just three weeks ago, is his sixth sideman in the last four years. Not only is Iceman not going to *Ang-Land*, but he just gave up a regular gig on the South Side "because that lady don't like to pay nothin'."

A few minutes after 9 P.M., Iceman and his combo climbed the stage and burst into a rhythm that galloped like the Broadway Limited. The Iceman cut through the heat of that August night with some biting leads—icepick piercing that recalled the guitar work of Albert Collins and B. B. King. On the slow numbers, he looked down at the guitar strings with a hard grimace, and then a weary look like he'd just been hauling cow carcasses all day.

I glanced around the dark expanse of Rosa's and saw maybe a dozen people, including the two oblivious props at the pool table. One man who had been sitting against the side wall—he was wearing a green windbreaker on this eighty-eight-degree night—tried to get up and walk, but was so inebriated that his weight almost carried him onto the stage. He had tried engaging the bass player in a mid-song conversation before Tony came up to restore order.

Now the band was playing an instrumental shuffle, and Steve—the Iceman's sixth rhythm-guitar player—was pumping up the volume and gradually edging toward the front of the stage, slowly upstaging the Iceman. The Iceman threw Steve a glance that carried the sub-zero chill of an Arctic air blast, and from our table Adam and I could see the stage was being set for sideman no. 7. I sensed that this was a typical night in Rosa's—a place for the glorious chaos of the blues.

It was the place that Tony Mangiullo had imagined from the dew-covered produce markets of Milan and that I had imagined in the backseat of a Galaxy 500 from the high safety of the Chicago Skyway, the working blast furnace of rock 'n' roll that will still be filling the American sky with its wonderful pollution long after the tall weeds have devoured Gary.

Chapter 5

....

Jukebox Hero

It was just before eight o'clock Monday morning when I awoke with a ringing in my ears. I thought it was some kind of hangover from Iceman Robinson's guitar solos at Rosa's the night before, until I realized it was just the hotel wake-up call—time for a day I had been planning for more than a year, a tour of the Rock-Ola jukebox factory.

After a quick visit to the drive-thru window of the Rock 'n' Roll McDonald's for a breakfast biscuit, we were funneled onto the Kennedy Expressway, the route toward suburban Addison, Illinois. From the overpasses and underpasses of the highway, the modest brick houses of Wicker Park, including the shutters of the Riptide Lounge, were a blur as we raced toward open field and then the shimmering expanses of a new city arising along the runways of O'Hare International Airport. The land around O'Hare is a kind of antimatter version of Gary, Indiana, or Chicago's southeast corner: O'Hare is a constant swarm of jetliners, where Gary is a tangle of slow-moving freight trains; O'Hare is the light-reflecting glass clarity of a Hyatt Hotel, while Gary is the opaque blur of a USX steel mill. Yet it was amidst this pristine setting that we were searching for the company that, for the last sixty years, has virtually come to define the jukebox in America.

After a couple of wrong turns down wide suburban boulevards, Adam and I were cruising through a faceless brick industrial park that looked exactly like brick industrial parks that I have
seen in Ronkonkoma, New York, Peoria, Illinois, and just about
everywhere else in post-industrial America. In the center of the
park, at 313 S. Rohlwing Road, we found a 1950s-style building
of white brick and long metal window frame, a structure that
might be mistaken for a Baby Boomer junior high school, with
a wide lawn and a few lonely trees out front. A sign—printed in
a half-modern, half-Gothic typeface—merely said Rock-Ola
Manufacturing Corp. There was no indication that this small
company has produced about one million jukeboxes since the
1930s, bringing everyone from Bing Crosby to Bell Biv Devoe
to America's ears.

Likewise, the modest front entrance, with its glass-
windowed reception area, had a Rotary Club feel, right down to
the American flag that had been flown over the U.S. Capitol by
Rep. Henry Hyde, an anti-abortion fanatic, and presented to the
company for display in its lobby. On the wall near the flag was
an artist's sketch of the original Rock-Ola factory, which was
located in the heart of a working-class neighborhood on the near
West Side of Chicago, the same general area as Rosa's blues bar.
In contrast to the lifeless industrial park, the old plant was six stories tall and seemed to stretch on indefinitely, until only its bound-
ary of the omnipresent rail tracks of Chicago could contain it—
it had a raw industrial power, like the Italian futurist paintings of
the 1920s. I yet again felt that Rear Guard Baby Boomer pang
of loss and regret, as Adam and I were summoned into the office
of Art Kareff, Rock-Ola's vice president.

"What can I do for you?" asked Kareff, a stocky, middle-
aged Chamber of Commerce type who sat behind a giant desk
in a beige-carpeted, wood-paneled office, sparsely decorated with
a couple of Rock-Ola promotional posters.

Art Kareff spent much of the next two hours trying to help
me, but he couldn't do the one thing that I really wanted, and
that was to bring back David Rockola.

*   *   *

Very early in my search for America's best jukebox, in my conversation with the flack for the Amusement Operators and Manufacturers of America, I had gleaned one useful—although outdated—suggestion: that I try to talk to David Rockola. Just a few days earlier, I had come by an article that discussed Rockola's role in the history of the jukebox, but that had been in the 1930s. It had never occurred to me that David Rockola was alive, not to mention interviewable.

"Oh yes," said the publicist, "he's in his nineties, but last I heard he was still going by the office."

There's a famous phrase in the newspaper business, credited to the *Washington Post*, about the file of "stories too good to check," and for me this became one of them; I waited a whole year to see if such an interview was indeed possible.

In the early summer of 1992, I called Art Kareff. I told him of my interest in jukeboxes, and made preliminary arrangements to tour the factory. At the end of the phone call, with some trepidation, I broached the subject of David Rockola.

There was a long pause on the other end. "That wouldn't be possible. Mr. Rockola hasn't come by the office for several years. He's in a convalescent home."

Too late. Missing something.

Instead, I got to read a few dog-eared clippings by writers who were fortunate enough to meet David Rockola, and that Monday morning I heard a few reminiscences from his most loyal employee, marketing chief Frank Shultz, and even from David's son, Donald Rockola. Although David Rockola was a Canadian native, his life's story was very American, fresh yet familiar in a Horatio Alger–ish kind of way—the saga of a real-life jukebox industrialist.

It was at the end of the nineteenth century—1897, to be exact—that David Rockola was born in Saskatchewan, Canada. Ambitious almost from the day he was born, Rockola grew up in an era when most folks didn't have the money or the patience for a formal education. By the time he was twelve, Rockola was working as a bellhop in a hotel in Saskatoon while at the same time seeking to learn about gasoline engines from the International School of Correspondence, a course he never finished. Instead, he opened a cigar shop in the Hotel Laurel in Medicine Hat, Alberta.

Years later, Rockola talked about his experiences to a high school student, LeeAnee Turbyfill, a writer for an amazingly slick student newspaper from a place called Kentland, Indiana, who produced the best story that I have read about Rockola.

"I went into the cigar business in this hotel and of course, like a fool, I worked all day and all night," Rockola told the young interviewer in 1987. "I ended up in the Medicine Hat hospital because I worked too many hours. I had diptheria fever. They took my cigar store away from me."

From then on, Rockola looked for ways to make money that wouldn't land him in the hospital. He moved to a bigger town, Alberta, and opened another cigar shop, this one in the St. Louis Hotel. But this time, he hired an attractive young woman to work the counter, figuring correctly that her presence would increase sales dramatically. But then Rockola discovered something more profitable than a pretty girl: a machine.

A salesman came by with a device with the highfalutin' name of a trade similator, by any other name a gumball machine. The nickel device took in even more money than the comely sales girl, and in it David Rockola saw his future. He got out of the cigar-store business and went to work for the Mills Novelty Co., learning enough to move to Chicago (penniless, of course, as in every Horatio Alger story) and start his own business.

The Rockola story is highlighted by one amazing coincidence: his name, which virtually everyone who's ever seen or heard a Rock-Ola jukebox assumes is a natural combination of rock 'n' roll and Victrola, or merely a corruption of rock à la "Shinola." By now the name has become so famous, according to the legend in the company headquarters, that "Rock-Ola" means jukebox in a number of Latin American countries such as Venezuela, where the law prohibits a "Rock-Ola" from within 500 feet of a church. The fact that there is a real person named Rock-ola inspired syndicated Chicago columnist Bob Greene to write a widely reprinted column about the entrepreneur in the mid-1980s, giving David Rockola his obligatory fifteen minutes of fame.

Ironically, the people who work for Rockola don't think much of the name-coincidence thing. "There is that, of course," says company spokesman Art Kareff, "but the truth of the matter is the reason that Rock-Ola became such a legend is its perform-ance."

It would be nice to say that David Rockola planned to bring popular music to the unwashed masses from the start, but his mind was on weightier matters. In 1926, Rockola sold his first coin-operated device: A scale with the customer-flattening name of "Lo Boy." His firm was called the Peerless Weight and Scale Co.

"The scale was a very needed part of an arcade," said Frank Schultz, Rockola's longtime aide. "Scales were a big thing in drugstores, because it fit in with the strategy of the drugstores, which was health."

But David Rockola was always a keen watcher of trends, and he probably foresaw the widespread use of home scales, so he kept branching out. In 1933, he started selling what was then known as "a flipper game," a less electronic forerunner of what we call pinball. The game, with its baseball motif, was called "World Series." But Rockola wanted to make something more timeless, less trendy. In the early 1930s, he made his fateful de-cision to start selling jukeboxes.

It's hard to believe, but by the 1930s, jukeboxes had already been around for nearly fifty years. When Thomas Edison in-vented the phonograph, working out of his new laboratory in Menlo Park in 1877, he was essentially inventing the jukebox; record players were largely an arcade and tavern phenomenon for decades before people started buying them for the home. Al-though the first thing that Edison recorded on his wax cylinder was "Mary Had a Little Lamb," he thought the phonograph would be useful not mainly for music but for spoken dictation, such as business lectures from his industrialist pals like Henry Ford. But popular culture won out, and by 1889 an entrepreneur had placed the first coin-operated jukebox in a San Francisco tavern named the Palais Royale. According to legend, the device brought in $15 a week, a princely sum in those days, and the owner saved the cost of a piano player.

But for its first four decades or so, the record machine was largely an arcade item. Remember, the device was still a wax cylinder containing one song that was played over and over. There were no electric amplifiers, so only one person could hear the song at a time, although some early jukeboxes were equipped with listening tubes, tentacles that allowed three or four people to hear the song at once. The novelty of this device was already starting to wear thin in 1906, when John Gabel thankfully invented the "Automatic Entertainer," which played flat records and offered more than one selection. Surviving documents indicate that the jukebox enjoyed its first wave of popularity in these years—one survey of Brooklyn in the first decade of the twentieth century found thousands of jukeboxes in that one borough alone.

Yet, for the second time in its brief history, the coin-operated record machine soon grew stale. Then came the 1920s, and a quick series of fortuitous events: Prohibition—from 1920 to 1933—actually helped the spread of the jukebox, as thousands of illegal speakeasies demanded cheaper forms of amusement than hiring a big band. Then, in 1927, Automated Musical Instruments, Inc., or AMI, introduced the amplified jukebox, which for the first time could fill a crowded barroom with music. When the lifting of Prohibition gave rise to explosion of thousands of now-legal taverns, the country was in the midst of the Great Depression. The reality was that few people had the money for a Victrola, but most could spare a nickel for the jukebox.

"During the Depression, people who made $3 a week bought a nickel beer and put a nickel in the jukebox, or seven plays for a quarter, and that was their weekend," recalled Rock-Ola's Frank Shultz. "A person who made $50 a week went out to hear a band."

In 1934, a year after the end of Prohibition, David Rockola started making jukeboxes.

"In 1928 the Victrola music boxes played such beautiful music—they had such a beautiful amplifier," Rockola told a weekly newspaper interviewer in 1987. "I thought, gee, it would be nice if I could have something like this that you could put a coin into."

And so Rockola, whose engineering background was that unfinished correspondence-school course, developed his own version of a jukebox. It cost $198—cheaper than the typical $250 models of the era—and it had a whopping sixteen selections. It would be nice to say that David Rockola had a hidden musical agenda—that he wanted to introduce the music of Robert Johnson and Blind Lemon Jefferson to the masses—but that wouldn't be true. It was simply that Rockola saw pinball and dime-store scales as fads, while music was eternal.

"Music never goes out of style," he said years later. "Back then, if someone had a new song the first thing they wanted to do was get it on a jukebox because that's how everyone would hear it. It was the way people got to hear music—it was very important to them."

The first Rock-Ola jukebox was the Multi-Selector, a four-foot-tall boxy wood cabinet that looks like an inflated version of those old-time radios that families use to crowd around back in the 1930s, listening to *Fibber McGee* and FDR's fireside chats. Popular 78s back in that year were Bing Crosby's "Missouri Waltz," Tommy Dorsey's "Blue Orchids," and "Cherri Beri Bean" by the Andrews Sisters.

It was the same year, 1934, that the company, now christened the Rock-Ola Manufacturing Corp., moved into its massive headquarters at 800 North Kedzie Avenue in Chicago, a 600,000-square-foot behemoth covering four city blocks. The company was a stereotypical American industrial success story of the mid-twentieth century, employing as many as 3,200 laborers working around the clock shifts. In 1942, Canadian-born Rockola even did his part for the American war effort, converting his plant

from jukebox production to—the concept is horrifying today—
making carbines and ammunition devices. The plant didn't re-
convert to music machines until 1946.

It's clear from looking at some of Rock-Ola's promotional
ads from the company's six-decade run that the idea was always
to convince the so-called operators—the people who peddle
jukeboxes to taverns, malt shops, bowling alleys—that they'd
make more money from installing a Rock-Ola jukebox than one
of their competitor's: Wurlitzer, Seeburg, AMI, and Mills. Until
recently, many of the ads featured a busty young woman; the
1940 brochure, "Strike Up the Band," featured a drum majorette
on the cover. Inside, there is a promo for the Junior model, a
smallish countertop jukebox in bright plastic splashes of red, orange, and yellow. Behind the counter is a teenaged boy in a white,
well-pressed soda jerk's uniform, while a group of two men and
three women—all but one of the men is wearing a hat—ogle the
modern device. Operators are told the device comes in "two profitable installations."

Maximizing profits was still the goal as late as 1986, when
Rock-Ola was aggressively peddling its Nostalgia 1000 model, a
knockoff of the classic Wurlitzer jukebox of the late 1940s,
shaped like an upside-down U with brassy trim and a rainbow of
plastic colors. This flyer carried the advice that "selection prices
can be higher—for the Nostalgia is a collector's item, not a common phonograph." Furthermore, "a great percentage of the selections ('oldies') don't have to be replaced ever," saving the
greater money. (Of course, the Nostalgia jukebox discourages operators from helping to break out new, young artists like they
did in the 1940s and 1950s, but that's a story for later.)

Indeed, I got the impression from reading David Rockola's
interviews and brochures and from meeting his underlings that
the last fifty-eight years have been a constant struggle to stay
current. The book of Rock-Ola's promotional campaigns shows
attempts in the 1970s to adorn jukeboxes with post-hippie psy-
chedelia, or with the look of the then-popular home stereo console. In the 1980s, Rock-Ola jumped on the video game
bandwagon just as the fad was ending. Like many great American

companies, Rock-Ola has followed trends as often as it has created them.

Yet Rockola outlasted and outlived its competitors. Seeburg, which came out with the first 100-song jukebox in 1948, was the industry leader for two decades, but it filed for bankruptcy protection in 1979 before being revived. Wurlitzer, whose 1946 "Bubbler"—with those bubbles crawling eternally up the neon bend—created the classic jukebox look, is now owned by Germans. Rock-Ola survived, I believed, solely by the force of its founder's personality.

"Dynamic" was the word that Shultz used to describe his longtime boss, whom he said he idolized. "He worked seven days a week, sixteen hours a day. He ran this place with an iron fist," Shultz said. "We'd have a staff meeting, and he'd come in and say, 'Press number sixteen wasn't running, press number eighteen wasn't running, press number twenty-two wasn't running— Why?!' When he came in he walked through different floors every day. His eyes were always looking. I remember stories where he'd walk through the assembly line and see some part lying on the floor, and he'd say, 'Would you throw money away like this at home?' "

Indeed, the pictures I have seen of the ninety-year-old Rockola depict a little general of a man, balding and bespectacled but with a ruddy face that looked weatherbeaten from the winds of the Canadian Rockies and Lake Michigan and the accumulated strain of decades of trying to keep up with teenage fads.

There was one question that I really wanted to ask David Rockola, and to me and Adam, who in these three days had become seriously caught up in the jukebox chase, it was the most natural question in the world: What song, or songs, were Mr. Rockola's jukebox favorites? Yet to his longtime aide Frank Shultz, the company mouthpiece Art Kareff, and even his own son, Donald Rockola, the question, which we reformulated about five different ways, seemed to come from outer space. The notion of songs, of rock 'n' roll and rebellion, did not compute in this world of operators, locations, and profitability.

"I think in his mind, he loved to give people entertainment

at a reasonable cost," said Shultz. "He always wanted to create a machine that functions, and he sold them at reasonable prices."

The idea that I got from the interview was this: When I go into a restaurant and see a jukebox, the first thing I want to know is what songs are on it. David Rockola was more likely to buttonhole the restaurant owner to sell him on a new model.

His own son was even more blunt, after Adam and I had pressed the question several times: "I think he enjoyed music," and he paused, "but not in that way."

Funny thing was, despite evidence to the contrary, I didn't believe them—or maybe I just didn't want to. I couldn't help feeling that for David Rockola to have prospered for so many decades, he had to understand more than just the machinery. He must have heard the music, too. I was sure he would have told me so, if only I could have gotten to Addison, Illinois, in 1987 instead of 1992. If my life wasn't always running behind schedule.

Frank Shultz, who'd been there for the heyday of jukeboxes, seemed to feel Mr. Rockola's absence even more than we did. "He was pretty active until a few years ago," Shultz said at one point, and then his voice trailed off into melancholy. "It's a different story now."

In our own ways, both Frank Shultz and I realized something had gone wrong at the Rock-Ola Manufacturing Co.

We became aware of the troubles the minute that Adam and I sat down in Art Kareff's wood-paneled office, when Shultz warned that our visit to the Rock-Ola factory couldn't last long.

"The company has really not kept its archives up," Kareff said. "The other thing that's going on is that the company is in the process of being sold, and we're racing like crazy to get a number of things done."

The Rock-Ola Manufacturing Corp. was for sale?

Rather than telling this story in the disjointed, back-and-forth cadence of our interview, it may be easier to explain by going back to 1985. That was around the time that Rock-Ola moved out of that massive factory site on North Kedzie Avenue in Chicago.

At its peak, which would have been the early 1960s—that industrial nirvana I remember from the windows of the Broadway Limited in my infancy—the company was capable of producing as many as 125 jukeboxes in a single day, and it could ship as many 25,000 new jukeboxes in a single year. That had changed by the mid-1980s, when the company was making a mere twenty-five or thirty new machines a day. The problems were industry-wide; informal surveys have estimated that from 1935 to 1950 there were as many as 700,000 jukeboxes in America, and even in the "Disco Duck" year of 1976 there were still 500,000 or so, but by the mid-1980s, a mere 230,000 jukeboxes remained in play.

What happened?

"The jukebox business went down the tubes," Art Kareff said matter-of-factly early in our interview. "The market was saturated, and there was nothing new in style and performance." There is some truth in the glib explanations you hear. It's said that McDonald's, with its musicless sterility, replaced the juke-box-equipped corner malt shop, and that the advent of the cassette deck—which played albums, more popular than 45s by the 1970s—often replaced the record machine in trendy fern bars. A more important factor, rarely mentioned because it's economic rather than cultural, is that jukeboxes weren't so profitable for those all-important "operators"—record prices were going up, and yet customers used to the standard three-plays-for-a-quarter wouldn't pay higher prices. While a few customers were replacing old jukeboxes in the 1970s, Frank Shultz told us no one was expanding.

On top of that was another "problem," the same problem Agatha Upchurch had bought up a few short days ago in the 924 Club, and the same refrain that—though I didn't know it yet— I would hear from Virginia to Mississippi. The "problem": drunk-driving laws are now being enforced.

"I think some of the liquor laws that went into effect . . ."

said Frank Shultz, his voice trailing off. "Drunk-driving laws got a little stricter, bars started closing down."

Suddenly, a 600,000-square-foot factory was an industrial dinosaur. The jukeboxes had to be lugged from floor to floor by elevator, and that was time-consuming. And the heating bills! But that wasn't the kiss of death for the Rock-Ola factory. The death-knell was sounded because the neighborhood had changed in character. Like many urban blue-collar neighborhoods of the 1930s, the 800-block of North Kedzie Avenue was surrounded by a poverty-stricken black environment.

I learned this when I told Art Kareff and Frank Shultz I wanted to see the old plant.

"Is that building still there?" asked Kareff, who had been with Rock-Ola for just three years.

"They knocked it down and made a shopping center," said Shultz. "800 North Kedzie. It's a very tough area. Keep your doors closed."

I wasn't sure where 800 North Kedzie was, but I thought it might be in the predominantly Latino neighborhood near Rosa's, where we had been the night before.

"Is that a Hispanic neighborhood?" I asked.

"No, it's a black part of town," said Shultz. He described better where it was, and then repeated that "it's a very tough area. If you're going into that area, keep your doors closed."

It seems that security became a big issue in the 1980s— Rock-Ola had more than forty security guards, working around the clock, watching front doors, back doors, side doors.

And so Rock-Ola moved about twenty-five minutes west to suburban Addison, to a quiet industrial park with big lawns and shady trees and American flags and empty parking lots. Thanks to automation, a mere 105 people work for the company now, and although Rock-Ola makes more than thirty jukeboxes a day—the exact number is a trade secret—the number is considerably less than its peak of 125.

There was a major irony here, yet it seemed lost on Kareff, Shultz, and the people who make Rock-Ola jukeboxes for a living. In the office-park world of Addison and O'Hare Airport, there are hardly any jukeboxes. The places where jukeboxes still survive are the gritty neighborhoods like the one Rock-Ola left behind.

"Jukeboxes make most of their money in very ethnic locations," Shultz said earlier. "A person—let's use today's criteria—who makes $200 to $250 a week: where he hangs out is where a jukebox makes the most money. I can take you down Kedzie Avenue in Chicago, down to 22nd and Kedzie, which is a Spanish neighborhood."

The juxtaposition of those two comments—go to Kedzie to find jukeboxes, but stay away from Kedzie, it's dangerous—drew me to the odd conclusion that the executives of the Rock-Ola Manufacturing Corp. were afraid of their own customers.

In the meantime, the company has a problem on its hands: How to woo back the largely white and upper-middle-class establishments that were finding 45 RPM jukeboxes so unprofitable in the 1980s? The answer was, of course, the CD jukebox.

The key moment of the interview came when it was just me and Adam and Art Kareff.

"The CD jukebox has revived the industry," Kareff proclaimed, and then he was brutally candid. "The reason it has revived the industry is that the operators make more money. If they play 45s, you'll see two songs for a quarter. You put a CD jukebox in the same location, you're talking at most three for a buck."

Kareff then made a point which I am willing to concede, and that is that a CD jukebox means higher start-up costs for the operator, who must stock as many as 100 CDs at $12 or so apiece, as opposed to 100 45s at a mere $2 a record. Yet the higher cost of amortization doesn't explain the dramatically higher price to the consumer.

"The consumer knows what's going in, and he doesn't seem to mind paying twice as much," said Kareff. (CD jukebox selections cost nearly three times as much, but let's ignore that for a minute.) "It's the quality of the song—the CD delivers a better quality song."

Adam, who's a far more tenacious interviewer than I am,

immediately picked up on some double-talk. Kareff wasn't saying that the sound of a CD jukebox was better, but the "quality of song."

"You mean the sound quality?" Adam asked.

"The sound quality," Kareff said half-heartedly. "More selections. It's really the quality of song rather than the sound itself. If you are into music and you take a 45 versus a CD, there is a sound difference, but the question you have to ask yourself in a crowded bar is do you hear the sound difference—and the truth of the matter is that, no you don't.

"And so the truth of the matter is that it is a marketing ploy," Kareff said. Adam and I looked at each other in disbelief. We felt like we were successful prosecutors, like Tom Cruise getting Jack Nicholson to admit to ordering a "code red" in *A Few Good Men*, or Paul Newman locating that nurse in *The Verdict*. A major official of the jukebox industry in America had just confessed to what I expected all along, that the CD jukebox is a "marketing ploy."

Frank Shultz picked that inopportune moment to walk into the room, but a few second later Art Kareff was continuing with his explanation of the CD jukebox ruse.

"They buy CDs for the home, and they know they're much more expensive—so they have to pay more," said Kareff. To translate, people are willing to pay $12 for a CD for their home stereo—when they were used to paying $6 for an LP—because they know they are getting a better sound. Now they are paying *more* than twice as much to hear a CD jukebox in a crowded bar, where the sound is no better. In other words, the American jukebox customer is getting fleeced.

On top of that, the advent of the CD jukebox gave salesmen for companies like Rock-Ola a new marketing tool to use on their operators. When one tavern installed a CD jukebox, Schultz observed, everyone else in a one-mile radius had to have one, too. "It's the domino effect."

All this meant that the much-ballyhooed Nostalgia 1000 jukebox that Rock-Ola was peddling in 1987 was actually the dying gasp of an era—it was one of the last 45 RPM jukeboxes that Rock-Ola would ever market. In 1992, there were five major manufacturers selling jukeboxes in America—Rock-Ola, Seeburg, Wurlitzer, Rowe International, and NSM—and four were manufacturing only CD machines. Wurlitzer, the company who brought us the "Bubbler" was the last to manufacture a 45-RPM jukebox, and that was a nostalgia model, destined to be playing "In the Mood" into eternity.

So, the downward spiral of the 45 RPM jukebox in America was accelerating—there were only 180,000 or so left, probably fewer—while the CD jukebox was on the upswing. With the jukebox market expanding for the first time in more than a decade and with David Rockola's health now failing, there could be only one set of circumstances.

The Rock-Ola Manufacturing Corp. was for sale.

And it was clear that the prime mover behind this development was Donald Rockola, son of David.

Donald joined the four of us near the end of our interview, and it was clear that the man had none of the entrepreneurial, Horatio Alger–ish qualities I have ascribed, fairly or unfairly, to his father. His face seemed pale and drawn, with none of the ruddy, windbeaten charm of David's photographs. But what I remember most about Donald Rockola was not his features but his countenance—something like that of an elder in a harsh prairie congregation.

Donald Rockola looked like he had never heard a jukebox in his life.

To be fair, he was pleasant enough to sit down and chat with, but he seemed to have little of the native energy of his father. In particular, I asked him if he was the envy of all the other boys as a child, growing up around jukeboxes and working summers at 800 North Kedzie.

"I think they probably thought I was something of a putz," Donald said. Everyone laughed.

Still, Adam and I could never get a solid handle on why Donald Rockola was selling the family jukebox business. Donald was a soft-spoken man, so much so that my voice-activated tape recorder died out on him from time to time. And his reasons for

the sale were mumbled, something about other business opportunities, something about—curse the words—real estate ven-
tures.

"You're coming in on the tail end of the Rockola era," Art
Kareff said.

I wondered how Frank Shultz, after forty years of selling
Rock-Ola jukeboxes, felt.

"Is it traumatic?" I asked.

"It definitely is. Mr. Rockola went out there and said: 'This
is what we're going to do.' To have a person like that and to give
up like that, it's just not right."

Frank Shultz—as much as anyone I met during my jukebox
travels—understood the concept of Jukebox America, and how it
was barely clinging to life. Just a few seconds later, we had a
revealing conversation, about how representatives of the new de-
mocracies in Eastern Europe were now coming to America to
learn how to manufacture jukeboxes, a personal freedom that had
been denied under Communism.

"They weren't allowed to do that before," Shultz said.
"They weren't allowed to have them. I think you'll see at more
and more of the shows"—here he was referring to the annual
trade expos for jukebox distributors—"you'll find people from
the Communist countries looking at the business."

Adam piped up again. "As a symbol of personal choice and
freedom?"

"That's right," said Shultz. "That's exactly right. That's the
reason you play selections on a jukebox—that's your individual
choice. That's the reason you pay your 25 cents or 50 cents."

After seeing the outside of the nondescript factory building and
hearing about the death of the 45-RPM jukebox and how Rock-
Ola Manufacturing Corp. was up for sale, the tour of the jukebox
assembly line—an event I had been looking forward to for
months—proved something of an anticlimax.

In retrospect, I'm not sure what I expected a jukebox factory room to look like—maybe a giant assembly line of jukeboxes

rolling past me, one blasting "Tears of a Clown," the next one blaring "Strangers in the Night," all under a neon glow.

In fact, when Frank Shultz strolled back to the manufacturing area with Adam and me, it was 12 noon, lunchtime, and the place was largely deserted. Even if the plant had been fully staffed, only 105 people, including the white-collar staff, worked there—a small fraction of the workforce from North Kedzie. To someone like myself, largely ignorant about the industrial process, the Rock-Ola back shop looked a lot like any other plant. The floor was rock-hard concrete—poured especially to withstand the weight of all the jukeboxes and the pressing of the metal forms, Shultz said—and the room was a dreary twilight. The only sound was the steady drum beat of a machine stamping out steel somewhere in the distance. There were plugs and wires coming down everywhere, so that each jukebox could be tested.

The biggest disappointment was the new jukebox Rock-Ola was manufacturing in August 1992, a model called the Trilogy that the company was getting ready to unveil at the next big industry trade show in October. In the center of the plant was a row of ten or so, and they looked like the jukebox equivalent of Darth Vader, black and menacing and impersonal. Unlike most jukeboxes, which are contained in one solid-body frame, the Trilogy was a two-piece machine: a solid wedge of plastic sloped at a forty-five-degree angle for viewing the CD selections, and a bulky rectangular base for the sound components. At the front of the base was a silvery, psychedelic disc that looked like a relic from 1974 and was the only concession to color.

"In a semi-lit location this looks like it's floating," Shultz said. "We said, 'Let's make it not look like a cabinet,' and so this part and this part are separated."

"Oh, like stereo components," Adam said, while I gaped on dumbfounded.

The Trilogy jukeboxes, standing in a row, were plugged into the big black chords dangling from the ceiling. It would be interesting to say that they were all blasting Pearl Jam or Garth Brooks, but they all stood mute, their red digital numbers ever changing like some crazy slot machine.

"Why is it called Trilogy?" I asked.

"That's the name that we choose for it."

I gave Frank Shultz a look. He would have to do better than that.

"Trilogy—if you go back and look at the word, it has something to do with bars and the parts of music."

My four-day mapcap adventure in Illinois was almost finished, but after Adam's flight left I had about five hours to kill before the 8 P.M. departure of the Broadway Limited back to Philadelphia. I decided to ignore Frank Shultz's advice and visit 800 North Kedzie.

It was after six o'clock when I headed toward the old factory site, starting from the Loop and working west on the Eisenhower Expressway. The Bears—known to all as Da Bears in 1992—were playing their first home exhibition game at Soldier Field that balmy August Monday night, and so a long line of cars was headed in the opposite direction. I was going against the grain yet again. On the radio, a newsman was saying that thirty-five people—some kind of record—had been murdered in Chicago in the last month. I checked the door lock.

For some reason, Kedzie and Chicago didn't meet on my map, so I meandered through the West Side. Soon I was in the vicinity that Frank Shultz had warned me about, although it didn't seemed particularly threatening; it was just a working-poor neighborhood in a big city, worse than many sections, better than some. On every corner, broad-smiled nine-year-old boys were dancing under the spray of open fire hydrants, while beer-bellied middle-aged men watched from well-shaded front stoops. The only sight that alarmed me was a storefront up ahead on my right, the Unique Funeral Home. I wondered if business was good.

The street signs were poor, but I knew when I reached my destination: on my left was the only modern shopping center for blocks, with a railroad track cutting diagonally across the rear of the lot—just as in the artist's rendering at the Rock-Ola Manufacturing Corp. It was the kind of brand-new L-shaped strip shopping center you'd find in a suburb, with a gleaming white facade, but there was a noticeable lack of commerce for twenty-to-seven on a Monday evening. The parking lot was nearly empty, the only major activity a flock of gulls from Lake Michigan that was ambling around a large puddle in the asphalt. There was a food store with bright orange bunting, but the Rainbow Shops store was shuttered tight with an iron gate. The biggest trade in the neighborhood seemed to be in shoes—there was a Payless store and a Foot Locker—but there were no customers. I sat there for five minutes or so, trying to imagine the days when hundreds of workers cranked out 25,000 jukeboxes in one year, when David Rockola marched through six floors, ranting about missing parts—an image to replace that of the antiseptic brick building in Addison. The newspaper reporter in me told me I should investigate who—the Germans, the Japanese, Donald Trump—was buying Rock-Ola, but I dropped the idea. Finally, the silence was broken by a double-decker commuter train, whisking downtown office workers quickly and safely to some pristine suburb like Addison, leaving 800 North Kedzie in a blur. A young Latino man was dragging his son by the hand across the puddles. Then I started the car—and the twenty-four-hour-long journey home to Lower Makefield.

Almost six months later, David Rockola passed away—taking a huge chunk of Jukebox America along with him.

Chapter 6

....

Sweet Dreams

The weekend I finally got to
search for jukeboxes in Patsy Cline country came on August 15
and 16, 1992, and a gentle summer rain fell throughout those
two days, a misty-eyed, honky-tonk, 2 A.M. downpour.

The sad drizzle seemed most appropriate, for Patsy Cline's
death in a small plane crash in 1963 had been the silencing of
probably the greatest female pop singer of the greatest American
era, the happy-go-lucky years of Presidents Eisenhower and Kennedy. By all rights, a sixty-year-old Patsy Cline should have been
enjoying her fourth husband by now, appearing for two weeks at
the Trump Taj Mahal, showing up every blue moon on The
Nashville Network to sing "Crazy" for the 5,738th time.

Ironically, if Patsy Cline had lived to become a Tammy
Wynette–like elder stateswoman of country music, or even a
southern-fried, sequin-studded Barbra Streisand—the career path
not taken—she might never have become what she *was* in 1992:
the greatest jukebox artist of all time. That AMOA jukebox poll,
in 1989, had placed Patsy Cline and "Crazy" behind Elvis Presley
and his double-sided hit "Hound Dog/Don't Be Cruel," and my
immediate reaction was that a great injustice had been commit-
ted. Sure enough, a second survey in 1992 reversed the results,

and Patsy Cline was officially sanctioned as the Queen of Jukebox America.

That statistic didn't explain why Patsy Cline—much more so than any of the dozens of other great American music makers—has come to be associated with jukeboxes. My theory is that her best songs—and there are three that must be played thousands of times every night in gin joints across this great nation: "Crazy," "I Fall to Pieces," and "Walkin' After Midnight"—all share a common theme, a sense of transcendent yearning, a determination to get back to a certain place, the same yearning that motivates the lost souls who populate juke joints. And the reality of her death nearly thirty years ago, in the very prime of her career, makes that hopeless longing real: "This isn't just a 45," it says, "this is life."

Of Patsy Cline's three hit singles, it was 1957's "Walkin' After Midnight," her earliest, that I had taken as the unofficial theme song of my journey. It has more of a shuffling, country-and-western feel than the torchy "Crazy," recorded five years later. In "Walkin' After Midnight," the singer wants something bad—her lost lover—but she goes about it in a most improbable way, wandering out country back roads in the predawn hours, in the stubborn and impossibly foolish hope that she will stumble across him.

It was the unfocused desire of that song—there's something more out there, and maybe if I keep looking and looking I will find it—that had inspired me. Like Patsy, I hadn't found it right away, but, again like her, I'm quick to find signs of hope; just as I was inspired by a Nancy Sinatra cryin' from a jukebox, Patsy "stopped to see a weepin' willow/Crying on its pillow," and thought, "Maybe he's crying for me."

August 15 was the day that Winchester, Virginia—Patsy's hometown—was throwing a special party to celebrate the opening of a Patsy Cline exhibit in its downtown cultural center. That meant that her semilegendary husband, Charlie Dick—portrayed by Ed Harris as something of an alcoholic lout in the movie *Sweet Dreams*—would be there, and so would some of her friends. I also found out that one of the rural roadhouses where she performed, the Rainbow Road Club, was still in business . . . and had a jukebox.

My wife, Kathy, is a hopeless romantic, and so she, too, felt the pull of Patsy Cline. During our courtship, we would plug in a cassette of *Patsy Cline's 12 Greatest Hits* and dance around the semidarkness of her apartment in Philadelphia, or play "Crazy" on the jukebox at the 16th Street Bar and Grill a few blocks away. The constant playing of "Crazy" in 1989 had led not-so-indirectly to Kathy's condition in August of 1992: nearly seven months pregnant. And so, with a handy supply of crackers under the front seat, we climbed into my Honda CRX early on a Saturday morning and headed south. There was a traffic jam in northeast Philadelphia and tolls every two miles south of Wilmington, and it seemed as if we would never be free of I-95's ugly sprawl. But by lunchtime we were rolling across the bald pastures of western Maryland's horse farms and then zigzagging through the shadowy woods of Civil War killing fields. At the West Virginia–Virginia line was the aforementioned Rainbow Road Club, a spartan roadhouse with a neon arrow and a heart reading Home of Sweet Dreams. Then an apple orchard or two, and then a 7-11 that warned us civilization was reappearing. We crossed over I-81, the postindustrial main street of Winchester, Virginia, and were confronted with the inevitable Welcome to Winchester sign, in the shadow of a much larger Texaco sign. There were welcomes from the Kiwanis, the Rotary, the Elks, every fraternal group you could imagine, but right in the center, in small letters, it said: Welcome to Winchester—Hometown of Patsy Cline, Country Music Legend.

There was a story in that sign—although we didn't realize it yet—because Winchester is still a battleground. The combatants are not the Blue and the Gray, but the true friends of Patsy Cline versus the chamber-of-commerce types who had shunned her for nearly four decades. The battle concerns nothing less important than the revered memory of America's greatest jukebox singer.

*   *   *

The story of the Battle of Winchester—as we unraveled it—started with a short, wrinkled retiree, the jukebox man of Winchester, the man the chamber of commerce didn't want me to meet: Jesse Richardson.

The way I found Jesse Richardson is a long story: basically, I had called the chamber of commerce, who tried to steer me to the officially-sanctioned Patsy Cline Memorial Committee, who reluctantly gave me the number of the former mayor, who was willing to give me Jesse Richardson's name and number. It's unlikely any of these civic leaders would have even known about Jesse Richardson, but for the fact that they were having a wine-and-cheese reception to kick off the Patsy Cline exhibition on August 15, and they needed a jukebox. Jesse Richardson had been Winchester's jukebox distributor from 1954 to just a few months before I arrived, and he seemed like the perfect source of information for my search.

When I finally reached him by phone—it took several tries—I told him my idea. I wanted to revisit some of the old dives where Patsy Cline used to sing, and I needed his help.

"Most of the places she played were just country dives," said Jesse Richardson.

"What about the Rainbow Road Club?"

"That's where they made the movie," Jesse said. "It's just an old roadside bar—nothing special."

Then he started to tell me all about Patsy Cline, about how she had to play out of town, in Brunswick, Maryland, with Jimmy Dean back in the 1950s, to make a name for herself.

"Nobody thought too much of her around here," said Jesse, talking about Winchester. "She could cuss like a sailor, and this was an old conservative town."

It turned out that Jesse Richardson hadn't been just Winchester's jukebox man for the last thirty-eight years; he had also been a friend and confidant of the young Patsy Cline. He talked on for ten minutes or so about how he advised Patsy Cline on choosing an agent, about how she would have dumped her husband, Charlie Dick, if she hadn't died in that small plane crash in 1963. He mentioned that Patsy had had something of a bad reputation in town, and how his sisters wouldn't hang out with her.

"How come you know so much about her?" I demanded.

Jesse Richardson just laughed and laughed—a knowing, almost demonic laugh, as if he was mocking my naïveté.

"I was a little on the wild side myself," Jesse Richardson finally said with another gleeful laugh, suggesting a side of Patsy I hadn't planned to explore. "I've been known to tilt a few."

A couple of months later, we arrived in Winchester under that unforgiving drizzle. It was hard to discern when we were actually there, what with the endless sprawl of motels, restaurants like Fritters Restaurant and Gathering Place (specializing in margaritas) and shopping malls in this sprawling section of town.

I called Jesse from our hotel room; yet again, I suggested meeting somewhere with a jukebox, and yet again he rebuffed my suggestion. When I told him where we staying, he suggested the coffee shop at the Lee-Jackson Motor Lodge, a two-story Best Western across the road from our five-story Budgetel. I didn't have any better ideas, so I told him we'd meet there in a half hour.

I later learned from Jesse that back in the '50s there had been an old Esso service station on the site of the Lee-Jackson Motor Lodge, with a wild twenty-four-hour snack bar boasting one of his jukeboxes, so I guess it *was* an appropriate place to meet after all. Nowadays the coffee shop was kind of a dreary place, flooded with bright, institutional lighting, all done up in brown and beige, with fake flowers and folksy baskets all over the walls. Things improved when Jesse Richardson walked in.

Actually, it was more like a shuffle. He was not a tall man, maybe five-foot-five or so, but he had thick, brawny forearms from lifting jukeboxes and Budweisers his whole life, which was nearing sixty-seven years. His face was a jowly, rosy red; for a second I thought he might have tilted a few back that afternoon, but he sipped iced tea through our interview and proved to be a model of sobriety. He rested his sunglasses on his bald forehead, and his choice of apparel could be described as unique—sky-blue slacks, topped by a powder-blue dress shirt completely untucked.

In a high-pitched voice I immediately recognized from the phone, Jesse Richardson proceeded to hold court about two of my favorite subjects—Patsy Cline and jukeboxes.

Jesse Richardson was twelve years old when he moved to Winchester in 1938 from Danville, a cotton-mill town in southern Virginia. The woman we know as Patsy Cline was born just up the road in Gore, Virginia, neither Patsy nor Cline but Virginia Hensley. Jesse repeated his story about how his sisters, closer to Patsy in age, didn't want much to do with her.

"They didn't want to tarnish their reputation."

How so?

"If boys treated her right, she'd go to bed with them."

Kathy and I looked at each other. The interview was only about three minutes old. I wasn't sure what to ask after that, so I decided to shift gears, to ask where Patsy and other singers used to perform locally.

He said there was a popular amateur show before the Saturday matinee at the Palace Theater downtown, and that most of the live entertainment was at armories or veterans halls. Bars were where people heard jukeboxes, not live bands.

"Out of town there were roadside taverns, but not anymore," he said. "Back in the early years, it was pretty rough. It calmed down. That was Saturday night around here." There was a palpable sense of longing in his voice.

His theory on what was killing off the roadhouses was the same theory I heard throughout my jukeboxes travels—that it was stricter drunk driving laws. Cops were waiting outside taverns to arrest patrons as they left. "It used to be they didn't write you up unless you had a wreck," he said with some nostalgia.

Jesse Richardson was on a roll now. He started to wax rhapsodic about the Armory, just down the hill from the coffee shop, where Patsy used to perform on Saturday nights back in the 1950s, where they'd get 500 people for a dance.

"None of it, now," he said. "None of it."

Like most people his age, Jesse Richardson had served in the military in World War II and after, based in New York and California. When he came home to Winchester in 1946, he did plumbing and electrical work, eventually fixing pumps and compressors for the City Service Oil Co. He eventually went to work for the local jukebox concern, Frye Amusement Co., and in 1954 he bought the company when the owner had a heart attack.

How well did Jesse Richardson know Patsy Cline? After talking to him a few times, my guess is better than most people but not as well as some. He used to run around with a crowd of people that included Jack Fretwell, one of her musicians, and some other drinking buddies. He claimed that Patsy called him one night in the mid-1950s from a trailer park after a big fight with her first husband—the man who left her only with the name Cline—and asked him to pick her up. He said Patsy asked him for advice a few years later, after she sang "Walkin' After Midnight" on *Arthur Godfrey's Talent Scouts* back in 1957.

"Some guy wants to be my agent—Eddy Arnold—but he wants fifty percent," she said.

"How much did you make last year?" Jesse said.

"Zero," Patsy Cline said.

Jesse advised her that half of something was better than nothing.

In 1963, right before she died, she told him that she was fed up with her second husband, the fabled Charlie Dick, and that "she was going to dump him on his can." She was starting to play Vegas, to veer from country into steamy pop, and Jesse Richardson is sure that she would have been "big, big, big" if she had lived.

Earlier, Jesse had tried to help Patsy get played on jukeboxes.

"She gave me a bunch of old records to put on the jukebox, and I can't find none of them anymore," he said. Back in the 1950s it was common for local artists to cut a 45 just to get play on the jukeboxes in their home towns. "That's how you got heard," Jesse said. "There's people who were popular around here, you go down the road twenty miles and people have never heard of them."

I asked him if in recent years he had placed local artists on his jukeboxes.

"I just put one on for a local guy, but it didn't do nothin'." In the old days, thousands of artists would cut 45s, and if someone had a hit, he would get to record an LP, Jesse said; now the major labels were more likely to release albums first, pulling singles from the few that are successful.

I was curious about Winchester, especially since I had seen little more than I-81, the Budgetel, and the minimart. His answer took me by surprise.

"I don't like it like I used to. It's not my kind of town anymore. I liked it the way it used to be. It used to be a fun place. All these people would show up from the hills of West Virginia on a Friday or Saturday night. Nowadays, if someone starts a fight, they want to put him in jail. That's crazy! If we didn't have a fight before the night's over, something was wrong!"

Then he laughed—that same strange insinuating laugh from the phone call, conjuring up his and Patsy's wild old days. "I mean—there were some horses around here!" he continued. "There were some men!" He started talking about the Saturday-night dances, when he and another fellow from the American Legion were on hand, allegedly to keep order. Of course, a fight broke out, and his friend leapt up and declared: "If anybody's going to fight in this damn place, it's going to be me." By now Jesse's laugh was maniacal, straight out of some grade-B horror flick. "But now if a couple of guys get in a fight, we send in the cops."

I thought Jesse was ready for a change of scenery—I know I was—so we asked if we could take him up on an earlier offer to show us Patsy's grave, which was just about two miles away.

We walked out into the drizzle and I climbed into his car, a Ford Escort he proceeded to drive erratically—now I worried about a fender bender and a roadside brawl—while Kathy followed in my Honda. I was glad to get Jesse alone, man-to-man, so I could ask what was the deal between him and Patsy Cline.

"She was not what you'd call a pretty woman," Jesse said in the car. "She was big and horsey—a tall, big-boned girl—but she was a nice-looking woman. A lot of fun to be with. She'd give you the shirt off her back—I liked her."

"Did you, like . . . ever date her?"

"Oh—I'd go out with her, you know. I guess you could say I dated her, but I wasn't what you'd call her boyfriend. If I was going out for a couple of hours, I'd go with her.

"Actually, I was never her boyfriend or anything."

I was oddly relieved, but wasn't sure what to say next. I paused for a very long time. "How far out is her grave?"

On the left side of the road, the city fathers were trying to develop an airport industrial park, which turned out to be across the street from the cemetery. We turned in the entrance, near a modest green tower with three bells erected in honor of the grave-yard's most famous tenant; the first-ever venture of the Patsy Cline Memorial Committee. Before then, carload after carload of tour-ists had managed to find the resting place of Patsy Cline without any official guidance. Even on this day, despite the lousy, ceaseless drizzle, a couple of cars pulled up right behind us.

It was good that we had Jesse along, because there is no headstone for Patsy Cline, just a simple plaque on the soft green Virginia grass. There was a vase with about two dozen roses, a rainbow of red, yellow, peach, and off-white. I walked slowly toward the plaque, the way I approach anything loosely con-nected to mortality, when I saw something I found quite jarring.

The plaque read: "DICK."

Then, in much smaller letters, in the upper left, it listed the woman's second-ranking identity, her Christian name of Vir-ginia H. (for Hensley). Only below that is her third-ranking iden-tity—Patsy Cline—listed, and that name is bracketed by parentheses. I suddenly realized that there was a whole different way of viewing this woman, the hierarchy imposed on any thirty-year-old woman in Winchester, Virginia, in 1963. Virginia Hens-ley Dick was a wife, and that was the most important thing. Oh, yes, in her spare time she had this country-music thing going, this Patsy Cline thing. I had only known Patsy Cline through the prism of the 1980s, as the heartsick crooner whose voice visited the desperate juke joints of places from Birmingham to Albany; it had never occurred to me that at home she was still considered a wife, a woman of the 1960s.

I stared at the tiny bronze plaque, which said one other thing: "Death Can Not Kill What Never Dies," and then: "Love."

If you ever find cause to go to Winchester, Virginia, you might be interested in writing to the local chamber of commerce for information. In 1992, their literature bragged about Winchester's favorite son, Admiral Robert Byrd, who went walkin' after the midnight sun and reached the North Pole. Their brochures spoke quite a bit about apples like the red delicious, for an estimated 10 million bushels are still harvested every year in the vicinity, and told of how every May there is a gala Apple Blossom Festival which is said to boast, curiously, the world's largest parade of fire-fighting equipment. The material we received carried a full-page ad for the spanking new Winchester Medical Center, which like hospitals in many midsized American towns is now the largest employer, and steered visitors toward the eighty-four stores of the Apple Blossom Mall, on the other side of I-81 from the Budgetel.

You will not read one word about Virginia Hensley Dick.

That is because Winchester, though just about an hour and a half from that yankee state of Pennsylvania, is above all a prim, proper southern town, and Virginia Hensley Dick was anything but a prim and proper girl coming of age in postwar Dixie. You can still see the roots of the problem as you head into town—as we did that drizzly Saturday—from the Budgetel, the mall, the airport industrial park, and the graveyard. There was a lumber yard and a couple of old gas stations, and then, predictably, a single railroad track. A quick right, and we were in the neighborhood where little Virginia Hensley grew up.

The homes in the area could charitably be called antebellum, for they appear to predate the Civil War, but they are hardly plantations—the worst are two stories of rotting wood in long-faded yellow or blue, some with black shutters askew, some that look as if they have been unoccupied for decades, a four-alarm fire waiting to erupt. Poverty knows little prejudice in the South, and so the hilly neighborhood is somewhat black and somewhat white, whoever's down on their luck these days. On a corner near the top of the hill there is a white house with a newer coat of paint than most, and a decade-old tan Cadillac parked in front, and that is where Patsy Cline's mother, Hilda Hensley, still lives. About six houses down the hill and across the street is a sturdier but spartan two-story brick home with a front porch and a couple of planters, where a straw-hatted Virginia Hensley—as the *Winchester Star* stubbornly insisted on calling her, still—posed in front of her new home for wedding pictures with the white-suited Charles Dick on September 15, 1957.

Just like today, there were two separate societies in the post–World War II Winchester in which Patsy came of age. There was Patsy's World, and then there was the stable and permanent Winchester that erected that array of Kiwanis and Elks signs, which was the first thing we spotted on the border of town. Schools, weddings, social announcements in the *Winchester Star:* it is this world that has struggled for sixty years to catalogue Virginia Hensley Dick.

But Patsy Cline would never let them. I'm sure that many Americans from the wrong side of the tracks feel her kind of yearning, but Patsy and her mother focused hers into music, and it was music that set Patsy Cline free. She sang in an amateur show when she was just four years old, and her parents managed to give her a piano when she was seven, where she practiced her singing so she could perform for prayer groups and in church. In 1948, when she was sixteen, she dropped out of high school. She auditioned unsuccessfully for the Grand Ole Opry that year, but eventually took a job waitressing at Gaunt's Drug Store, a soda fountain that is still up and operating today, now wedged between McDonald's and a Midas muffler shop. One wooden booth there is still standing, near the Russell Stover candies and the Commercial Fax Center; there hangs a picture from July 1951 of the nineteen-year-old girl with wavy brown hair, standing in her backyard in her white waitress uniform. The fuzzy innocence of the picture is a striking contrast from Jesse Richardson's tales of bad language, boys, backseats, and barroom brawls.

The picture is signed "Virginia."

She might still have been Virginia by day, but she was already Patsy Cline by night. For three years, she sang almost every Saturday night at the Moose Hall in Brunswick, Maryland, with Bill Peer and the Melody Makers. She started recording 45s in 1954 for a small label called Four-Star and peddling them to distributors like Jesse Richardson—who took over Frye Amusement that same year—while continuing to take advantage of another outlet for music, a local radio station called WINC where she regularly appeared on Saturdays with a disc jockey named Joltin' Jim McCoy.

"When she first came into the station, she was just a youngster," said Phil Whitney, the general manager of the radio station, in an interview just a few hours after Patsy Cline was killed in a plane crash on March 5, 1963. "And very quiet. The wide-eyed type. She wasn't very good when she started out. Her inexperience was obvious. But she was willing to work, and work like the devil."

Like Elvis Presley, Patsy got her biggest breaks on TV. She had hooked up with Jimmy Dean in Washington, D.C., by the mid-1950s just as he was taking his radio show, *Town and Country Time*, onto TV. Now a local celebrity, Patsy Cline went national yet again on television, when she got a much coveted spot on *Arthur Godfrey's Talent Scouts*.

The song she performed on January 21, 1957, was "Walkin' After Midnight."

The rest of the story is familiar, especially to the millions who saw Jessica Lange portray the singer in the movie *Sweet Dreams:* the constant struggle between stardom and the pressures of troubled marriage; a serious automobile accident that almost derailed her career; a brilliant manager named Randy Hughes who steered her away from traditional country and toward pop and Las Vegas; and how it all ended in seeming mid-flight on that Tennessee hillside in March 1963.

A less well-known part of the story was the cold shoulder that, even in death, official Winchester turned to Patsy Cline. Here, she was never more than Virginia Hensley Dick from the wrong side of the tracks. Oh, there was a big write-up in the *Winchester Star* about the death of the hometown girl, and a massive traffic jam south on Route 322 for her funeral—but then Winchester tried to forget. The whole downtown was redeveloped with a Colonial period look, but no acknowledgment of Winchester's most famous daughter—no plaque, no monument, no street name, no instructions on how to find her house or her modest burial plot. And at first there were also but few tourists, except the few on I-81 who were headed someplace else and the few more from New York and Texas and Canada and everywhere else who insisted without any official help on seeing the grave of the woman whose sultry 45s had touched them back home.

Of course, the unofficial side of Winchester, that hard drinkin', fist flyin' contingent that counted Jesse Richardson as a member, never forgot. Bill Madigan, the man who took over Gaunt's Drug Store, remembered Patsy with a folksy barbecue every year around Labor Day weekend, which falls near her birthday, and believers from all over the United States came down. And there were others, like guitar-playin', beer-drinkin' Jack Fretwell, and a man named Al Smith who—as if fated by his political namesake—became a state representative.

You might think that official Winchester's policy toward Patsy Cline was merely one of benign neglect, but the truth was discovered by a middle-aged real-estate broker named Fern Adams. She moved to the town in the 1980s and—like me—knew Patsy Cline, the entertainer, but had never heard of Virginia Hensley Dick, the town tramp.

Like many people, Fern Adams knew little about the Patsy Cline legend until *Sweet Dreams* came out in 1987, but she was taken by the film. Not long after her arrival in the singer's hometown, Adams was developing a new subdivision just behind the Apple Blossom Mall, and came to the good idea of naming one of its new streets Patsy Cline Drive.

As any student of civics knows, naming streets is one of the main functions of municipal government in America—the New York City Council seems to do little else—even though most such votes are merely a formality.

The Winchester City Council's vote on Patsy Cline Drive was twelve to one.

Against.

The city burghers of Winchester hadn't forgotten that the greatest jukebox singer of all time—the only Winchester native whose name was known to most Americans—was really just that slutty waitress from the other side of the tracks.

But Fern Adams didn't give up. She discovered an obscure group in town called the Patsy Cline Memorial Committee, which had managed to erect the bell tower at the cemetery but little more. Taking over that committee and then wooing Winchester's elite slowly and professionally, she assembled the first-ever brochure locating the Patsy Cline landmarks, started a laudable scholarship fund for local young musicians, and, notably, got not one but two highways named for Patsy Cline.

This day—August 15, 1992—was to be Fern Adams's crowning achievement, a reception that would bring together the chamber-of-commerce crowd with the Saturday-night-fistfight crowd to kick off a month-long exhibition of Patsy Cline memorabilia at the Kurtz Cultural Center in downtown Winchester, with a "permanent display case" to remain in place. After meeting Jesse Richardson—who was thinking, with great reluctance, of showing up, if only to start a little brawl—I knew this was an event I had to see. And I was anxious to see the jukebox that Jesse had assembled.

When Kathy and I strolled into the Kurtz Cultural Center that afternoon, there was the usual five seconds of silence, and then Jesse Richardson's jukebox blared out the slide guitar intro to "Walkin' After Midnight."

The Spirit in the Sky was becoming almost predictable.

Under the exposed wood beams of the Kurtz Cultural Center, a turn-of-the-century food warehouse converted into public space, I raced past the inexplicable drek of the gift shop—Confederate and British flags, Australian knickknacks—and past a blur of Patsy Cline album covers, a microphone stand, and a sequined dress to see the jukebox that Jesse built. I was beginning to wonder if I'd be needing a new category in my one-man jukebox contest—best museum jukebox.

I was looking at a Rock-Ola jukebox, Model #448, which Jesse later said was from 1974. Like most 1970s jukeboxes, it was a triumph of function over form, a low-rider with a plain glass top harboring the selections and a base of bluish-black fuzz that probably looked neat in the pitch-blackness of a tavern, which the Kurtz Cultural Center clearly was not. One thing I liked about Jesse's jukebox—as distinguished from the museum jukeboxes in the Chicago library or the Rock 'n' Roll McDonald's—was that it played, and it played on quarters, not for free, an economical seven plays for a dollar. I guessed that Jesse was keeping those quarters, a small token of fiscal revenge on official Winchester.

Most important, though, Jesse Richardson's jukebox was what I had come to Winchester to see, and that was the world's greatest Patsy Cline jukebox, albeit one especially created for an exhibit. The first twenty-six A-sides and B-sides were all Patsy Cline standards (her biggest hits, "Crazy," "I Fall to Pieces," and "Walkin' After Midnight" were included twice). The all-important #100 selection—I have learned in my jukebox travels that the first selection is always the operator's favorite song—was an offbeat choice, a four-song EP of religious tunes, including the ironic (and inaccurate, considering the plane crash) "Life's a Railway to Heaven." Next came "I Love You, Honey," a pre-feminist tract that celebrates using rich men with nice cars, and then most of the other Patsy Cline songs you'd want to hear on a jukebox, including covers of everything from "Your Cheatin' Heart" to "Love Letters in the Sand." There was also her posthumous duet with Jim Reeves, "Welcome to My World," and a song by Marsha Thornton called "Patsy Cline and a Bottle of

Wine." The rest of the jukebox was pure country—Hank Sr. and Jr., George Jones, Merle Haggard—and all of it was worthy of the Queen of Jukebox America.

For me, the jukebox was the centerpiece of a decent collection of Patsy Cline stuff, even though one highlight, that sequined dress, was worn not by Patsy but by Jessica Lange in the movie. There were some priceless pictures of Patsy in those cowgirl getups, parading through the streets of Winchester in an open convertible for the Apple Blossom Festival and singing with groups like the Kountry Krackers. There was a replica of the booth at Gaunt's Drug Store, including the "Virginia" photograph, and the "permanent display case," which was a little light (among its items was a fur stole that Patsy had given her mother-in-law) but featured some neat 45s, like "A Church, a Courtroom, then Goodbye" on Coral Records, and cover slips for singles like "Tra Le La Le La Triangle." They had been collected by Fern Adams's Baby Boomer son, Kevin.

But Jesse's ad hoc jukebox seemed to be the star attraction, and I noticed a funny thing in Winchester that I had also seen with the other museum piece jukebox, in Chicago, and that was this: There are millions of Americans, middle-aged people who've been busy raising families, who haven't set foot in a corner tavern for decades, and they all seem to think that the jukebox is extinct, a relic of Americana equal in trivia value to the Packard or a string of Burma Shave signs.

A teenaged girl took a look at the rather nondescript jukebox frame and proclaimed: "Boy, is this pretty." A minute or two later, an older woman in a white sweater and blue jeans—it may have been her mother—dropped in a couple of quarters and lit up like she was playing some illegal basement slot machine in Little Italy.

"I haven't done this in years," she said gleefully.

Maybe that was because the grand poobah of this event, Fern Adams, did not appear to be a jukebox person. She was a middle-aged woman with attractive, Waspy features, a gold-and-diamond necklace and a modest, appropriate khaki suit, and she looked like the heroine of a Century 21 real-estate ad. Although she came from another world, she seemed earnest about her effort to pay homage to Patsy Cline, and I admired her for that. At the same time, I couldn't help put think that the support she was finally getting from official Winchester was motivated not by a love of Patsy Cline or music, but by a yearning for the tourist dollar that in 1992 was forsaking Winchester for the bed-and-breakfasts of the Shenandoah Valley.

Kathy and I talked to her briefly, and we learned that the turning point in her drive to recognize Patsy Cline was a government report prepared by a local economic development corporation for Winchester and surrounding Frederick County.

Fern Adams told us that the economic-development report suggested "that the legacy of Patsy Cline hasn't been—I don't think they used the word 'exploited,' at least I hope they didn't—but that's the word that comes to mind."

And so now, in August 1992, the mayor of Winchester, the former mayor, the head of the local council on the arts, and other suits were all on hand to honor Patsy Cline, all so her memory could be "exploited" sufficiently to fill the empty rooms in the Budgetel and the Lee-Jackson Motor Lodge out by the interstate.

Luckily for the memory of Patsy Cline, some of the folks who really remember the singer, who had tossed back shots with her at the Rainbow Road Club, were still around, and thanks to what seemed to be a Fern Adams–arranged truce in the Battle of Winchester, they were on hand for the reception, too.

Jesse Richardson—after expressing a great deal of hesitation about attending the soiree—did decide to drop by, without bothering to change his outfit.

Indeed, the true friends of Patsy Cline were easy to single out. There's a great debate in American studies over whether this great nation is really a "melting pot" or a "salad bowl" of distinct ethnic groups, but I would have to describe this party as "cheese and crackers": The big cheeses, the mayors and developers stayed on their side in their wool and cotton suits, while those semiretired barroom brawlers in a pastel rainbow of polyester, also kept to themselves trading off-color jokes.

One of the true friends was Jack Fretwell, a strapping six-foot septuagenarian with greased-back hair who wore a sky-blue blazer. Fretwell was a comedian back in the 1950s who often shared a stage with Patsy Cline during the Jimmy Dean TV show period, and he fancies himself a comedian still.

"I'm seventy-seven years old, and I've never needed glasses," Fretwell said to some nervous titters from the suits, who seemed to view him as a loose cannon. "I drink out of the bottle."

Another true friend was the above-mentioned Al Smith, the state legislator, who by virtue of his standing was entitled to hang out with the suits, if he hadn't been such a man of the people, such a Huey Long type. It turns out that the sixty-four-year-old Smith grew up a few doors away from Patsy Cline, and he never forgot whence he came.

"What people forget is that forty or fifty years ago, there weren't too many people who would admit to liking country music," said Smith. I tried to find out more from Smith about what Patsy Cline was like, but he seemed obsessed with discussing how great Patsy Cline sounded on a car stereo, especially his own. He told us he played her tapes every week as he drove from Winchester to the state capital of Richmond, and insisted that we go to his car. We headed out the door but never made it to his blue Lincoln, because the star of the affair was walking past, and that was Charlie Dick.

When I was hatching my plan to visit Winchester, one of my crazier ideas had been to look up Charlie Dick and take him out to some juke joint for a beer. Then I learned that he lived in Nashville, not Winchester, and that he was something of a music-world big deal, so I gave up on the scheme—but now here he was at the Kurtz Cultural Center. I don't want to belabor this point, but meeting Charlie Dick was the only real disappointment of our trip to Winchester. For one thing, I was expecting the right-stuff masculinity of Ed Harris, but Charlie Dick looked more like a drawn-faced version of Bob Uecker, the buffoonish sportscaster and Lite Beer pitchman. I'd had no luck finding out what kind of music David Rockola like on his jukebox; now I had the same question for Charlie Dick about his wife, but I got no great answer from him, either; all he offered was that she liked big band music, even the records of Sophie Tucker. I also asked him if he could recall the places where Patsy used to sing around Winchester, and he mentioned a couple of roadhouses, most notably the Armory in Berryville, about ten miles northeast. Mainly, though, Charlie Dick was an entrepreneur, and he wanted to talk about a documentary that he was producing on Willie Nelson.

Charlie Dick had moved onto his next project.

It was left, instead, to the unlikely duo of Jack Fretwell and Fern Adams's son, Kevin, who cut quite a contrast from Fretwell in his navy suit and mod floral tie, to honor Patsy Cline in a brief ceremony. In a variation on Patsy's cemetery plaque, Kevin declared, "A person is not dead until forgotten." He asked for a moment of silence, and then Fern handed him a boom box. He pressed the play button, and on came "Sweet Dreams," slower and sadder than ever.

The whole room, cotton and polyester, swayed ever so gently. Then the song ended, and a line formed for soft cheese and chardonnay in a back room. Fern Adams had achieved her truce, the banishment of Virginia Hensley Dick was officially over, and we were there to witness it. And yet I couldn't help but think that this was only temporary, like the ceasefire in Vietnam before Saigon was overrun. In time, after Jesse Richardson and Jack Fretwell and Al Smith make their last trip down the Patsy Cline Memorial Highway, who will be the keeper of the truth—the tales of barroom brawls and backseat rumbles that inspired the music? All that would be left would be the "exploiters," the economic developers, with their T-shirt shops, CDs, and "Walkin' After Midnight" double-deck-bus tours.

But I didn't want to dwell on the future that night. I had a roadhouse to visit.

After a whole afternoon of learning about the longtime prudery of official Winchester, it was refreshing to have to drive twenty miles out of town—clear out of Virginia, in fact—to hear another jukebox.

Our destination was the Rainbow Road Club in Rippon,

West Virginia, a roadhouse with a confusing past. For years it was called the Orchard Inn, and it was one of the places where Patsy Cline used to sing, although how often was a matter of dispute. Back then, as Jesse Richardson had said, it was just one of a bunch of roadhouses in the rolling apple hills outside of Winchester, but by 1984 most of the competition had closed down. That was fortuitous timing, for that's when the makers of the movie *Sweet Dreams* pulled into town and declared they needed a roadhouse where Patsy Cline/Jessica Lange could sing, get picked up by Charlie Dick/Ed Harris, and fool around in his classic car in the parking lot.

When the film came out a year later, the movie-bar was called the Rainbow Road Club, after a long defunct gin joint closer to Winchester. Not one to miss a chance for a dollar, the owners said, in essence, To heck with the Orchard Inn, and re-named the place the Rainbow Road Club in real life. In case anyone missed the connection, there was a slightly tacky red heart next to the front door that declared this tavern to be The Home of Sweet Dreams.

With that damned rain and with the total blackness of a West Virginia hillside night, we got lost once on the rural back roads, and the thought occurred to us halfway there that going to the Rainbow Road Club might be a giant mistake. The seven-month-old creature in Kathy's belly was kicking up a storm, and we were both exhausted from a long day of driving and reminiscing. But then we pulled onto that dirt parking lot where Jessica and Ed made out, and where Patsy Cline—if Jesse was to be believed—might have done more, and we were reenergized with the jukebox fire of the Spirit in the Sky.

It was a little after nine o'clock when we strolled in. There was a tiny front room with a pool table and a blindingly bright light, overdressed women in suit jackets and underdressed men in NFL merchandise, and an older man who took $5 from each of us. Then we were in the main room, cavernous and dark like the West Virginia night, illuminated only by a widely scattered beer sign or two.

The first thing I really noticed, when my eyes were able to focus, was the guns.

All along the center beam of the barroom was a small battery of firearms—predominantly muskets from the Davy Crockett days, but this was a Saturday night in a back-country roadhouse, and thinking back on Jesse Richardson, I couldn't help but worry if one or two of the relics might still work. This was clearly alien ground for a native New Yorker, for the Rainbow Road Club was solid Hank Jr. territory, a place where what mattered was God, country, Monday Night Football, and country music, and not necessarily in that order. Hanging over the dance floor was the black-and-white POW-MIA flag, something I'd never noticed in any East Village bars.

The jukebox reflected all this. As Kathy and I entered the back room, it was playing one of the few contemporary country songs we knew, Randy Travis's "On the Other Hand," an ode to the hardships of marital fidelity that Virginia "Patsy" Hensley Cline Dick probably would have understood. I looked to see where the music was coming from, but it took me a minute or two to find the damn thing. It turned out that the jukebox at the Rainbow Road Club was something called a "Consolette," one of those space-saving wall units with no concession to style or color. If you haven't already forgotten the summer of 1992, you won't be surprised to learn that the all-important #100 selection was the inescapable Billy Ray Cyrus, and "Achy Breaky Heart"— same as at the 924 Club in Banner, Illinois, the week before. After that, things improved. There were four Patsy Cline songs—the three obvious choices and "Crazy Arms"—as well as modern stuff by Garth Brooks and Travis Tritt, classics like George Jones's "He Stopped Loving Her Today," and, unfathomably, "Let's Get Rocked" by Def Leppard. Kathy—who had missed most of the jukebox-hunting trips and felt rather deprived—was in charge of the selections, and we settled down at our bar stools to take in some more Patsy Cline and Randy Travis.

I needn't have worried about the guns.

It turned out, as we watched a steady trickle of customers

approach the bar, that beer and tequila in tandem were the drink of choice in Rippon on a drizzly Saturday night. Soon no one would be able to point a musket in the right direction, let alone aim properly. The pregnant, Coke-drinking Kathy (Nutrasweet was deemed perilous, and forget about Coors Light) and me with my lonely Budweiser were relative teetotalers. Unlike my other jukebox stops, where I asked a lot of nosy questions, in this rugged roadhouse I was happy to just eavesdrop.

A minute or two later, a blur of feathered haircuts and cheap perfume was on its way to the Ladies' Room.

"It'll be fucked if they don't play 'Achy Breaky Heart,' " squealed one, discussing the country-music combo that was slated to take the bandstand in a couple of minutes.

"They said they're not going to play it!"

"I could play Billy Ray Cyrus all night long!"

Then the two young women, barely past the legal drinking age, slipped out of earshot. But a minute or two later, they had rejoined their two other friends on some stools in a far corner of the bar. They were having an oblivious good time— one was wearing a frayed T-shirt that said "Achy Breaky Heart" in big letters, while another's T-shirt had a caricature of none other than Billy Ray himself. I couldn't hear all their conversation, but they seemed to talk of nothing else, and soon, inevitably, the four girls started singing their favorite song at the top of their lungs.

Luckily, the clock had struck 10 P.M., and the band was tuning up on stage, beneath a giant velvet rendering of the Billy Ray Cyrus of the 1950s, Elvis Presley.

"We're Fallen Timber," the leader leaned into a microphone, "and we'll be here until 2 A.M., playing country music." There was a jaunty riff on the rhythm guitar, a wah-wah from a steel guitar, and then he leaned into the mike again.

"Don't rock the jukebox . . . "

Soon, the woman with Billy Ray Cyrus's face on her chest was swaying on the dance floor with her tight-jeaned female friend, and a minute or two later they were joined by an older man with in a black cowboy hat and pointy boots, who with his glitter-studden partner could two-step more gracefully than anyone on TNN. Kathy and I looked at each other and her baby-bearing belly, and we knew that for us there might never be another chance at a Saturday night in a West Virginia roadhouse again. Soon the two-and-a-half of us were out on the dance floor, as I stumbled my way into a three-step, or maybe a nine-step, swaying to a steel guitar.

I was no big fan of Billy Ray Cyrus—he seemed more a product of cable television and the Nashville marketing machine than anything real—and so it was tempting to dismiss the Rainbow Road Club and its patrons, to say that I found nothing left there of Patsy Cline or her legacy. But my heart leaned to the contrary. With all the cussing, the shot-drinking, the dirty dancing, and all that music on the jukebox, I have no doubt that she would have loved the Rainbow Road Club in 1992, that she would have been ordering tequila for those four young women, maybe even joining them in singing along with Billy Ray. Jesse Richardson was wrong to dismiss the Rainbow Road Club—it was merely younger and a little more TV conscious than he'd probably enjoy, and the only thing missing was a good brawl.

And it seemed like even that could be arranged. On our way out, Kathy and I checked out that bright front room with the pool tables, which had a few faded Patsy Cline clippings and album covers. As I read one of the stories on the wall, Kathy strayed too close to one of the billiard games, where a young punk spoke from underneath his tractor hat.

"So who knocked you up?"

I guess Jesse Richardson would have grabbed a pool cue and started swinging right there, but my first thought was to make like the Charlie Daniels character in "Uneasy Rider," to hit the parking lot and start kicking up some gravel in my Honda CRX with the New York license plate.

And so Kathy and I drove back through the drizzle—away from the West Virginia frontier and back into the law-and-order state of Virginia Hensley Dick. My mind was a jumble of happy thoughts—of Patsy Cline and "Walkin' After Midnight," of Jesse Richardson and his jukebox, of drinkin' and fightin' and those Billy Ray Cyrus girls—and the idea that death cannot kill what never dies.

Chapter 7

....

''Allons à Lafayette''

We were approaching Picayune, where the seemingly endless scrub pine of the southern Mississippi forest gives way to a soggy world of reedy bayous, alligators, and bait shops.

I had to go to the bathroom. The blue sign on Interstate 59 said there was a Burger King at Exit 4, and that seemed as good a place as any. Mississippi Exit 4 looked just like most other small-town interchanges in the Deep South—a couple of fill-ups and a couple of fast-food joints carved out of the piney woods. I was anxious to go the last four miles into Louisiana, so I hurried out of the men's room, to find Bob inside the eating area, licking on a vanilla-and-chocolate frozen yogurt cone.

"Take a look at this," Bob said.

I looked to the far side of a typical Burger King, on the other side of the salad bar, and saw something I had never seen in a run-of-the-mill fast-food joint before: a jukebox. And it wasn't a spanking new CD model either, but a real relic—badly faded blue and aqua green, a dented AMI High Fidelity model that had to be from the 1950s. To give you an idea of how old it was, the 45s were listed under the following five categories: Rhythm & Blues, New Releases, Country Music, Old Favorites, and Polka. Amid the freshly scrubbed tile and the clutter of Formica, the record machine looked highly out of place, but my only thought was that this great old jukebox in a Burger King confirmed what I had believed for a long time—that Louisiana and Mississippi were going to be a peek at Jukebox Heaven.

"We like old antiques," said a stout man with a pink shirt and a tie clip who identified himself as Allen Hunter, the assistant manager. He pointed over to another relic from the 1950s, a forty-eight-star flag. I was momentarily disappointed; could it be this was yet another jukebox museum piece?

"Oh, it's operational," Hunter said, fumbling for change. "Let me get a quarter." The jukebox, which had been purchased secondhand in nearby New Orleans, still played three songs for twenty-five cents. Hunter hit three songs at random, and one of the few modern selections—"Night Vision" by Suzanne Vega (I guess this was a New Release and not Polka)—came on, so scratchy and slow she sounded like a man. The next song was "Hello, It's Me," not the hit version by Todd Rundgren but the seminal 1968 acid-rock version by Rundgren's original group, the Nazz. If the Burger Kings in the Deep South have such wild jukeboxes, what about the juke joints?

I wandered about while the Nazz sang slowly, sounding like about 39 RPM. There was a tackboard of business cards, and I saw one for a company called St. Tammany Games and Amusement Co. The card had a picture of the old Wurlitzer Bubbler jukebox, and the company provided pool tables, pinball, and foosball as well as record machines. It also gave the company slogan: Shoot Pool, Not People.

I got a bit of a chill at that: I'd expected that hanging out in the juke joints of Louisiana and Mississippi would be exhilarating—I hadn't counted on it being dangerous.

Bob and I seemed unlikely candidates for a hazardous assignment. When we first met in 1982, I was a twenty-three-year-old cub reporter in Birmingham, Alabama, and Bob was a twenty-four-year-old copy editor there. Our first couple of years as friends had their share of walks on the wild side: Bob was a key member of the kick line the night I discovered "New York, New York," and there was that time at the stodgy Birmingham Press Club we broke a mirrored wall slam-dancing to the B-52s and Jim Carroll's "People Who Died." But even then Bob was already in the process of trading in his Mazda RX-7 for a VW Rabbit and a marriage license, and when I left three years later to make a brand new start of it in old New York, Bob—now an award-winning reporter—was hunting for a home for himself and his wife, Tondee, who was three months pregnant.

And so on the morning of August 21, 1992, after a 5:30 A.M. flight from Philadelphia to Atlanta to Birmingham, I found myself at Bob's new home, just purchased and bigger than the first. Bob now had a six-year-old daughter, Holly, and a two-year-old son, Derek. I was anxious to get on the road to Louisiana, which was still an eight-hour drive, but first we had to drop off some books he was giving to Holly's elementary school.

When we finally hit the road, it was a strange combination of old times and new. We made the traditional stop at the world's greatest barbecue joint, the Dreamland Drive-In in Tuscaloosa, for a slab of ribs (at 10:45 A.M.) and blasted the latest obscure but hip rock groups from Bob's boom box. But the talk was not so much about concert-going anymore as it was about child-rearing. In particular, we talked for a long time about his son Derek, a hyperactive but lovable toddler who insisted on dancing around their house with an open umbrella. Bob was still one of the hippest Rear Guard Baby Boomers I knew, but it was clear he had made the transition from slam-dancer to superdad—and now here he was, coaxed along on a half-crazy search for great jukeboxes. At one point, he gazed out the passenger window at the red soil of western Alabama.

"I feel as guilty as hell," Bob said.

So did I. I wasn't sure which of us had done worse: Bob leaving behind two kids, or myself leaving one wife, seven-months pregnant. A few moments later, a song by a Canadian group called the Odds, rang out of Bob's boom box. It was called "Domesticated Blind."

Makin' babies,
Buyin' a house,
French guy's name is on my trousers,
Used to be such rabble rousers,
Before the world revolved around us,
I've been domesticated blind,
Family fills my mind,
I've been domesticated blind.

This Louisiana trip wouldn't get us nominated for Fathers of the Year. But—at least for me, with a little one less than ten weeks away—it seemed there might never be another chance to visit the one bar in America I had always dreamed of seeing. That was Fred's Lounge in Mamou, Louisiana.

Like most everyone, I had never heard of Fred's Lounge until the early 1980s, when Charles Kuralt called in an *On the Road* report from Louisiana's Cajun country. His opening shot was of a place called Fred's Lounge, video of a packed barroom, people swilling beer and dancing the two-step, and I can still remember what Kuralt said: "This is Mamou, Louisiana at 9 A.M. on a Saturday morning—Miller time!" I remember those words because I thought a packed barroom at 9 A.M. looked like the most fun I had ever seen. As a young adult, I always nurtured an unhealthy and unrealized fantasy about walking into a bar, preferably one with a great jukebox, in the dead of night, and walking out into the blinding sun of morning.

Fred's Lounge opened at sunrise: the next best thing.

Not too long after seeing that show, I—along with a bunch friends, including Bob—took a longstanding shine to the music of Louisiana. On weekends, we'd cook shrimp Diane or jambalaya and listen to the latest sounds from the bayou—white Cajun fiddlers and rub-board strummers like Beausoleil or black accordion-squeezing zydeco players like Buckwheat Zydeco or Clifton Chenier. By the early '80s, independent record labels like Rounder Records out of Boston or Alligator out of Chicago were recording the top Louisiana artists on LPs.

But like all great forms of regional music in America—Mississippi Delta blues, Tennessee hillbilly, Texas swing—Cajun music was first and best heard on single records—78s and later 45s—that were intended for jukeboxes. In 1928, Joseph Falcon and his wife Cleona recorded the first Cajun record, "Allons à Lafayette" as well as a follow-up 78, the standard "Jolie Blonde" (spelled "Jole Blon" in most later incarnations). While white Cajuns like Dennis McGhee and Auguste Breaux were also cutting seminal records, a black accordionist named Armadie Ardoin released a record in 1928 called "Valse de Guedon" that author Philip Sweeney notes was quite similar in style to the white recordings. By the 1950s, the black and white cultures and musics had diverged, the black pioneers like Clifton Chenier, who had moved to Texas to work in the oil refineries, pioneering the R & B–inflected zydeco music. In 1954, Chenier went into a radio station, KAOK in Lake Charles, Louisiana, and cut his first 45 for Elko Records.

My guess was that Louisiana, with its rich and still ongoing tradition of local music, would have some of the best and most original jukeboxes in America, filled with obscure zydeco and Cajun hits. I knew that Cajun country—the swampy lands an hour or so west of New Orleans where French and French-Canadian refugees, the Acadians, came to settle—was a hard-drinkin' place for ruddy-faced men with French accents and tractor hats, still suffering the damaging effects of the oil slowdown of the 1980s. Another American place in transition, prime Jukebox America.

That border incident—the unexpected Burger King jukebox in Picayune—seemed to presage a treasure trove of jukebox riches in both Louisiana and our next stop, the Mississippi Delta. And so it was with both excitement and trepidation that we crossed the Big Muddy in Baton Rouge at about 4:30 P.M. Then something incredible happened—for the next twenty miles or so the highway, Interstate 10, became a concrete ribbon in the sky, a seemingly eternal viaduct riding fifty feet or more above a swamp underworld, a mysterious and wet landscape of soft Spanish moss, insects, snakes, and gators. Whipping past on I-10 or on rail tracks below were massive lumber trucks and chemical cars, the vessels of man's effort to tame the swampy beast. Then came the strange signs—for Green's Cajun Mart, serving hot boudin, and for Breaux Bridge, "Crawfish Capital of the World"—and we began to pick up the sounds and scents, once again, of Jukebox America.

It was almost dinnertime when we arrived at the Super 8 Motel in Lafayette, the capital of Cajun country. After checking in, Bob and I cruised the city streets and found that Lafayette looked on the surface a lot like any other small city in Wal-Mart Land, with a couple of notable exceptions. One was the pawn shops—at least four in just the short drive from the Super 8 to the Cajun diner where we went to eat. I've noticed pawn shops before in America, but always in the seediest of neighborhoods; not so in Lafayette. In fact, one of those I saw was wedged into a brand new strip shopping center—this was surely the only place in the country where the pawn shops are spanking new, high-tech enterprises. But that's nothing compared to the other phenomenon in Lafayette and sprinkled elsewhere in Cajun country, and that is the drive-thru daiquiri stands. There was one every few blocks or so, and several looked clean and new, like McDonald's without the arches. No wonder they call Louisiana "Sportsman's Paradise."

Several dozen crawfish and shrimp later, we were on our way to our first official stop—El Sid O's, reputed to be the home of the best, if not the only, zydeco jukebox in America. We had some crude directions, but it turned out that El Sid O's was just three minutes from the Super 8, across the main railroad track in town. It was hard to miss, with a sign like a beacon—bright yellow, suspended forty feet in the sky, like some interstate Shell station where the fuel was "Zydeco & Blues." The building was your basic all-American cinder-block roadhouse, but El Sid O had gussied his up with brick trim, a yellow-and-white canopy over the entrance, and an oversized accordion. We had come to the right place.

Bob and I paid a cover charge and entered a cavernous room, with a band stage in the back left and a well-stocked bar to the right. It was just after 9 P.M.—about an hour before a band called Nathan Williams and the Zydeco Cha-Chas were to hit the stage—just enough time to check out the jukebox, which was straight to the back. It was a low-lying basic black floor console, an unspectacular relic from the late '70s or early '80s. But as with all great American jukeboxes, it was the music and not the hardware that mattered. The all-important #100 selection (which had been Billy Ray Cyrus in the two other roadhouses I had visited) was the old Hank Williams classic "Jambalaya," performed by Clifton Chenier, the widely acknowledged King of Zydeco before his death in 1987. Next was "Goin' Go Rockin' Tonight" by Buckwheat Zydeco, the closest thing to a successor, and that was followed by 45s by Rockin' Sidney, Zydeco Force, Boozoo Chavis, and Nathan Williams and the Zydeco Cha Chas, as well as blues standards from B. B. King, Z. Z. Hill, and Tyrone Davis.

I put in a dollar—good for a whopping eleven songs—but somehow the jukebox effect seemed lost in such a large room, like a basketball game in the Rose Bowl. Besides, the music wouldn't come on until a guy onstage in a wild aqua-blue floral shirt and big white cowboy hat—riffing away on an accordion and shouting something in French every now and then—finished his sound check. When that was done, we listened to two or three of our jukebox selections, and then asked a bartender how to find El Sid O himself.

"He's over at the One-Stop," said the bartender. "It's just across the street and down the block."

When we arrived at El Sid O's One-Stop a minute later, we realized that when we crossed those railroad tracks we were in a Lafayette far different from the Kmart roads we had seen at twilight. Rows of shotgun shacks stretched back into the darkness, and about seven or eight pickup trucks were circled around the small cinder-block convenience store, each truck with a cluster of three or four young men sipping from a paper bag.

We hurried inside, and were immediately face-to-face with the man known as El Sid O—the very same wild-looking accordion man from the sound check. His real name was Sid Williams, and he was the older brother of Nathan Williams, the zydeco star. El Sid O was a walking Fort Knox—he wore a solid gold watch on his left wrist and a gold bracelet on his right, a diamond dangling from his neck just above his crucifix, and four massive gold rings, including one that was a replica of an accordion. A sturdy black man with a goatee, El Sid O was forty-one, not much older than Bob or I, but he had clearly made it on his own terms—America's only zydeco entrepreneur.

"It all started weeth this leettle store," El Sid O said.

"It all started with this little store?" I repeated. I was straining to hear El Sid O, partly because of his accent, which—not unlike the quirky rhythms of zydeco music—was a strange brew of African American and French, and partly because of its soft delivery at machine-gun speed.

"About fifteen years ago. I built the store—built it with my own hands."

El Sid O's father had died when he was just eighteen, but the young man was a fast learner when it comes to matters of the wallet. He worked in construction and oil, but after an injury in 1974 he was the first to see the need for a semi-modern convenience store in Lafayette's black community. When he moved in across the street in Lafayette from Stanley Dural—better known to the world as Buckwheat Zydeco—El Sid O decided to get into promoting a few concerts. At first he was reluctant to build his own nightclub, but around 1986 erected El Sid O's, again from the ground up.

By then, his younger brother Nathan, who moved in with El Sid O and his wife at the age of six, was becoming an accordion virtuoso. El Sid O bought his younger brother an accordion from his friend Buckwheat, and then did something that recalled the jukebox glory days of the 1950s—he formed his own record label, El Sid O Records. He went into the studio and produced two 45s with Nathan's band—ES-100, "Everybody Calls Me Crazy (But My Name Is Nathan Williams)"/"I Got the Zydeco Blues (Down in My Shoes)," and ES-101, "Bye Bye My Little Moma/Louisiana Waltz." The records never made the Billboard charts—small independent records never do anymore—but they probably helped in some small way, for by the late 1980s Nathan Williams was appearing on TV shows like *Good Morning America*, playing clubs in New York City (I saw him at one, Tramps, in 1989), and recording for a respected independent label, Rounder Records. El Sid O, the band's manager, said a Rounder CD was due that fall.

"Why no 45s anymore?" I asked.

"If you got something good on an album, they'll take it off and make it a 45," El Sid O said.

I complemented him on his jukebox back at the club, and asked if it got a lot of use.

"I got it for the old people—old people like a jukebox."

"Why the old people?" I asked. "Old-timers, old habit?"

"Old Memory Lane," said El Sid O, tersely and very quickly. "Wonder where you're goin', but don't forget where your comin' from."

El Sid O was talking so fast—he conducted our whole rapid-fire interview standing up in a small alcove between a Galaga video game and a deli counter that offered smoked tasso and hog head cheese—that Bob and I got the impression he didn't have much time for us, and began to think we ought to head back to the club. But then El Sid O took us to a little stockroom in the back, with liquor boxes stacked every which way. He kicked aside a black accordion case and handed me and Bob copies of the two 45s that he had produced for El Sid O Records, at a cost of $3,000. On the plain white cover slip, he signed: "Sid."

"I believe in two things—God and the dollar," El Sid O told us. It seemed Sid Williams wanted everyone to know not only how far he had come but how hard he worked to get there, how he hustles weekdays peddling cigarettes at the One-Stop and tends bar at the zydeco club on Friday and Saturday. "People are full of sheet," he said in that strange accent. "They forget where they came from. I told Nathan: 'If you're gonna get too damn big, I'm gonna quit right now.' I made ten million dollars in my lifetime, cash, in my hands, and I've never forgotten nobody." On Labor Day, he throws a free cookout in his parking lot for hundreds of people from his side of the tracks, and he said he financially backs anti-drug programs. But he also realizes that zydeco philanthropy has its limits.

"The neighborhood is tough—that's why I carry this." He lifted up that funky floral aqua-blue shirt to reveal the cold steel handle of a revolver thrust into his pants. Suddenly I realized why his shirt was untucked. "I keep them in order . . ."

"Do you ever use that thing?" I asked. I really didn't want to know, or even to carry on this line of conversation, but I wasn't sure what else to say. El Sid O mumbled an answer so fast that I couldn't understand it anyway, but somehow it raised the issue of whether white people ever go to his nightclub. "I got tour buses coming in, full of tourists . . ." El Sid O said. "Nobody here's gonna put their hands on white people." He paused. "Because you know what's gonna happen to them? They're gonna have to deal with me!"

Bob and I laughed heartily. I knew El Sid O was trying to reassure us, but I began to wonder if even America's premier zydeco jukebox was worth the trouble. Still, we had already been inside the nightclub, and by the looks of its early customers, parking lot guard, and steep cover charge, El Sid O's looked like a safe haven. And, to be quite honest, there was little to worry about after all. At about 10:30, a slightly younger looking version of El Sid O—this would have to be Nathan Williams—hopped onto the spartan stage with a bulky white accordion, and soon he was trading lightning riffs with the band's saxophonist. By eleven o'clock, there were forty people on the dance floor—working women in their floral-print Friday best dancing with men in orange T-shirts, a mix of old and young, black and white (as El Sid O promised), including one spectator in a tweed jacket who looked to be about seventy-five. A man from the black neighborhood, wearing an impeccably tailored suit, was running for district judge and he made the rounds of every table in the joint.

Bob and I were drinking beer and tapping our hands on our table, lost in Nathan Williams's raging current of accordion riffing; our earlier guilt was long gone, as it was way past our wives' and children's bedtimes anyway. By midnight I was swept away by this tiny corner outpost of Jukebox America despite my lone black 1950s-style Washington Senators cap among a crowd of Stetsons.

Eight A.M., a decade after watching that Charles Kuralt report, we were finally en route to Mamou and Fred's Lounge. It was less than eight hours after our safe passage from El Sid O's, and as we headed north on Interstate 49, the flat swamps and forest of the bayou country were enshrouded in a thick fog that added an air of mystery to the whole strange affair. As we veered off the interstate toward Eunice, Louisiana, an intermediate point, the drive-thru daquiri stands were preparing to open for business, and several small taverns were already surrounded by pickup trucks.

First, we made a quick pit stop at another Cajun shrine—the Savoy Music Shop. As with some of my other stops, the purpose here was not to find a jukebox, but to get a glimpse into the culture between the grooves of those 45s. The Savoy is a few miles before Eunice on U.S. 190, located in a big green prefab industrial building that looks more like the local auto-body shop than a music mecca. It was a little after 9 A.M. when we arrived, and we had to park up on the highway, behind a row of four or five pickups.

As we approached the front door, we heard a muffled cacophony of fiddles and squeeze boxes. Sure enough, inside the Savoy music shop there was a cluster of fifteen people standing around in a crude approximation of a circle—seven or eight of them sawing away on fiddles, their bows shooting every which way, a few more strumming guitars or banjos. Seated in the center of the cluster there was a weatherbeaten man in a gray shirt, pants, and hair, wearing a white cowboy hat and squeezing an accordion. Near him was a fortyish fiddler in a white shirt with bushy eyebrows and a five o'clock shadow—this was Marc Savoy, the prominent Cajun musician who owns the store and cooked up the idea for a Saturday morning music jam in the late 1960s.

The music chugged along like a freight train, some folks

singing along in French, and every few bars one of the old-timers would yell out, "Ow-oooh," like an old swamp dog. At the edge of the circle, there was a tiny red-headed girl who couldn't have been more than nine or ten, laboring to keep pace on her fiddle.

In the center of that awkward circle was a case of Miller Lite—I guess 9 A.M. in south-central Louisiana really is Miller time, just like Charles Kuralt said.

Bob and I stood about ten feet from the cluster—spectators are more than welcome, but somehow it felt awkward to be there without a giant accordion strapped around our shoulders. Marc Savoy shook our hand, directed us to a box of steaming hot boudin, a Cajun rice-filled sausage, and went back to his fiddling. I studied the guitars and banjos dangling from the tackboard of the music shop and came across this sign:

DO NOT REPLACE FAMILY TRADITION WITH MEDIA-IMPOSED CONVENTIONS.

I thought Bob and I were intruding, that we should hurry up the road to Mamou and Fred's Lounge, but first I buttonholed an older man in a bleached white shirt who was leaning against the keyboard in the back of Marc Savoy's shop, taking a Miller Lite break from the music. A few beads of sweat rolled down from under his tan straw hat and onto his ruddy face. He said his name was Joseph Bertrand and that was sixty-one. He was a retired state highway man, and he told me that he started playing the accordion in 1955, when he was already twenty-five years old.

"It took me four or five years to learn to play," Bertrand said. But he said that outsiders often find they can never get the hang of playing Cajun music. "If you're not in it—do you know what I'm trying to say. We're with it every day. There's a difference, we're with it every day."

I remarked that in Louisiana there must be a lot of opportunities to perform and to practice.

"Just about everywhere you go, there's an accordion, or somebody playing the accordion, or they let you play," he said. "One thing they got a lot of near Lafayette is jam sessions. Last night they had one at Noonan's in Eunice—that was Friday, and on Thursday night they got one at the Gumbo House in Eunice."

I wondered why jam sessions were so popular.

"A lot of people are apprentices—that's where they learn to play," Bertrand said. He then pointed out four people in the cluster of musicians who were apprentices—a couple of the men looked old enough to be Bertrand's father.

"I don't play too much anymore," he continued. "I used to play all the time."

"When's the last time you played?"

"Last night."

We traded some small talk about the sorry state of the economy in Louisiana—he said a nearby plant that employed 250 people making drilling bits for the oil industry was going to close at the end of the year. "It's gonna hurt," he said, "but we're used to it." I had one more important question for Joseph Bertrand, one that had been on my own mind for the last twenty-four hours: What did his wife think about his hanging out and drinking beer at the Savoy Music Shop, at an hour when most husbands were mowing the back lawn?

"She's not too crazy about it."

I had thought so.

I'm not exactly sure what I had expected downtown Mamou, Louisiana, to look like all these years after I first heard about Fred's Lounge—a bunch of wood cabins on stilts, perhaps, above a crawfish-infested swamp. Instead, it was a bastion of pre–Wal-Mart forgotten small-town America, with a main street about as wide as Broadway on Manhattan's Upper West Side, and dust-covered one-story buildings—either faded brick or cinder block—on either side of the street. The shops on the left side of the street were mostly boarded up, except for the two-story Hotel Cazan at the end of the street. On the right side there was Bill's—the Cajun concept of a department store with "$1 Jewelry and Hair Accessories"—amid a row of seedy bars called Casanova's and Infatuation and Diana's Brass Rail. A Schlitz beer sign hung from a nearby telephone pole, and then a barbershop with a red-, white-, and blue-striped pole, and then, on the corner, in red brick with those thick, opaque glass windows to hide Saturday-morning beer guzzlers, was Fred's Lounge.

At long last.

Bob and I, in some kind of twisted jukebox foreplay, snapped a couple of pictures of the outside before we opened the thick black door. When we entered, we could barely squeeze our way in—there had to be seventy-five people compacted into this tiny bar the size of a middle-class family's living room. We stepped aside to dodge a middle-aged couple—a man in a white polo shirt and a woman in a blue sundress—who were sashaying quickly to the Cajun music right in front of us. Right in the center of the tiny joint was the band—an accordion player, a guitar player, a steel-guitar player and a drummer—chugging away at a breakneck pace. All around them about ten couples were dancing wherever there was a square foot of open space, and others were swilling down beer—all kinds of people, geriatric cowboys in stitched-up shirts and faded blue-jeans, fraternity brothers in loud Hawaiian shirts. Somebody was recording the whole chaotic affair on one of those hand-held video cameras.

The music stopped and a man stepped up to the microphone.

"We want to thank Australia!" he shouted. "What do you think about this place?!"

Sure enough, a man with a Down-Under accent grabbed the microphone. He had traveled halfway around the world for the privilege of drinking beer on Saturday morning. "I think it's fantastic!" he shouted, as seventy-five people whooped in response. "Great music, great people, and great beer!"

It seemed like everyone had been here for hours, and that most were already three-quarters tanked. I glanced down at my watch. It was 10:30. A midmorning, mid-August sun was beating down on the bayou on the other side of that thick black door.

"Uh-oh—look," Bob said, pointing to the right of the doorway. There it was, the jukebox that had been touted in advance as the best in all of Cajun country. Not only was it shut off—that's to be expected when a live band is performing—but a blue-and-white tablecloth had been stretched across the glass top, obscuring the selections. And that tablecloth was covered with the flotsam and jetsam one might expect from a bar where people have been partying nonstop since 9 A.M.—a dozen Miller Lite cans, a couple of Coors and Coors Light cans, a Miller bottle, two Coke bottles, a yellow plastic cup, assorted napkins and drink stirrers.

I had two thoughts. The first was: "Why would anyone downing beer at nine o'clock on Saturday morning worry about drinking Lite instead of regular?" And my other thought was about the jukebox: "Shoot, I was afraid this would happen."

I knew in advance that Fred's Lounge had live music on Saturdays, but I had hoped that there would be time to hear the jukebox, too, if only between sets. My original idea was to see Fred's Lounge not only on Saturday but at another time, maybe Friday night, just for the jukebox. In the week or two before the trip, I had called the number for Fred's Lounge over and over—morning, afternoon, and night, and there was never an answer. It didn't make sense, because a co-worker from New York City had just been there a few months before. Finally I called a man named Barry Jean Ancilet, who is a professor at Southwestern Louisiana University in Lafayette and an authority on Cajun culture.

"If you're looking for a good jukebox, you should go to Fred's Lounge," he said.

"What's the deal? I've been calling there all week, and no one answers."

There was a pause. "Fred died."

In researching the Louisiana portion of my odyssey, I learned that Fred Tate had been quite ill for the last couple of years, and there was no one else prepared to run the joint full-time. So Fred's Lounge was locked shut all week, only to open on Saturday, not only for the regulars and for the tourists from all over the world, but for the weekly radio show on KVPI (1050 AM/93.5 FM) out of Ville Platte, Louisiana, "The Voice of Cajun Country." Fred finally succumbed in July 1992.

Ironically, the wild scene at Fred's—the video cameras, the Hawaiian shirts, the tourists from Australia—was not at all what

Fred Tate had in mind when he and his twin brother, Alphan, opened the tiny corner bar in 1946, upon returning from World War II. Fred Tate was one of those classic American bar owners who lived to trade jokes with his steady customers—his most frequent remark, his friends say, was the unremarkable: "That's a good one."

But with the arrival of the 1950s, there were dark forces at work in Cajun country. This was the dawn of the era of American assimilation, of network television and Top 40 radio, of golden arches and those wild green-and-neon Holiday Inn signs. There was cultural pressure for Louisiana's Cajuns to speak English instead of French, to listen to Patti Page records and not the Alley Boys of Abbeville.

In 1950, Fred's nephew Paul Tate, a small-town lawyer, opened an office across the street from Fred's Lounge. Paul Tate and his friends began to hang out at Fred's, cooking there with dashes of cayenne pepper and listening to the likes of Cyprien and Adam Landreneau fiddle away into the balmy night. They had the rare foresight to realize their culture stood on the brink of the abyss, and so they started small—using Fred's as a base for a revival of the wild Cajun spring festival, the Courir de Mardi Gras, now an annual happening in Mamou. It was Paul Tate and his friend Revon Reed who contacted a prominent talent scout for the Newport Folk Festival in 1964 and urged him to book a genuine Cajun band featuring the locally renowned Dewey Balfa—paving the way for Louisiana music to reach the intelligentsia and, indirectly, for the popularity in the 1990s of such younger musicians as Beausoleil and Zachary Richard. And in 1968, it was Paul Tate who led a successful drive in the Louisiana Legislature for creation of the Council for the Development of French in Louisiana—government working to preserve the Cajun culture, not destroy it. Around that same time, KPVI started broadcasting from Fred's Lounge on Saturday morning, eventually with live bands, and the crowds followed. Soon famous people were knocking on Fred's door, not just Charles Kuralt but actors Dennis Quaid, who studied Cajun accents here before filming *The Big Easy* with Ellen Barkin.

Now, at 10:30 A.M. on August 22, 1992, on a beautiful sun-baked Saturday when the Spirit in the Sky had surely intended His children to be outdoors, Bob and I were wedged into this darkened cubbyhole with pink walls, raging accordions, and beer-chugging grandpas in cowboy hats, and all I could think was: "Is this a great country or what?" Bob and I ordered beers; behind the bar, a gray-haired woman in a purple T-shirt was swilling Miller from a bottle, moving from customer to customer in a kind of frenzied two-step.

I looked down the bar. I didn't know who I expected to find in a bar on Saturday morning, but I didn't expect the two women in the two stools in the near corner. They were trim, well-dressed and well-coiffed, like somebody's youthful grand-mother—they were at least in their fifties—and if I hadn't known better I would have guessed they were on a shopping trip to New Orleans and had taken a seriously wrong turn. One of the women, who told me her name was N. R. Smith, was wearing a blue-studded shirt, big white earrings, and ruby-red lipstick, while her friend, who refused to identify herself, wore a bright red sweater. She had gray hair, and every once in a while she took a long chug from a can of Lite.

"How often do you come here?" I had never said that to a woman in a bar before, but in this case it didn't seem inappropriate.

"About two or three times a year," said Mrs. Smith. It turned out they had come all the way from Monroe, Louisiana, a couple of hours to the north.

"Where did you hear about this place?"

"In *Southern Living Magazine.*" I tried to imagine Fred's Lounge sandwiched between a pictorial on the mansions of Natchez and a recipe for pecan-chocolate pie. "It's because our ancestors are Cajun," she continued. "We used to go as kids and sit at a bar at nine in the morning. It's all family tradition—it's passed on. You work hard, you play hard, and you're at Mass on Sunday."

I introduced myself to the sometimes-gyrating woman be-hind the bar, whose name was Sue Vasseur—she had been Fred's ex-wife and mother of his two children, and it was largely she who had kept the Saturday-morning tradition alive. We chatted for a minute when a jowly man—seemingly the oldest of the many old-timers in the bar—rapped me on the shoulder, hard. His name was Pascal Fuselier, and he was the columnist for the local paper, the *Mamou Acadian Press*. He was also something of an unofficial historian of Fred's Lounge. When Fred's opened, Pascal was a twenty-one-year-old, just old enough to drink. Now he is sixty-seven, and still comes by every Saturday. He remembers those early days—the just-ended war, the birth of television, and the completion of the modern roads started in the 1930s by populist Governor Huey Long.

"There's just one culture like ours—the Amish," Pascal told me, punching my shoulder once again. That seemed both right and ridiculous—I tried to imagine Fred's Lounge in Bird In Hand, Pennsylvania, surrounded by horse-drawn carts instead of Chevy pickups. "My brother's child cannot speak English." *Pow!* "But now we're losing the culture." *Whap!*

Every two minutes or so, Pascal would walk away toward the front door, and I would turn away, only to feel another hard shot to the right shoulder. "All my friends come to Mamou on a Saturday morning," he declared, and he introduced me to one, a man about my age, solidly built and wearing a New Orleans Saints cap.

"He's a deaf-mute," Pascal said with another pound.

The man handed me a slip of paper. "Do you want a drink?" he had written. "No, thank you," I wrote on the bottom, although I thought more alcohol might numb my throbbing right shoulder.

Besides, my real thirst—to get out there and drink a beer on a lazy Saturday morning in Mamou before both Louisiana and I faded into middle-aged, Middle American conformity—had been largely quenched for the moment. What I needed was food and a chance to hear that Cajun jukebox. Bob and I swung by what seemed to be the only restaurant in Mamou, Jeff's, where we ordered a $2 chicken gumbo and were handed a bowl of spicy brownish goo, with a drumstick plopped down in the middle. When we returned to Fred's Lounge at about 1:30, the blue-and-white tablecloth had been removed; I felt a rush, as at the unveiling of a commissioned sculpture.

It was the kind of record machine, wonderfully dated, yet too ugly to be an expensive antique toy, that I have come to expect and enjoy in Jukebox America—a hulking, boxy, gleaming Seeburg model that appeared to date back to the *Saturday Night Fever* days of the late 1970s. The base of the jukebox was fiery red, tinged with a little gold: the color of Tabasco sauce, the perfect hue for the Louisiana bayou. Near the coin slot was a blue sticker: QUARTERS ONLY.

A Cajun fiddle was sawing away from the speakers, and the "Selection Playing" lights read #123—"Down at the Twist and Shout" by Mary Chapin-Carpenter, my omnipresent Rhode Island college classmate, who had borrowed Cajun music for her first hit. But much of the rest of Fred's jukebox was a treasure chest of hot-pepper Cajun hits on obscure record labels. The #100 selection was "La Chanson de les Mardi Gras" by the late Dewey Balfa, and then there was "Pine Grove Blues" by Nathan Abshire, "La Valse de la Vie/Maurice, Fait Pas Ca" by Paul Daigle, "Happy Cajun Man" by Jimmy Newman, as well as a couple of zydeco selections like "My Toot Toot/Jalapeno Lena" by Rockin' Sidney. About half the jukebox was Louisiana music and most of the rest was the best of contemporary country—Alan Jackson, Travis Tritt, Garth Brooks, and, of course, Hank Williams Jr., singing "Big Mamou."

I put in fifty cents and punched out the numbers for Nathan Abshire, Jimmy Newman, and the Texas Tornados. Only then did I have another look around Fred's Lounge, and it was as if the whole wild fiesta had turned into a pumpkin when the clock struck one. There were only about ten people standing around in a couple of clusters on the now-deserted dance floor, and it looked like they were the ones too intoxicated to find the front door.

A tall young man with a beard and long hair—he looked

like either the local methamphetamine dealer or a rock musician (it turned out he was the latter)—was tossing a shot of a crimson liquid into his mouth.

"Hot damn!" he exclaimed.

"What's that called?" asked Bob, who was standing next to him.

"Hot damn," he said. That was the name of the drink.

One of the few people still around was Sue Vasseur, Fred's ex-wife. I wanted to ask her more about Fred and the bar, and we stepped outside into the blinding midday sun. We stood in a vacant lot next to Fred's Lounge on the corner, and Sue leaned against an oil drum. She had short permed gray hair, and the age lines crinkled around her narrow eyes when she smiled, which she did frequently, but her skin had the healthy pink glow of someone who had danced and served cold beer every Saturday morning instead of shopping for peanut butter.

"He was a wonderful man—he always looked for the good in people," Sue said. She had been married to Fred Tate for fourteen years and had given birth to their two children, and even after their marriage dissolved they remained close friends. During those painful last three years, it was Sue Vasseur who was a frequent hospital visitor, administering insulin shots to her dying ex-husband. And it was Sue Vasseur who reopened that padlocked bar every Saturday morning at 8 A.M., helping to keep the French Acadian culture alive for another week.

Now Vasseur, who worked as a legal secretary in Mamou during the week, had a difficult decision to make—she couldn't operate Fred's on a Saturday-morning-only basis forever. She said she would have to sell Fred's Lounge and its forty-six years of history.

She had shown Fred's Lounge and was on the verge of a deal with prospective buyers, who had suggested that the bar wouldn't be profitable unless it expanded into the vacant lot where we were now standing. "They're going to put up a restaurant—not hamburgers!" she said, explaining that the menu would be Cajun. "I'm going to stay with the new owners—I want to stay. Hopefully, we'll sign a contract and I will be the manager."

Still, it was clear that Sue Vasseur was worried about the future of Fred's Lounge, about whether it would become cluttered with video games or maybe a tacky souvenir shop, worried that any sale "would ruin a unique atmosphere."

It was now after 2 P.M.—Bob and I were supposed to be well on our way to the Mississippi Delta, and Sue had to close up for the day. She turned the key on that thick black door, and Fred's wonderful Cajun jukebox—which I had heard for a painfully short fifteen minutes—was gone for another week, and probably gone, for me, forever.

Bob and I walked slowly down the main drag of Mamou for one last time. We stuck our head in Diana's Brass Rail, and now—on an early Saturday afternoon—there was yet another Cajun band sawing away, a cluster of twenty never-say-die revelers swaying tipsily to the music. I imagined a constantly moving party of beer-bellied Cajuns, moving to Infatuation and then to Casanova's and then down Louisiana Route 13 to Eunice, and then to Grand Coteau and Lafayette, until everyone ended up passed out in the hot-pepper fields of Avery Island on Friday, and it was time to head back to Fred's Lounge and start all over again.

With my whirlwind night-and-a-day in Cajun country coming to a close, I wondered at the vagaries of the Spirit in the Sky. It was exactly the kind of night-and-a-day I had envisioned when I had set off—I couldn't imagine a more Bacchanalian twenty-four hours of sheer fun, just the kind of adventure I would have missed if I had stayed in front of my green marble fireplace in Lower Makefield. I will never forget the music, that magical zydeco squeezing and sawing—or the people: El Sid O in those lizard boots, Pascal Fuselier assaulting my collar bone in the name of preserving French culture. If Bob and I felt guilty for leaving family behind, at least it was guilty fun.

And yet I also realized that I had made a mistake in thinking I might find America's best jukebox in Louisiana. The miraculous Burger King jukebox of Picayune had been a false sign; as appealing as it was on the surface, it was merely an effort by a faceless interchange along I-59 to invoke a 1950s malt-shop culture that had never been there in the first place. In Lafayette and Mamou and the sunrise watering holes in between, the music is something real and altogether different, something that arrived with the French refugees in the eighteenth century and with the African Americans who came—against their will—not much later. Here, the music has never gone away.

Where I grew up, the somnambulent suburbs of Westchester County, New York, real musicians were unique—most of us lugged a saxophone around in the fourth grade, and then dropped it for a hi-fi and a record collection. In the Louisiana bayous, almost everyone had the music inside of them, so that it was nothing for either Ed Sid O Williams or Joseph Bertrand— two men from very different sides of those railroad tracks—to each pick up an accordion at the age of twenty-five and learn that most complicated of instruments. Sure, they had great jukeboxes in Louisiana—how could they not, with all that music all around?—but no one ever bothered to listen, because every bar, every restaurant, every wedding, every town was a jam session waiting to erupt.

In my other stops, from Hoboken to Chicago, the problem was that Jukebox America was under assault from modern technology, from the compact disc and Nike Town and the Rock 'n' Roll McDonald's. In Louisiana, the problem was different—this was a time warp, where itinerant folk musicians and not Thomas Edison and his talking machine are still the primary means of making music. As much as I love jukeboxes, I came to the odd realization that if things ever changed in south-central Louisiana, if no one could be found to take the place of Nathan Williams and the Zydeco Cha Chas or Marc Savoy—if that music became solely a jukebox phenomenon—then a terrible tragedy would have taken place.

As Bob and I headed north on Route 13 just after two, five

hours from the jukebox mysteries of the Mississippi Delta, I noticed that there was a chapel called the Word of God Church on the outskirts of Mamou, and that there were about fifteen cars already parked in the lot. I guess when your Saturday night starts at 8 A.M., the Lord's day comes early.

Chapter 8

....

It's a Man Down There

If Satan himself opened up a restaurant, it would probably be something like Doe's Eat Place in Greenville, Mississippi, a monument to my favorite of the seven deadliest sins—gluttony. It all starts when a bright-eyed waitress comes by and asks what in the world you would like to eat—maybe a sixteen-ounce rib eye, maybe a one-and-one-half-pound T-bone, maybe a four-pound sirloin, and how about some barbecued shrimp and a hot tamale or two to wash that down.

There is nary a mention of price.

Within a few happy minutes, you are devouring a well-charred carcass of cow, with no thought to cost, passage of time, or the limitations of mortality. Then, gorged to the point of nausea, that bright-eyed waitress comes back with a bill—for more than a week's eating would cost you anywhere else in Jukebox America.

Nothing in Doe's Eat Place seems in earthly order—the creaky wooden floor slants in odd directions; your dining-room table has been warped into the curve of a U from the infernal heat. The air moves about in waves of dry heat, cascading from massive cow crematoriums, where unrecognizable slabs of bovine matter are being incinerated. Through the visible heat, you begin to make out The Others—bankers, accountants, insurance men, each in his own splash of madras, married to a helmet of long blond hair, arranged in foursomes that will be verbally dissecting the Mississippi State football program until the Judgment Day.

On my day in Hades-on-the-Mississippi, a Man in Madras emerged from the Hellfire.

"Hi there," the figure said. "My name is Charles Jordan. Where are you from?"

It was my damned notebook, which I had pulled out somewhere between the Shrimp Massacre and the Cow Slaughter. So I confessed to the very worst: I was "a writer from New York City."

By now, Bob and I were surrounded by four of them—two madras, two blond—but Charles Jordan wanted us to know he came in peace. And so when I told him we were looking for juke joints, they nodded knowingly—another crazy Yankee, here to chase the black man's music. I learned that an open-minded Charles Jordan had been to the Mississippi Delta Blues Museum ("a disappointment," however), and I got some friendly advice: to drive rather than walk the four short blocks down crime-ridden Nelson Street to our next destination, a blues bar called Perry's Flowing Fountain.

Then Charles Jordan made another kind offer.

"Are you going to be in town on Monday? I work in a bank in downtown Greenville. I have this old picture from the 1930s or so that you really have to see. It's this old blues band, and they're all standing in front of this great old jukebox. It might help your research."

I told Charles Jordan that I appreciated his offer, and that I would think about it. Then they vanished, traces of pink and green and blond that faded slowly into the sticky darkness of an August Saturday night in Mississippi.

I couldn't confine my search for America's best jukebox to freshly swept museum corridors or a two-dimensional photograph in some air-conditioned bank vault. I wanted to get my feet muddy, to feel the alluvial silt of the Mississippi under my feet. I wanted to bathe in my own salty sweat in some tin-roofed steam bath of a juke joint in the middle of a godforsaken cotton patch. I wanted the stench of cheap malt liquor and vinegary barbecued chicken flaring through my nostrils.

I wanted to touch the blues. I wanted to get dirty.

For anyone who loves jukeboxes, the Mississippi Delta is a kind of mecca. The actual machines can be something of a disappointment, collapsing affairs from the late 1950s that are missing parts or that play selection #C9 if you press #A1. But as in any ancient holy land, there are still ghosts—Charley Patton, Robert Johnson, Son House—and the rotting sharecropper shacks where they performed, and then left behind their scratchy 78 RPM "race records" for the jukebox, seem likely still to stand.

Like most other newfangled technologies that slowly reach the plantation lands of the Mississippi Delta, the jukebox was a product of Yankee ingenuity, invented in Edison's Menlo Park, built in faraway factories in places like Chicago and North Towanda, New York. Jukeboxes didn't show up in the Delta in noteworthy numbers until around the time Prohibition ended, but the timing proved exquisite. Starting around 1920, record companies such as Okeh, Columbia, and Victor had began recording race records at 78 RPM, and blues historian Paul Oliver has estimated that about 500 were released each year during that decade. But in a place like the Mississippi Delta, most blacks eked out a grim subsistence as migrant farm laborers or sharecroppers; they couldn't afford a phonograph or a record collection, but on a Saturday night, most anyone could go to a juke joint and drop a nickel to hear the latest song by Blind Lemon Jefferson.

Today, the most famous of those Mississippi bluesmen is Robert Johnson. An intinerant musician making his way among the labor camps and juke joints of central Mississippi, Johnson was taken to San Antonio, Texas to record in 1936, and eventually cut eleven 78s, including "Terraplane Blues" on Vocallion Records, which were heard in smokey dives all across the South. Johnson's career was short-lived; in August 1938, they say, he sidled up a little too close to another man's woman in a Greenwood, Mississippi, juke joint—and was apparently poisoned by the jealous lover.

Until the device reached Mississippi, it wasn't even a *jukebox*, just an automatic record machine, little evolved from an arcade novelty.

There are at least five or six theories on how the jukebox got its name, but all are rooted in the gin joints of the Mississippi Delta. One theory is that the name is a corruption of *jute*, a Delta crop used to make rope, and that on Saturday night the workers hung out in *jute joints*. Some scholars say the roots of the word go back to preslavery Africa, possibly to a word for dancing, *jugue*, or to another word, *juba*, that was used to describe a chugging kind of rhythm played by early blues pianists. The theory I've heard most often is that *jukin'* was a Delta term that described dirty, suggestive dancing, and so the party shacks became *juke joints*. One Pittsburgh record distributor told me a *juke house* was a Carolina whorehouse.

The theory I like best, though, is the most outlandish one, espoused in a book by Marc Eliot entitled *Rockonomics*, and given little credence by music scholars. In 1877, the same year that Thomas Edison invented the record machine, a writer named Thomas Dugsdale published a book, now long-forgotten, in which he claimed that heredity was the root of most crime and depravity; his research purported to show that many of the crimes in an upstate New York county were carried out by people from the same gene pool, a fictional family that he called, for whatever reason, "The Jukes." Dugsdale's theory—eventually discredited for his shoddy research methods—held sway through the 1930s, when bulbous-nosed politicians and huffy preachers offered speeches and sermons against poor, uneducated sharecroppers who wasted their few dollars on demon rum and the suggestive records played on "jukeboxes."

That was one thing that intrigued me about Mississippi and its juke joints—they were such subversive affairs, tributes to the ability of human beings to be free spirits even in the face of oppressive poverty and discrimination. Monday through Saturday afternoon was the white man's time, but from Saturday night through Sunday the black folks of Mississippi achieved a kind of freedom—limited, but joyful—to create that sad but uplifting music that became known as the blues.

The other thing that intrigued me was that, even though they were born of the 1920s and 1930s, southern juke joints still exist. I had never even heard the words *juke joint* until 1989, when I wandered into a poster shop. On the wall was a print that almost made my heart stop: It showed a living, breathing Mississippi juke, with a couple of guys playing on a rickety pool table in a run-down bar, a crude mural of a buffalo painted on the wall. The poster carried the caption "Juke Joints of the Mississippi Delta," and I soon learned that an entire book had just been devoted to a collection of like pictures—all in bold splashes of primary color, with splintered wood planks for tables and peeling walls and ceilings, each revealing beat-up jukeboxes filled with Elmore James and Howling Wolf records.

Ever since seeing that picture in the Main Line poster store in Philadelphia, it had been my goal to see a real juke joint in person. So many other great bars, I'd learn, were no longer around in 1992—the taverns where Sinatra sang with the Hoboken Four, or the West Virginia roadhouses that Jesse Richardson wistfully recalled. But there were still juke joints in Mississippi, and now I was going to see them. I guess that's why Charles Jordan's well-meaning offer in Doe's Eat Place had bothered me.

I didn't want to see any more pictures.

Unfortunately, Perry's Flowing Fountain—a Pepsi Cola–signed oasis surrounded on either side by posses sipping from brown paper bags—didn't bring me as close to the Juke of the Covenant or to those Birney Imes photographs as I had hoped.

That was a shame, because Perry had himself a killer jukebox—by Mississippi standards a relatively modern NSM machine with 240 red-hot songs and the most heavy-duty pair of speakers that I have ever seen, master-blasters on either side of the jukebox that started on the floor and went all the way up to my armpits. Like any great American jukebox, it was chock-full of 45s by local artists, in this case Little Milton ("I'm at the End of My Rainbow"), Roosevelt "Booba" Barnes ("Going Back Home," an ironic song for a man who had just abandoned Greenville for the greener pastures of Chicago), and Clarence Carter ("It's a Man Down There," a song I saw on every jukebox in Mississippi). Then there were the big timers like B. B. King, Bobby "Blue" Bland, and Albert King. It was truly one of America's great jukeboxes. But—like the (almost) all–Frank Sinatra jukebox or the blues box at Rosa's in Chicago—it was one I was fated not to hear.

When we strolled through the front door, a man asked us for a $2 cover. That seemed strange, until I saw that it was a disc jockey, and not the jukebox, that was spinning Tyrone Davis's, "If I Could Turn Back the Hands of Time." The jukebox was shut off for the night.

The long front barroom—illuminated by a bright string of red and green Christmas lights—was clean and the bar stools looked comfortable, like a place you might find in a working-man's neighborhood in Albany or Philadelphia, the clientele solidly middle class. The owner, Perry Payton, was working the bar. Then sixty-five years old, he looked out of place in a blues bar, a little bit like . . . well, like the mortician that he is. He spoke in rich, earthy tones and somewhat matter of factly, as if the irony hadn't struck him that he may be the only man in America who runs a funeral parlor in the daytime and a juke joint after sundown.

Soon, Bob and I soon found ourselves in a cavernous hotbox adjacent to the main barroom—a sign on the wall called it the Disco Club Room—listening to Perry Payton's life story. He grew up on the same block in Greenville as the famed bluesman Little Milton, and as a young man started promoting blues concerts, promising friends like B. B. King from nearby Indianola a $350 cut to play at some sweaty lodge hall. The very week that we met Perry Payton, B. B. King was playing for GOP fatcats at the Republican National Convention in Houston, while Perry's Disco Club Room, where he books bands on occasion, sat dark.

Perry's voice rose as he remembered the old days. "You know what," he said, his words rushing with enthusiasm. "Ray Charles! I booked him, at the old Elks Club. He was getting $350 a night. James Brown! He was with the Midnights, and he had one little old song out, and he was runnin' around. All these guys, years ago, they was trying to make it out there."

I enjoyed talking to Perry Payton and hearing his thoughts on the blues, but about halfway through we were joined by one of Perry's contemporaries, a man with black eyeglass frames and a well-trimmed mustache who looked like a younger Thurgood Marshall.

Perry told me the man's name but I quickly forgot it, so I apologized and asked his name again.

"Lucas. L-U-C-A-S. Like Prentice Lucas."

"That's your first or last name?"

"Like Prentice Lucas."

"So Prentice is your first name?"

"No. *Like* Prentice. The Goddess of Money."

I let out a huge laugh. I had no idea what he was talking about.

"Same name. Lucas Lucas."

"Lucas Lucas? Really? That's pretty wild."

I didn't believe that Lucas Lucas was his real name, and I had some serious questions about everything else he told us that night. At first he said he was a financier, but he later explained that he had played for the Count Basie band for about five years during the 1950s, and he spun some tales about his travels to New Jersey, Australia, and other destinations far from Greenville. Perry Payton told me later that he was an official at a nearby penitentiary.

"I think that blacks are looking to black roots, whites are looking to white roots," Lucas Lucas said. "I think we got a really renaissance thing that might have happened in Eastern Europe a long time ago—around Leipzig. You know everyone around there went for the symphonies, and all the concertos and what have you, and all of a sudden you start looking for something else. They looked to Leipzig University!"

It was time to regroup for Sunday afternoon—prime time for Mississippi Delta blues.

We stopped to say goodbye to Perry Payton on the way out, and he walked us outside, something that he said he always does for "strangers." Perry stopped to chat, and he sat on the hood of his big gray Cadillac. After the steamy disco room, the eighty-degree Delta night felt like central air conditioning. And being near Perry Payton gave me a strange sense of serenity, even with the crack dealers just a block or two away. I had the strange thought that if I died, I would somehow like Perry Payton to arrange my funeral.

We asked him about a tip about a real authentic juke joint that was out in the country, a shack called Little Blue's Cafe. Perry gave us some typical Mississippi directions—it was "close to Ray's store," he said. He also pointed to a dilapidated shack hard up against the railroad track and said we might hear some live music if we came back at 2:30 P.M. on Sunday.

I wanted to know if Perry's Flowing Fountain would be open, so I could play his jukebox.

"I'm going to open around four," Perry Payton said. "I've got a funeral tomorrow."

Mississippi 1 is straight and flat, and the horizon seems endless except for the gentle slope of the Mississippi River levee—hiding the unseen force that shaped the Delta and the blues—off the passenger side of the car. The drive starts out in the dismal New South of Charles Jordan and his white banker pals—new Saturn dealerships, a red-brick subdivision called Country Club Estates, broken up by the sturdy white chapels of the Methodists and Southern Baptists and their peppy roadside message boards: You Can Understand the Bible if You Know the Author.

But the lay of the land changed as we got farther away from Greenville: There were no more Toyota dealers or Pizza Huts, but every couple of miles or so we saw a service station/general store hawking Live Bait.

"We should be getting near Longwood," I said after we

had been driving for fifteen minutes. There was only the green rise of the levee on the horizon.

Then we saw a cluster of midsized grain silos and a string of about five or six low-lying ranch houses extending off to the left, the only sign of civilization for a few miles. "You know, this could be it," I said. "It's not a very big town on the map."

I had barely finished speaking when we saw a small green sign that read Longwood. But there was no sign of anything resembling a cafe—no Coca-Cola or Busch signs, no gravel parking lot or ice machine. So we drove south another 100 yards or so, until I noticed the rear of a small sign on the other side of the road that looked strikingly similar to the Longwood sign that we had just seen on our side. I slowed down and twisted my head.

Sure enough, we had just traversed the entire width of Longwood, Mississippi, in about six seconds. There was a dirt road, the rust-red color of clay, that meandered aimlessly to the right, but Bob and I agreed that we would have better luck back near the silos.

The few hundred yards that comprise the town of Longwood are a fantastic study of southern social strata. It starts with the local industry—in this case the C. D. Steele Farm, a chaotic array of big rigs and farm tractors parked every which way off the road. Just past the cluster of silos is a large, leafy magnolia tree next to a small pond green with algae, shading a stately two-story home with a white-lattice porch from the scorching Mississippi Delta heat—the grand plantation house that no doubt belonged to Mr. Steele. The next four or five houses were quite modest and mercilessly exposed to the high noontime sun.

In a matter of seconds, we had reached the end of the line— a ramshackle house, no wider than the length of a pickup truck, with a rickety front porch supported by three bright blue columns. There were four or five vehicles, pickup trucks and vans, scattered about the property; a couple of them looked roadworthy, but two were surrounded by tall grass around the wheel wells. Parked hard up against the side of the shack was a run-down school bus, painted in a tone that once was a summer-sky blue but now was faded like a dim December afternoon.

"I don't know why, but I think this is it," I told Bob.

"I think you're right," Bob said. Then he pointed to the old battered school bus and some lettering in the back that was so badly faded that we could just barely make out what it had said: "Little Blue."

We had found Little Blue's Cafe.

There were six people on the front porch. There were three squirmy children, and a middle-aged man who was sipping from a sixteen-ounce can of malt liquor. There was a woman who seemed to be the lady of the house, in a blue sundress that hung loosely over her thin body. Then there was the patriarch, a grim-faced black man wearing a baseball hat with the word "Captain" inscribed upon it. More striking, however, were his teeth, testimony to the things that those of us who who aren't poverty-stricken lifelong residents of Mississippi take for granted, like dental care. There was a large gap in the center of this man's mouth, a crooked, diagonal gap right there in the center of his face.

This man, he told us, was sixty-one years old. He murmured his real name, but it wasn't really important because everyone called him Little Blue, the proprietor of this two-room shack called Little Blue's Cafe.

Bob and I received a few waves of hello as we approached the porch, but Little Blue just sat there, his jaw locked in what seemed like a perpetual grimace of disdain.

"Hi there," I said. I had dispensed with my long and awkward rap about jukeboxes.

"Hi, how y'all doin'," said Little Blue.

"Is there going to be music this afternoon, or . . ."

"There's supposed to be, right, there sho' is."

I asked Little Blue what time the festivities were supposed to begin.

"I told the guys to all be here by four o'clock." I found out, through Little Blue's rather reticent responses, that somebody named John Horton was supposed to perform that day, along with a band that, well, would probably consist of whoever else bothered to show up around four o'clock. The malt-liquor

man had wandered inside and come back, and I introduced myself, saying that I was from "up around New York."

"You're spectatin', huh?" said the malt-liquor man.

"Yeah, that's right, I'm spectatin'. I don't think I'll be playing today." The woman in the too-large blue dress let out a
laugh. I laughed, too, since I hadn't touched a musical instrument
since some disastrous after-school saxophone lessons in the
fourth grade.

But music ran in Little Blue's family. Little Blue said he
played the drums, and we might get to see him perform when
we came back at four. He told me that he had a son, who was
also called Little Blue and who used to perform with the senior
Little Blue but now played around Greenville in a band called
FM Stereo.

"I thought you were Little Blue?" I said.

"I'm Little Blue," said Little Blue. "They call him Little
Blue 'cause we're so much alike."

"They should call you Big Blue."

"No, my daddy was Big Blue."

"Did he play the blues, your daddy?"

"No, I don't think so. He liked it a lot, but he never
played."

It seems the blues-music scene in the Mississippi Delta,
while famous the world over, is really a small and insular affair.
There are maybe a couple hundred people or so, mostly old-
timers like Little Blue, and Perry Payton, and Booba Barnes, who
all know each other, and frequent the same slowly shifting circuit
of little clubs and juke joints. For example, I mentioned Perry
Payton and the Flowing Fountain.

"I think I seen y'all last night," said Little Blue. "I was up
there in that truck right there."

I began to wonder if Bob and I would begin to become the
talk of the Mississippi Delta, if word might spread from the liquor stores on Nelson Street to the churches on Route 1 to
Charles Jordan's county club, about the crazy Yankee with the
paisley shirt and his bearded friend, the two nuts who drove all
this way looking for a jukebox—a goddamn jukebox!

But for the moment my mind was on Little Blue's Cafe, jukebox or not. Little Blue told me that Little Blue's Cafe, at least this incarnation, was about to become history: in two weeks, he would pack up and open a bigger club in a place closer to Greenville called Freedom Village. Little Blue said that his new club would be bigger, and I figured it would probably have a jukebox.

I launched into a delayed version of my awkward rap about the jukebox search, and how "nowadays I guess it doesn't seem like you see as many. I mean, Perry has a good jukebox, but . . ."

"Well, I'm gonna put one out there," Little Blue said.

"Yeah?" I said, my interest level on the rise.

"I got one in there," he said, pointing to the little shack, "but it's old, and it ain't operating right now. There's something wrong with it."

I was exhilarated and disappointed at the same time. "If it's not too much to ask, could I see your jukebox?"

"Yeah," said Little Blue, adding with slight disgust, "It's old."

I didn't care. I rushed to the trunk of the car to get my camera. All the while Little Blue had been talking with me and Bob, I didn't really believe there could be a jukebox inside that tiny shack. Now I was going to see a real juke joint, a real-life Birney Imes photo.

I bounced up the front porch steps, while Little Blue opened the door. After seeing the almost neon Birney Imes photos in *Juke Joints of the Mississippi Delta*, I had expected a blast of primary colors; the truth was something different—the inside of Little Blue's Cafe was so dark and dingy that, after the blazing noontime sun of west-central Mississippi, I could barely see.

"Maybe we could turn the light on?" I asked Little Blue.

"It is on."

As my eyes slowly adjusted to the lack of light, I saw the one dim bulb he meant. It was hot, not the searing heat of Doe's Eat Place but more like an old steam bath. I didn't even see the jukebox until Little Blue pointed off to the side, and moved away a rickety old bench—it looked like the seat of a school bus, supported by an old tire rim and by two blocks of wood—that was blocking all access.

To appreciate Little Blue's jukebox, it is important to take any notion that you might have about what comprises a great jukebox, and throw it out the window. The idealized jukebox, the one that any graphic artist will conjure up for a million-dollar ad campaign to sell Ritz crackers or Budweiser, is a late 1940s Wurlitzer, the one that's shaped like an upside-down U, with those red, green, and blue tubes of neon light with those tiny bubbles slowly heading north, one with happy white songs like "In the Mood," with Elvis imploring "Don't Be Cruel," with Patsy going "Crazy."

Little Blue's jukebox was nothing like this. For starters, it was brown, deep brown, like the silty soil of the Delta itself. This jukebox was one of those ancient console models, designed to look like a home hi-fi of late '40s, with a heavy brown lid that was pulled open and a big speaker in its base. It was set back in some crevice that was once probably a food pantry, under some shelves that were now barren except for an empty Miller beer bottle and an old windbreaker. There was no red, no blue, no green, no neon—in fact, no hue at all in the humid darkness of Little Blue's Cafe.

Nevertheless, I was enthralled. I glanced down to see what songs would appear on an authentic juke joint jukebox. I widened my eyes, still baffled by the loss of sunlight, and bent down close to the glass cover. My eyes were two inches away, but I still couldn't make out a word. Little Blue's jukebox was covered with a thick layer of dust. Suddenly, I felt like the archaeologist Heinrich Schliemann, digging into the brown dirt of Hissalik and discovering the stone walls of ancient Troy.

Between the dark and the dust, it was impossible to make out the 45s in Little Blue's jukebox. That's why the selections had been inscribed on four yellowed pieces of paper loosely stuck onto the brown console lid with gray tape. The room was so dark that my flashbulb didn't work much better than my eyes, and so I quickly scribbled down some of the selections.

There were a lot of local Mississippi folks, like Artie White ("Words on How to Love Your Man"), Z. Z. Hill, Tyrone Davis ("It's a Miracle"), and Clarence Carter. There were the usual blues heroes, Muddy Waters ("Got My Mojo Workin' "), Albert King, Freddie King. There was a Christmas 45, and even, inexplicably, wonderfully, a single from Milli Vanilli. At least that's what was written on the four fading sheets of paper, anyway.

As I looked at Little Blue's colorless, dirt-encrusted jukebox, in a cramped 200-degree oven of a run-down room, with its sagging school bus seats and a wobbly ceiling fan that was threatening to decapitate me or Bob at any second, I had just one thought:

This was the Juke of the Covenant. I had found America's greatest jukebox.

Except for that one nagging problem, the fact that it didn't work . . . at least not in the conventional way a jukebox is supposed to work, where you drop in a quarter and select a record.

Instead, Little Blue had strung a couple of wires across the room, up along the ceiling and then dangling down loosely behind the bar. They were connected to a bunch of appliances that were crammed underneath, into a kind of Mississippi-Delta home-entertainment center that included a cassette deck, an eight-track tape player (still a popular accessory in Mississippi, I was later told), and an old phonograph. I glanced down onto the turntable, and there was a dusty old Albert King 45 from the late 1960s, the classic "Crosscut Saw."

While I had been jotting down some of the songs on the jukebox, Little Blue was telling Bob about his job, driving a truck for the rich white man, C. D. Steele and his son, hauling rice and cotton to market. It was interesting stuff, but I wanted to hear the jukebox.

"Can we hear it?" I asked.

Without pausing, Little Blue pressed a button on his tape deck. I think he was trying to play me a tape of his own blues band performing at a club, but, quite frankly, I'm not quite sure what I was listening to. When the music blasted out from that giant jukebox speaker, it had to be in violation of some federal noise pollution standard—105 decibels at the least. The distortion was incredible: it was a racket like riding the F train under Queens Boulevard at the height of rush hour, with motors rumbling, voices shouting, melodies bursting in and out. It was the most god-awful blast I had ever heard.

I loved every second of it.

I think the reason I liked Little Blue's jukebox so much was that it was so subversive, so different from the 1990s notion of a jukebox—spinning Elton John's greatest hits on compact disc in some suburban shopping mall—that the Amusement and Music Operators of America wanted me to see. Little Blue didn't have the money for Rock-Ola's new Trilogy CD jukebox; he didn't even quite have money or the wherewithal to fix the old relic that he owned. But he was determined to play music for the folk of Longwood, Mississippi, even if it meant risking electrocution by stringing wires all over his juke and hooking them up to an eight-track tape deck. If it hadn't been for Mississippi men like Little Blue and their jukeboxes, blasting the devil's music at ungodly levels, I might have grown up listening to Harry James instead of Tommy James and the Shondells.

I asked Little Blue how long he had this jukebox, and he told me he'd bought it secondhand, maybe four years ago, maybe six.

"Who did you buy it from?"

"It was Mr. Moe's friend."

"Really? Who is Mr. Moe?"

"He's the one who they sent to the penitentiary for selling dope."

It didn't really matter much to me who had sold the jukebox to Little Blue, but he paused for a second, and, like a witness in the final four minutes of a Perry Mason episode, he suddenly recalled the truth.

"I believe it was Mr. Moe that sold it to me."

The truth was ironic. It wasn't news to hear of a convicted felon in the jukebox business; it's pretty well understood that La Cosa Nostra had controlled most jukebox distribution in the Northeast and Midwest for decades; now a crack kingpin in

Greenville, Mississippi, was peddling jukeboxes on the side. I've never understood how the money from jukeboxes, which give people such innocent pleasure, so often ends up with criminals; the thought threw a small splash of cold water on my excitement over his jukebox. Nevertheless, Bob and I were looking forward to returning at four.

We climbed back into our boat of a rental car for the straight, sunbaked drive back into Greenville, to find lunch and that dilapidated railroad-siding juke that Perry Payton had tipped us off about the night before. On the ride back, the car radio, scratchy and bass-heavy, was playing Sunday gospel music. The music gave way to a Bible-thumping preacher.

"Now who do you think it is that is holding the moon and the sun in place?" the preacher thundered. As we pulled back into Greenville, I scrambled to write down those words on the back of my receipt from the Hampton Inn.

Back on Nelson Street, 2:30 P.M. The little joint that Perry Payton had pointed to on Saturday night had looked funky in pitch darkness, but the bright and all-revealing Delta sunshine of a Sunday afternoon made the little bar look like what it was: a dilapidated mess. It was hard up against a railroad track—there was a new set of railroad tracks slashing through the black section of Greenville every three blocks or so, as if some white railroad baron had plotted to bring as much smoke and noise to as many poor people as possible.

It was just a little cinder-block building, with a red-brick front and a lot of graffiti scrawled on the side facing the tracks. There were two front windows, with a neon Lite beer sign in one, but many of the smaller windowpanes had been knocked out over the years and replaced with unmatching shades of blue or green, or just plain cardboard. There were a couple of those green Newport cigarette signs that you tend to see in black neighborhoods, with well-dressed African American couples happily puffing their way toward chemotherapy, although one of the signs had been knocked sideways. On the sidewalk right in front was parked a van, where a couple of guys were setting up a steel drum and getting ready to barbecue for the afternoon. Above the entrance was a barely faded powder-blue-and-white sign, barely readable, that said: Blue Note. It wasn't clear if that was still the name of the bar.

As Bob and I walked down the slight incline to the entrance, we could hear the muffled thumping of a blues beat, but I was beginning to wonder already whether the Blue Note—if that, in fact, was its real name—was such a good idea. I had to open a series of two doors to get in, and both appeared ready to fall off their hinges. The handle to the second—made of rotting dark-brown wood in various stages of erosion—almost came off in my hand, but I was able to push it open. Then, magically, I beheld the panorama of a Mississippi juke joint.

That split-second when I stood on the threshold of the Blue Note is one of those moments so frozen in my memory that I can still conjure up its sights, its sounds, its smells, today.

I remember the drummer, a goateed man, tall and skinny—maybe six-foot-six and about 180, if I had to guess—and the way he was pounding an old brown beat-up drum kit, muffled by old newspaper and held together with masking tape.

I remember the tiny little barroom, its walls of simple, mostly undecorated navy-blue and white cinder block, brown and watermarked in a number of places, covered by a ceiling that—well, I'm not really sure how to describe it, except to mention the large haylike bushels of asbestos-like matter dangling down in some spots.

I remember the bar itself—this, I especially remember—and the bar stools. Well, you couldn't really call them bar stools. What they were was a row of five metal bar-stool bases, and four had no cushion at all, just the round metal seat; the fifth was somehow missing even that, so that any patron dumb or drunk enough to sit there was in for a spikey surprise. No one seemed particularly alarmed by this state of affairs.

I remember the patrons. There was a thirty-something man with a backwards baseball cap pulled tightly over his head, round-rimmed sunglasses sunk down to the tip of his nose, and a gold earring—like a pirate, except that he was sipping from a Styrofoam cup. Seated next to him was a gray-haired woman in a blue polka-dot dress, who might have been his mother; she was pouring malt liquor from a thirty-two-ounce bottle. There was a man leaning against the bar in a gas-station attendant's uniform, a couple of crusty guys absorbed in a pool game near the back, and a gray-haired guy in a silky, contemporary shirt that you might find in SoHo or somewhere, and a woman in her flowery blue Sunday best.

I remember the star performer, a man who strummed the guitar and sang in a low, guttural moan, sporting a black fedora with a silver band, a long gold chain, and a gold pendant. With his mustache and oversized, bushy eyebrows, he looked like Greenville's answer to Leon Redbone.

But there's one thing that I really, really remember, and that is what happened as Bob and I stepped down into this den of malt liquor, sweat, and blues: the way all heads turned toward the door, the way the steady drumbeat seemed to stop, the way the black-skinned Leon Redbone stopped strumming, looked up at us, leaned into his microphone with a broad grin, and said:

"Hellooooo, white folks!"

Unsure of exactly how to read that welcome—warmth or warning?—Bob and I pulled up chairs at a shaky Formica table and tried to focus on the music. Bob, thinking it a wise idea to contribute some of our money to the proceedings, got up and returned with a couple of sixteen-ounce Budweisers from the bar.

The music itself was raw and refreshing. It turned out that the guitar player sang under the stage name of T-Model Ford; he was a local bluesman whose act was well-known and whose talent was the subject of frequent debate. He had that low moan, that often indecipherable whine, that makes for great blues music, although occasionally I could pick up a phrase like "I'm going home / Got nowhere to go," strummed over the "Baby Please Don't Go" riff. The tall guy was banging away on his patchwork drum kit, although the beat was loose and muffled, not the clear crack of a professional drummer.

Every once in a while, T-Model Ford would stop in the middle of a song to berate the drummer.

"You're running off with yourself," T-Model shouted at the tall guy as one song fell all apart in the middle. I guess, in layman's terms, the problem was that he was hitting his drums too many times. "You ain't got to do all that!"

That's the way a Sunday afternoon seemed to go in the Possibly Named the Blue Note bar, an informal affair where songs seemed to come in second to barroom banter.

"I'll tell you one thing," a man, his opinion very much unsolicited, nevertheless shouted out from somewhere around the pool table. "That man right there sure knows how to play the drums!"

"One man got a record out says He's coming around the mountain," T-Model said a minute later, in an apparent non-sequitur. "Ain't no thing comin' round the mountain!"

The biggest thing that was slowing down the performance, however, was a condition that was afflicting T-Model—the condition of his throat.

"I got a catch in my throat!" T-Model shouted at the end of one of his songs, throwing a glance toward the woman in the blue Sunday dress, who was evidently his wife. "Give me a drink! I've got to clear my throat."

The woman in the blue dress threw him a grimace, but eventually dug into her purse and pulled out a bottle of some kind of whiskey—I couldn't make out the brand—that had the amber color and the consistency of motor oil. She gave the bottle to T-Model, who took a big swig and who flashed another wide grin.

A song or two later, he was at it again. "I got a catch in my throat! I want to howl some! Ow-ooooooh!"

Despite all the back-and-forth, nobody asked Bob or me for our opinions, which was probably a good thing because we were still in something of a daze. Looking around the room, I noticed that one of the few barroom ornaments, a 1992 calendar showing an idyllic shot of a river flowing between some forested mountains. The calendar was an ad for the Redmon Funeral Home. Why were funeral homes such a big business in Greenville?

I was also studying the jukebox, which, typical of my Mississippi misadventures, was turned off in favor of the live music. I was beginning to think I would traverse all of northern Mississippi without hearing a jukebox.

Then I got a lucky break—literally. T-Model's guitar string snapped, and he had to take a breather.

The older woman near the bar—she was apparently the owner of the Possibly Named the Blue Note—got up, and flipped a switch on the jukebox, and hit a couple of buttons. A gravelly voiced soul singer started belting away, singing that "You're like Mom's apple pie." In fact, the song was called "Mom's Apple Pie," and it was by local favorite Tyrone Davis.

Emboldened by the turn of events, I got up to check the jukebox out. Like the other two I had seen—but not heard—in Mississippi, it was chock-full of local blues artists. Mom's apple pie aside, there were lots of songs about adultery: "I Didn't Take Your Woman," says Lou Pride. "Cheatin' Is Risky Business," says Little Milton. "I Didn't Take Your Man," says Ann Peebles. And so on.

Like the record machine at Little Blue's, this jukebox was something of a cultural artifact. It was a Seeburg Discotheque model, and it clearly bore the stamp of the mid-1960s. Above the list of selections was a painting of what looked like the Manhattan skyline, with the names of long-forgotten dances like the bossa nova, the go-go, and the frug interspersed among the skyscrapers. It was a time and a place far from the one-story shacks and the malt-liquor reality of Mississippi; no one danced the frug in Greenville.

My jukebox time was short-lived. By the second selection, T-Model Ford was tuning his new guitar string over the noise of the record, creating a quite a racket. He played one more tune, but then yielded the stage to a younger man—he looked to be in his fifties—and sat down at the table with his wife and the bottled motor fuel.

I was sitting at the next table, and soon we struck up a conversation. T-Model Ford told me that his real name was James Floyd, that he was sixty-eight years old, and, most incredibly, that he hadn't picked up a guitar until just ten years before. Before T-Model Ford played the blues, he merely lived it.

"I can't read or write," T-Model said, a sad fact but unfortunately common for those who grew up in separate-but-unequal Mississippi before *Brown* v. *Board of Education* was enacted. "I used to be a saw-mill man," said T-Model, dragging out the syllables. "I was a truck-drivin' man. Then I was a sand-blastin' man."

I only got to talk to T-Model Ford for twenty minutes or so, and a lot of it was shouted over the music, but what I heard was honest. There were a lot of things T-Model Ford didn't do, and he was happy to tell me so.

He said his life of hard factory work was "the reason I'm drinkin' whiskey. I don't fool with beer." He said he didn't drink gin, or wine, and added, as an afterthought: "I'm an old man—I can't fight." Out of vanity, though, T-Model Ford dyes his hair.

"I'm still a playboy," he said.

I wondered whether T-Model Ford had any children.

He said he did. There were twenty-six, to be exact.

Most of T-Model Ford's talk about his vastly extended family, or his premusician careers, was the result of my prodding. Mostly, he wanted to discuss only two things. The first and foremost was the ongoing crisis over the catch in his throat and his need for constant medication. The other thing was his music. Sometimes he got so excited about his music that he grabbed my shoulder and pushed, hard.

He said a few years back he had played with Willie Foster, a locally well known bluesman, but lately it seems T-Model has been on his own, and he's been plagued by the same problem facing Iceman Robinson back in Chicago and hundreds of other small-town musicians in Jukebox America: lack of good sidemen.

Or, as T-Model puts it with a dose of Delta subtlety: "My drummer's messed up."

Truthfully, I thought that drummer was doing pretty well, given the fact that his taped-up, newspaper-filled drum kit looked ready to burst with every rim shot. T-Model said he and the drummer had been playing together for a while, at VFW clubs and juke joints around Greenville and Indianola, the nearby birthplace of B. B. King.

"Really," I said. "What's the drummer's name?"

"Spam."

"Spam." It seemed like an odd nickname for a man so tall and lean, more like a breakfast sausage than processed meat. "What's his real name?"

T-Model Ford had jammed with Spam a number of times, and was quick to berate the poor man, but it had never occurred to him to ask Spam his real name. He looked up at the drummer, who was right in the middle of a song with the new guitarist. He walked right up to Spam in mid-riff, and leaned over close.

"What's your real name?" The music scene in Greenville is not too big on formality. Spam replied—never has a cliché been more apt—without missing a beat.

"His real name is Tony Miles," T-Model proclaimed as he returned to our table. And on a hot and lazy Sunday afternoon on Nelson Street, the beat went on.

I think it's safe to say that, before me, few men in American history had deserted a seven-months' pregnant wive to travel around the lower 48 with the express purpose of listening to jukeboxes. So, faced with the looming accusation of total lout-hood, I made Kathy some special promises. I would call her three times every day, so that she knew my whereabouts constantly. (In the year 2092, when some forager leaves his wife to look nostalgically for the best vintage CD jukeboxes in America, will they have perfected the electronic tracing device?) That bargain had proved easy to keep, but my second promise—to stay away from dangerous neighborhoods, pretty logical for a man about to father a baby girl—had proved more difficult. There were crack houses on Nelson Street, to be sure, but after Beale Street in Memphis it was the most famous blues street in America, and I don't think I would have found Clarence Carter's "It's a Man Down There" on the jukebox at the Ramada Inn on U.S. 82.

I wasn't about to lie—not only did I feel morally obliged to tell the truth, but there was a practical consideration: I planned to write an honest account of everything I saw on Nelson Street, after all. So when I stopped to call Kathy from a pay phone on Highway 1 on our way back to Little Blue's Cafe, I felt some trepidation. When I reached Kathy, my fears seemed justified.

She could have started by telling me about the $140 speeding ticket she had received that morning, but I wouldn't learn about that for another two weeks. She could have started by telling me she was mad at her lovable-but-absentminded father for getting lost between Philadelphia and Wildwood, even though he's driven between the two places 500 to 1,000 times before. She could have started by saying she was justifiably angry with me for running behind on painting the baby's room and countless other household chores.

I was sure I had it coming, so I tried heading her off at the pass: I told Kathy how much I loved her, and that in just a couple more days I would be home again, never more to go chasing some far-flung jukebox—at least not without her by my side. I put the best spin possible on the day's events, telling her about T-Model Ford and his twenty-six children, and about how we were off to hear another band in a real juke joint. I don't believe I mentioned the ambiance of the Possibly Named the Blue Note bar, the incredible cushionless bar stools, or the problem with the catch in T-Model's throat. I'm sure that I didn't say a word about the "Hello, white folks" incident.

Despite my cheery account of the day's events, Kathy seemed unimpressed.

"Isn't the whole point to listen to jukeboxes?"

I had been afraid she would ask that question.

"No, you don't understand—we're seeing lots of jukeboxes down here," I said, trying feebly to mask my own concern over the very same issue. "We just heard a really cool jukebox back in Greenville."

That was true, though I neglected to say I had only heard two songs, and one of those two songs was inaudible because of T-Model tuning up.

"And you should see that jukebox at this place we're going back to now, Little Blue's Cafe. It's one of the most amazing jukeboxes I've ever seen, a real relic."

That was true, although I carefully omitted the part about how the jukebox had been broken for so long it was covered with a layer of sediment, and about how it only made music because Little Blue had wired it to some 1950s phonograph.

"Well, okay," Kathy said grudgingly. "If you say so."

I hung up and got back in the car—thoroughly depressed. No wonder that frigging beer commercial got pulled off the air— "Who says you can't have it all?" Nobody said it, but it's true. When I was home with my loving wife, I was constantly wondering what it was like at a juke joint. Now I was on my way to probably the most authentic juke joint in all of America—feeling guilty as hell.

And where were the jukeboxes? A couple of years ago, when I was single and covering the state legislature in Albany, New York, I went to a place called the Hill Street Cafe almost every week night, placed a $5 bill in its CD jukebox, and listened to eighteen songs. Every night. Now I've been in Louisiana and Mississippi for almost three full days—with the sole purpose of listening to jukeboxes—and I hadn't heard eighteen jukebox songs in all that time. This wasn't really what I had envisioned that night with Nancy Sinatra.

But I had learned by now that the greatest jukeboxes in America are not the ones you expect. Most, it turned out, were a matter of mind over machinery. That CD jukebox in Hoboken that played virtually nothing except Frank Sinatra was a state of mind. Raw American musicians like Iceman Robinson still begging to record a 45 and get on a jukebox in 1992 were a state of mind. Dale Evans, the Human Jukebox, was a state of mind.

Now, voices as loud as God's or the Devil's were emerging through a dust-covered, dysfunctional jukebox in the middle of a rice field in a Mississippi town so small that it doesn't belong on a map, and so what if some loose electrical wires and a phonograph were involved in the process? It was real American music, it was noisy, it was subversive, and it came from a jukebox.

In 1992, some of the best jukeboxes in America were the ones in your mind.

And, so, feeling a little hope and a lot of guilt, I pulled the car onto the gravel shoulder of Little Blue's Cafe.

In utopian Jukebox America, I would have found this: a rollicking blues band—perhaps, as I had been forewarned by local blues expert Jim O'Neil, standing on the back of a pickup truck—blasting Muddy Waters out toward the levee, with a couple of steel drums of barbecued ribs and chicken blazing away while a crowd of maybe 50 or 100 people watched, some dancing wildly, some coolly sipping from a can of beer.

What we found was this: a motley crew of about six or seven people—no more, really, than we had found at noon—either lollygagging on the wood front porch or standing around the front yard. The woman in the blue dress—Elvira, Little Blue's wife—was still there, but there was no sign of her husband. There was no band. In fact, it was so gosh-darned quiet you probably could have heard the boll weevils eating through the cotton patch.

Elvira walked out the front door. Bob and I had a lot of questions.

"Where's Little Blue?" we asked. "What happened to the music?"

"He must be on the way," said Elvira, her voice flat and unconcerned. "He went to go pick something up." She tried to reassure us that some musicians were, indeed, on the way.

So there was nothing to do but wait. I surveyed the handful of people. There were two people who appeared to be our age, early thirties or so, leaning up against a Buick Phoenix. One was a young black man in jeans and a white shirt; his name was Robert, and we exchanged some unmemorable small talk with him.

The other young man was—surprise, surprise—the only white man we encountered in two whole days of Mississippi jukin'. Bob and I couldn't figure out what his story was, but he looked like the kind of southern white male you'd find at a Molly Hatchet concert, with long frizzy hair that came to his shoulders, a sleeveless Guns 'n' Roses T-shirt, and a khaki baseball cap. He looked like the type of person, frankly, that a Yankee, out of earshot, would call a redneck, and—since he never opened his mouth—there was no way to disprove the theory. All the time we spoke with Robert, he not only didn't speak, but he crossed his arms and glared at us the entire time like we were carrying a stack of Mantovani records or something.

Later on, Bob and I exchanged a few theories about the white guy, the unfriendliest person we met in Mississippi—by far. My guess is that he had a lot vested, emotionally, in the Greenville blues scene and that he resented a couple of yuppified white guys breezing into Little Blue's for a few hours and acting like we deserved to be there. We didn't fit within his vision of musical democracy.

There were a few other folks cruising in and out: one in particular I took to be a much older man, possibly in his early seventies. He had a shock of whitish gray hair that, with a beard, ringed his entire face, and he wore a dirty old pair of blue pants and a freshly bleached white shirt that was untucked and buttoned only at the middle two buttons. I was scribbling a few notes in my ever-present notebook when his glassy gaze met mine.

"I'm on the run," he said.

I looked over at Bob. He was trying to sit peacefully on the porch, but a hornet was attacking his legs. "Don't fight it," Robert said.

In the meantime, a new customer for Little Blue's had arrived. His hair was a richer gray than the alleged fugitive's, but his face was sharply lined, and he looked to be in his sixties. He wore a military-style camouflage outfit, including the hat, and looked like he was stopping by for a malt liquor on the way home from a survivalist weekend.

The white-haired man knew him. "Tell that man your name," he said, gesturing toward me. The man in the fatigues said nothing, but his white-haired friend kept right on talking. "His name is Mad Dog."

So this is how things were going in Longwood, Mississippi. There was no music, but now I had a swarm of hornets, a mute and hostile Guns 'n' Roses kid, a fugitive on the lam, and a guy named Mad Dog to entertain me. It was looking like a long afternoon.

In the meantime, Elvira had cranked up the jukebox speaker inside, playing something that sounded like a batch of songs taped off the radio. I listened to the music, watching as Robert and the white-haired man made some feeble small talk about music. It wasn't just me, I thought, nobody here is communicating, and, in a strange, selfish way, I felt better.

A man who looked like the identical twin brother of Mad Dog—which he was, I later learned—had arrived in a mechanic's navy blue shirt and pants and an olive green hat from a Greenville factory that read: Safety First. Since the conversation between the two young bluesmen and the three older malt-liquor drinkers was going nowhere, the white-haired man turned his attention toward me.

"Hey, what are you writin' down?" It was a legitimate question. I looked like a revenuer from the IRS.

I told him, vaguely, that I was looking for jukeboxes. I was leaning on an old green Cadillac, about twenty feet away or so, and I was obviously keeping my distance.

"Come over here," he said. "I ain't gonna bite."

He had a good point. So I moved over near the porch, and the fugitive and I started conversing—slowly, of course, at first, but gradually finding some common ground. He wanted to know where else I had been on my jukebox travels, and so I told him a little about my trip to Chicago. During the 1930s, '40s, and '50s, hundreds of thousands of Mississippi blacks took the Illinois Central north, in search of decent factory wages. Many black people in Mississippi have relatives in Chicago, and a good number have tried living in the Windy City themselves. Sure enough, the white-haired man had just been back in Chicago a couple months ago, visiting his brother.

We agreed that the South Side of Chicago was a troubled place. "You can't even sit outside out there," he said—a serious drawback for someone from Mississippi, where porch sitting is an art.

By now, I felt a lot more at ease hanging out on the front porch of Little Blue's. Soon, I found myself talking to Mad Dog's brother, the man in the blue service-station suit. He seemed to be fixed on one issue, and one issue alone: bragging on his family. He especially wanted me to know that his two kids were both recent graduates of Delta State University in nearby Moorhead, Mississippi.

"My baby just got out of college!" said the man in navy blue.

Now, one might reasonably ask, if this man was so enamored with his family, what was he doing at Little Blue's, alone, drinking malt liquor, listening to the devil's music, and rapping with a man who quite possibly was a fugitive from justice?

He had a good explanation: His wife and daughter were on a weekend trip, visiting some family in Dallas. In fact, just before he left home his wife had just called from Texas to check in.

"I love my family," he said. And Mad Dog's brother kept it up, explaining more and more about his life, about how he'd been a pretty wild young man, about how he wasn't yet married to the woman when they had their first child. Not only that, but he was something of a bluesman, playing around in little juke joints like Little Blue's. Then one day he decided it was time to settle down. He married the woman and gave her a proper home in a country town called Hollandale, Mississippi. And he went to Greenville and got a job at the Cleveland Brooks boiler factory, and—except for one layoff—he's been working there ever since.

"I love my family," he said again. I had jotted that down the first time he said it, but he gave a look that made it clear I should write it down again.

"Pay attention," he said. "I love my family."

It was like a mantra. He soon fell into a pattern. He would speak a sentence or two then repeat: "Understand one thing. I love my family."

Maybe—because I was taking down a few notes, something that's not normally done at a Mississippi juke joint on a Sunday afternoon—Mad Dog's brother was afraid, that somehow his words and activities at Little Blue's would get back to his wife when she returned from Dallas. But I don't think that was the reason for his pronouncements. I think that, in meeting a writer from the city, the man saw a chance to impart the main piece of wisdom he learned in life, and that wisdom was no more than this: "I love my family." He had played the blues, and he gave it up for a steady job and a home, and now he wanted the world to know that he had made the right choice.

The circumstances were certainly different, but it was basically the same choice I'd made on that snowy night on the Upper West Side eighteen months before, when I said good-bye to the Raccoon Lodge and hello to Lower Makefield. I told him how I was now married myself, and about to be a father. "I love my family," I told him proudly.

The man wanted so much for me to get his words down right that he did something a little bit unusual—he pulled out his driver's license so I would get the right spelling of his name.

"Ezell Landrum," the Mississippi driver's license said. "Route 1, Hollandale. 1-6-35."

I scribbled this down, and then did some quick math. Ezell was just fifty-seven years old, a good ten years younger than he appeared. Born on the same day was his brother Mad Dog, whose given name, confusingly enough, was Izell. They were born triplets, and their sister, whose name is . . . Mary, lives in California.

Then the white-haired man, who had claimed to be on the run, pulled out his driver's license, too. His name was Ronald Hill, and he was just forty-eight years old—or about twenty-five years younger than he looked.

Then I looked at my watch and realized it was already 5:55. The sun was finally starting to drop toward the levee to our west, and the crowd outside had swelled to thirty or so. Now a pickup truck of young musicians was backing right up to the shaky wood porch, unloading drums and electric guitars. The band was going to set up shop right there in the front room of Little Blue's Cafe, a cramped space about the size of the kitchen in a New York City apartment.

Bob and I moved to the tiny front room, which seated maybe five or six people at two wood-plank tables. I sat down on one of the seats Little Blue had torn out of his old school bus, and sank down into the cushion. It was surprisingly comfortable, but the air inside the tiny room was stagnant, and hot as the inside of a barbecue pit. There was an electric fan in the room's one tiny window, but it was huffing and puffing to no avail, and my body was covered in sweat.

I was staring at a handwritten sign on the wall that read PLEASE NO DOPE ALLOWED. NO BEER FROM OUTSIDE ALLOWED. NO FIGHTING IN THIS PLACE. THANK YOU.

Then there was a blast from John Horton's guitar, and his simply named Special Occasion Band starting playing, a rollicking, uptempo sound, the kind of contemporary blues one might hear today from Son Seals or Lonnie Brooks. Soon the tiny sweatbox of Little Blue's front room seemed more like a revival tent—albeit one with posters of bikini-clad blondes—as people started swaying to this higher cosmic source.

A few feet away, on the school-bus seat perpendicular to mine, a middle-aged woman in a blindingly bright red, pink, and purple blouse rode up on the cushion and started to sway, hard and fast, to the music. She would cross her arms way high over her head and then gyrate wildly to the music, oblivious to the narrow confines of the Formica table or the tight seating arrangements. Several times I was sure she would topple the little table that we shared, along with my beer and a quart bottle of malt liquor that she was sipping with her companion, a young woman who might have been her daughter. Every couple of minutes she stopped to catch her breath and looked at me, rolling her eyes as if her soul was headed straight for Jordan. Somebody once told me that this was called "getting happy."

The first song broke to a hard stop, and then John Horton leaned over the microphone. "Goin' to Detroit," he proclaimed, and then he and his Flying-V guitar were off the ground yet again. The woman next to me was thrusting her pelvis like the King on Ed Sullivan; John Horton was leaning into the mike, singing "Gonna get me a job on that Cadillac assembly line." The overheated air in the room hadn't moved for minutes, but I could feel the electricity of the sound waves. Bob was standing near me, checking out the room, and every so often he would lean over and shout in my ear, "This is incredible!"

Sitting on the other side of the room—which was only about seven feet away—were Ronald Hill and Izell Landrum. Every so often, in mid-song, I would look over at Izell, and he would look over at me. Each time, we smiled broadly, and we dramatically, emphatically pointed at each other. It was a gesture of fraternity—for this one day he was sharing their well-kept secret with Bob and me.

Just when I was getting used to the house-rocking of John Horton and his Special Occasion Band, and to the threat of a large, gyrating woman toppling over onto me, a beer-bellied man in a white T-shirt and a white hat walked slowly up toward the band with the help of a metal cane. He was holding a plastic bag, as if he were stopping by to hear some blues on the way from the drugstore. I thought he might be a casual heckler like some of the customers back in Greenville, but then he pulled a harmonica from his pocket. Soon he was leaning into the mike, wailing away on his harmonica, still holding that bag. He was called Old Blind Jebby, I later learned, although in truth he is only fifty-two, and he has some vision.

The band raced though a version of the old blues standard "They Call Me the Rocker," then played a slow, scorching number, with Old Blind Jebby singing lead. "Yeah, you used to make your own paycheck, baby, and brought 'em home to me."

I wanted to catch every second in that stagnant air and clutch it forever. But even with the accelerated passage of time, the images from that hour or so are still white-hot—and indelible. Midway through the set, a white man with thinning blond hair, wire-rimmed glasses and a polo shirt—he looked like a missing member of Charles Jordan's golf foursome—walked into the center of the little room, stood there for about fifteen seconds, and left, never to be seen again. Old Blind Jebby blew a mean version of Slim Harpo's "Baby Scratch My Back" on the harmonica. The gyrating woman left her school-bus seat and tried her dance moves right in front of the band—only to collapse in a heap, causing a brief intermission.

Then I stopped taking notes. Then—too soon, far too soon—it was over.

When I came outside, it was about quarter past seven, and the sun was finally starting to nosedive toward the low slope of the Mississippi River levee, the highest point for miles. Elvira had cut the record machine back on, and a fuzzy Clarence Carter was singing his 1980s jukebox hit, "Strokin'." There were maybe thirty or forty people standing around in Little Blue's front yard, huddled aound pickup trucks in clusters of five and six, drinking Bud and talking about music and stuff.

I found Bob sitting up on the back of that old green Cadillac again. On his left was a thirtyish woman, with almond skin, in a yellow blouse and a white ball cap with the bill flipped up. She was drinking from a quart bottle of Colt .45, and her eyes had a glazed look, like she had been doing so for some time.

"Hey, you, take my picture," she said.

While I was snapping her picture, Bob was talking to another woman, on his right. She also looked to be in her thirties, and, with a spanking new pair of acid-washed jeans, a green blouse, a leather purse, and a stylish short hairdo, she was clearly the most fashionable woman in all of Longwood. She didn't want to tell me her name when she saw I had a notebook, but she worked about an hour away in central Mississippi, at a factory that built trailers for eighteen-wheelers.

Bob was asking her about Roosevelt "Booba" Barnes, whose name was still invoked by everyone in the Greenville area even though he had moved to Chicago.

The woman didn't think Booba was so great. "He let all us black folks down," she said.

She said it was getting harder and harder to find good juke joints in Mississippi. I asked her what she thought of the music scene on Nelson Street in Greenville.

She threw me a scowl. "Nelson Street is a hard place," she said. "That's a hard rock."

After a while our conversation took a probably inevitable turn toward the subject of race. It had been thirty-eight years since *Brown* v. *Board of Ed,* and yet social segregation, from the dry white heat of Doe's Eat Place to the earthy sweat of Little Blue's Cafe, was still the rule in Mississippi.

"Mississippi is a prejudiced state," she said, and Bob and I glumly nodded.

We talked about Alabama, where Bob has lived and worked for two decades and where I lived briefly. There was progress there, but not enough; in 1982, the year I moved there, the voters returned former segregationist George Wallace to the statehouse, while a tour guide at the state museum in Montgomery told me that Martin Luther King, Jr., had been "an outside agitator from Georgia" who didn't belong in the museum.

"Alabama is a prejudiced state," we all said in unison. Race was a depressing topic. But the acid-jeans woman took a longer-range view of the problem.

"One God is all that we serve," she said. "And one God will deal with all of us."

It was probably the most meaningful conversation I ever had with someone who wouldn't tell me her name. But if you'd been there to see it, the scene would have looked pretty silly: that's because we two white boys were the only ones dumb enough to wear shorts to a Mississippi Delta rice patch. As the sun dropped below the levee, thousands of little bugs—chiggers, no-see-ums, whatever—swarmed from fields and made a beeline for our ankles. At first, Bob and I were scraping one ankles with our sneaker every few seconds; eventually we were frantically hopping from one foot to the other in a futile and awkward dance step.

It was time to leave Longwood, Mississippi.

I still can remember saying goodbye to the unknown blues

woman in the Delta twilight. We shook hands, but she grabbed my fingers with a hard grip, and held on for at least five seconds or so. None of us wanted to let go of Longwood, or that afternoon.

Still, I felt an unusual sense of completeness. For much of my jukebox journey, I had always felt like I was running a little late, missing things that had been there just days, months, or years before. Now I had seen Little Blue's Cafe and a Mesozoic jukebox—just eight days before Little Blue was scheduled to move on to a less picturesque setting.

I was finally on time.

It would have been fitting for our day to end right there in the sunset over Longwood, but life is never that simple. For one thing, we had promised Old Blind Jebby a ride back into Greenville ("Just drop me off at the Flowing Fountain," he said).

Jebby talked a lot about music, and about some successful gigs that he played in the early 1970s with white musicians. We talked about the movie *Crossroads*—a Ralph Macchio vehicle about a white suburban kid searching, ahem, for the blues—that was filmed in Greenville in the late 1980s. There was even a part for a blind bluesman, but Old Blind Jebby didn't audition because he was looking after his dying wife in a Greenville hospital.

We told him we'd met another Greenville musician, T-Model Ford, that day.

"T-Model!" Jebby said. "That guy's crazy."

"He sure is," I said. "You know what he told me? He said he had twenty-six children."

"Oh. Well, that's a fact."

By now we were almost back to Nelson Street. It was about half past eight when we pulled up to the front of the Flowing Fountain, and we walked Jebby inside. I figured this was my chance to finally hear Perry Payton's jukebox. Instead, a man at the door asked us for $1. That damned disc jockey was back for another night. The fabled jukebox of the Flowing Fountain was indeed one I was destined not to hear.

So instead Bob and I swung through the Wendy's on Highway 82 for a grilled chicken sandwich, and then there was about an hour on U.S. 61—the fabled blues highway that Bob Dylan revisited—before our next destination.

"I wonder what Charles Jordan would have thought of all that," Bob said.

Then we fell silent for a long stretch, as if pausing to remember the face of every person, the sound of every guitar riff, and the smell of every Colt .45 from that incredible day. There were long stretches of open cotton fields, and the flat horizon was so dark that the moon and the stars burned with more white heat than this city boy has ever seen.

Chapter 9

....

The Wonder of You

It was Elvis Presley's fifty-eighth birthday, and I was running an hour behind schedule.

It was 11:30 A.M. on January 8, 1993. I should have been on the other side of Philadelphia already, whipping past the hole that used to be John F. Kennedy Stadium on I-95 with Elvis blasting "In the Ghetto" from what one might tactlessly be called the ghetto blaster that substituted for my stolen car radio. Instead, I was still in Lower Makefield, walking around in a continuous loop with the attractive young woman who had managed to take over my life in a mere sixty-nine days—my new daughter, Julia Elizabeth.

The whole schedule was unrealistic. Julia's first two nighttime feedings—this was foremost among my many new household responsibilities—had run long, and so I overslept, as I almost always did, while Kathy took over the predawn shift. Then I had to run out to the Thriftway to buy food for four New York friends who would be making a pilgrimage the following day, bearing gifts. Now Kathy had to get dressed while I was still around to watch little Julia, or spend the next twelve hours in her bathrobe. We hadn't gotten our mail—the mailbox is seventy-five feet from our front door—for three days. Julia started to wail. I hoisted the twelve-pound monarch onto my shoulder, and made yet another circular lap—there had easily been 7,000, at 100 per day—on a track that consisted of our living room, dining room, and kitchen.

I was struggling to leave the Queen for less than a day, to pay homage to the King.

For Julia Elizabeth was clearly the Queen of our townhouse, in every good and bad sense of the word. It was the Julian-Elizabethan era in Lower Makefield, Pennsylvania. At ten weeks, Julia was bald but beautiful, with big eyes the color of a crystal-blue prairie sky, soft pale cheeks, and a cockeyed smile—executed with one eye half shut—that looked with her hairless pate like a hilarious imitation of Marlin Fitzwater. Her struggle with colic, which dominated the first six weeks of her life, had made many of our first nights together a sleepless hell, but we worried more about her cramped intestines than our bloodshot, bedraggled eyes. I wouldn't trade Julia or that crooked smile for all the jukeboxes in America.

And yet . . .

And yet there were many nights after Julia had fallen asleep at 7 P.M. when Kathy and I, numb on our couch, too exhausted to even grab the channel changer to expunge *Wheel of Fortune* from our screen, dreamed of getting away, anywhere, and—to paraphrase U2—with or without her. We spent hours debating whether an infant can drink formula made from the water in France, or how we might shield her from the midday sun of Las Vegas. We researched vacations for couples with infants, and we got the impression that parents who even considered such a brazen scheme were just a step up from that *Home Alone* couple that was arrested in Chicago (although there is a Club Med that can cope with infants, located on a river—not a beach, mind you, but a river!—in Florida). And the next morning, we were always back on that couch, trying to strike a pose in which Julia wouldn't scream.

And what about jukeboxes? Ha! Needless to say, my search went on hold for those sleepless months, but I couldn't call it quits, because I still felt that neon buzz of longing in my soul. I had already made some discoveries—the world's greatest Frank Sinatra and Patsy Cline jukeboxes, and that dust-covered artifact in a Mississippi juke joint that might well have been the Juke of the Covenant—but I knew there were others. There was all that territory west of the Mississippi that, except for my brief Louisiana incursion, was still untouched. I hadn't even been to a truck stop. And, as Martha Reeves once said, can't forget the Motor City. I should have been out there, cruising Montana in a four-wheel drive, getting directions to the nearest rodeo bar.

But much of that was jukebox fantasy. Jukebox reality would be twelve hours in Baltimore.

That's because today was Elvis Presley's birthday, and I was making a pilgrimage with two special purposes. One was to hear an Elvis jukebox, for one simply cannot say he's searched for America's best jukebox without tithing the King. But my second purpose was trickier: I felt I couldn't really appreciate the Elvis Presley jukebox until I came to grips with the legend himself. Just like Charlie Brown, so bombarded with Yuletide commercialism that he didn't know the True Meaning of Christmas, I had a hard time fully relating to the birth of the Savior of Rock 'n' Roll. Maybe that's because I was a Rear Guard Baby Boomer who had only known two Elvises, or Elvii, in my aware lifetime—fat Elvis, who played nostalgia concerts for housewives while my teenage friends and I were grooving on Bad Company, and dead Elvis, who seemed more like a registered trademark than a rock 'n' roll star. I loved his music—especially and strangely his "comeback" songs, like "Suspicious Minds" and "In the Ghetto"—but couldn't understand the hype. I thought his fifty-eighth birthday was time to come to grips with Elvis.

And so I was off to Baltimore.

Baltimore?

When I hatched my jukebox scheme in 1991, I had it in mind to look for Elvis in his hometown of Memphis, but others warned me to stay away, that after fifteen unabated years of Elvismania there was no stone there not unturned. In August of 1992, I did visit the other major Elvis landmark—Tupelo, Mississippi; the two-room shack where Elvis and his ill-fated twin were born still stands, in the midst of a newer working-class sub-division, in a part of town some call Elvis Presley Heights. The place was interesting but artificial, for the relics—funky floral wallpaper, a picture of Elvis and his parents, the poem "If" by Rudyard Kipling, a rendering of Jesus on the nightstand—are not the original decor of the home, but somebody's best guess. In spite of this, the tour guide there bars any picture taking, as if this secondhand shack were the Sistine Chapel. The tour takes only three minutes or so for even a real gawker, so visitors are steered toward a museum and gift shop, where Elvis decanters go for $175 but a book of Elvis matches (which we still use for cookouts and our green marble fireplace in Lower Makefield) was just thirty cents. But those matches and a refrigerator magnet that I brought home to Kathy brought me no closer to the True Meaning of Elvis.

The truth, when it came, was in the spirit of the *National Enquirer* and the words of the Mojo Nixon song: "Elvis is everywhere." After all, unlike some of the other jukebox heroes that I was chasing, Elvis Presley could be anywhere in Jukebox America: L.A., Vegas, even Kalamazoo. The all-important tip that set me on the trail was that the best Elvis Presley jukebox in America was located in neither Memphis nor Tupelo but in the blue-collar burg of Baltimore, in a corner dive officially known as Miss Bonnie's Elvis Shrine Bar and Literary Salon. And that was just perfect, for I had long wanted some excuse to go jukebox-chasing in Baltimore. For me, it was a city that had always been on a par with Chicago as one of the industrial giants of Jukebox America, awe-inspiring and more than a little mysterious; the first five or six times I saw the city, from the soaring overpasses on I-95 that suddenly descend into the Harbor Tunnel, I thought the Baltimore Harbor was beyond belief, its skyscraping cargo-unloading cranes and building-block stacks of freight containers and tangled-piped chemical plants stretching eastward for miles to the Great Atlantic. In the 1980s, I got to visit Baltimore, but most of my trips were limited to that tourist belt from the new Oriole Park at Camden Yards to the Aquarium, leaving me to wonder about the ubiquitous row houses and corner bars that seemed to fill the gaps between cargo cranes.

Now, in the name of Elvis, I would finally get to find out. Miss Bonnie was planning an official birthday party for the day after, but I figured that a true believer would show up on the real birthday. And so, a few minutes before noon, I left our Lower Makefield town house and headed straight into a January drizzle, a chilly reminder of the same unrelenting weather Kathy and I had encountered when we headed down the same stretch of I-95 toward Winchester five months and light years before. Most of my Elvis music is still on vinyl, so I listened to my only cassette of the King, a collection of his post-1968 comeback singles. My theme song for the day was "Kentucky Rain"; like my Patsy Cline heroine in "Walkin' After Midnight," the singer is caught up in an impossible quest—"searchin' for you—in the cold Kentucky rain." I wasn't the only pilgrim that day: twelve hours earlier about one thousand zealots had risked pneumonia in the cold Tennessee rain to buy the first of the much-ballyhooed "young Elvis" twenty-nine-cent postage stamps. Twelve hours to the east I was driving through that same cold rain shower, past the fast-food havens of the Delaware House and the Maryland House and the Chesapeake House, in search of an Elvis Presley jukebox, and soon those beautiful cargo cranes loomed in the distance.

I exited I-95 before the tunnel and the endless port, but those freight containers were stacked under every odd overpass, and when I saw the headquarters of the Container Corp. of America I knew I was on the right track. Soon I was in a blue-collar American that I thought only existed in newsreels from the 1950s, a world of prehistoric food joints like Chilly Willy's Sno Balls, United Steelworkers union halls, rail underpasses, and dozens of identical and seamless brick row houses, jutting off on sidestreets at odd angles. I decided then and there that Baltimore should be declared the capital of Jukebox America. In less than ten minutes I'd found the three Red Square–like turrets of a brand new stucco Ukrainian church—a key landmark in my search—and a cargo crane hanging like a beacon down the side street. Around the block, on a street with a dozen two-story stone rowhouses on either side, across a narrow alley from Polish Veterans Association of America Post #112, I found Elvis Presley.

Well, to be perfectly honest, it wasn't Elvis in the flesh, or even his Holy Spirit. It was a fifteen-foot-high, twelve-foot-wide image of the King, which a Baltimore middle-school art teacher named Raphael Pantalone had painted in one day about a year before, and it adorned a windowless brick expanse on the side of Miss Bonnie's Elvis Shrine Bar and Literary Salon, located at 2422 Fleet Street. The mural represents a very young Elvis, the Sun Records Elvis, with a red knotted kerchief and his black hair (but for one rebellious strand) slicked back, staring down at the Polish veterans hall.

Elementary school was already out for the day by the time I reached Baltimore, and there were two ten-year-old boys Rollerblading up and down the narrow alley, oblivious to the drizzle. Two girls in down jackets, seven or nine years old, were watching the Rollerbladers in apparent boredom, and when I took out a notepad to describe the mural I must have seemed more interesting.

I asked them if they knew that today was Elvis Presley's birthday, and of course they did—they had even announced it over the loudspeaker that morning in school.

"I think Bonnie is having a birthday party," said the older girl, a blonde.

I was taken by surprise. In most towns tavern owners are considered a friend of the devil, but in the row houses of Baltimore even the grade schoolers seemed to be on a first-name basis with their neighborhood barkeep. I was already falling in love with this town, and I hadn't even seen a jukebox yet. The little girl spoke again. "Once you go in, you'll see how much she loves Elvis."

I was indeed anxious to enter the Elvis shrine, to meet Miss Bonnie, to hear the Elvis jukebox, but I stopped to admire the painting a little longer before the early January nightfall. I was particularly impressed with that one stray strand of hair—how one tiny gesture could convey such raw sexuality—when the little girl spoke again, and pointed right at that runaway hair.

"If you can see," she said, "there's one place where they messed up."

Actually, it was Miss Bonnie's next-door neighbor, one Florence Chenowith, who thought the whole painting was messed up, and that's what touched off the chain of events that brought me to this row-house corner of Baltimore in the first place. For ironically, the existence of the world's greatest Elvis Presley jukebox—a fact that should have been screamed from every newsstand and television monitor in this great nation—would have gone unreported were it not for Florence Chenowith and her bitter feud with Miss Bonnie, a battle that was waged before the zoning boards, the liquor boards, and finally in the national media, most notably the *Washington Post* and *A Current Affair*. (The feud is complicated, and I'll explain it all in a minute.)

To be honest, when I read in the *Post* about Miss Bonnie, the Elvis Shrine, and the feud, my first thought was that this was something out of one of those movies that the warped film director and Baltimore native John Waters shoots in his native city. I'm not sure if I expected Miss Bonnie to be blimp-sized or a cross-dresser or what, but when I went inside she proved to be quite normal . . . for someone who had assembled a shrine to Elvis Presley.

She had just been to the "beauty shop" that morning, and her auburn-colored hair—unlike the King's—was perfectly coiffed in a medium-length do. She had told me on the phone the day before I arrived that she has suffered a heart attack and three strokes, but she gave the appearance of good health, trim, with a complexion that looked younger than her sixty-two years. She wore a blue corduroy jacket and a light blue blouse studded with pearls, and with her rounded eyeglasses she looked fairly tame, more like a grade-school teacher than like a woman who used to sing country-and-western tunes, owned a couple of taverns, married five different men six times, and collected velvet wall hangings of Elvis. Her real name was not Bonnie at all, but Lavonda Hunt, and she hailed originally from Savannah, Georgia; her words were sometimes harsh but tempered with an accent like a Gulf Stream breeze. When I entered, the tavern was on the empty side: just her behind a bar and what seemed to be a scruffy-looking man in a black-and-white flannel shirt and a case of five o'clock shadow that contrasted with his boyish smile. The jukebox, over to the side, was shut off—TNT was running an Elvis film festival—but about seventy-five other Elvii were staring at me from pictures laughing in every corner of the bar.

There was only one obvious question: Why?

She said the corner bar—which from a distance looks like literally dozens of other corner saloons that I saw in just my cursory drive around eastern Baltimore—had been a run-down joint called Nadine's when she bought it in 1981.

"I had a lot of stuff, and I put it in here," she said, a massive understatement given the platoon of Elvises, or Elvii—velvet, watercolored, and ceramic—staring down. "And people gave me a lot."

Miss Bonnie is like a lot of Elvis fans in her simpler, biblical faith in the King.

"I've always loved Elvis, and one day I said, 'Well, I'm going to have an Elvis shrine,' and everybody says, 'Aw hell, are you crazy?' and I says, 'I ain't crazy, but I'm going to have an Elvis shrine,' and sure enough, I did."

Was she always an Elvis fan?

"I kinda grew up with his music," Miss Bonnie said. "He's fifty-eight, and I'm sixty-two."

"I noticed you talk about Elvis in the present tense. Do you think he's still alive?"

"Everybody asks me that question. Who knows? Nobody don't know but the Lord above. I wisht he was."

"What would he think of this place?"

"He'd love it."

It was about 3:30 P.M., and there was nobody else around; I thought for a moment that Elvis Presley's fifty-eighth birthday was going to be a long afternoon. I learned some interesting facts about Miss Bonnie, however: about how she once traveled around South Carolina, Georgia, and Florida, singing country tunes with a group called Bunny Livingston and His Girls, and about how she had five husbands—including a couple of "Balto-morons"— but none at the moment. I saw the pictures behind her bar of her two sons—one, beefy with sideburns, looked uncannily like the 1977 Elvis—and her five grandchildren. I learned that her favorite Elvis song was "My Way" (I tried to point out that wimpy Paul Anka had written it, but nothing would dissuade her) because, "That's the way I did it: 'My Way.' " Then I learned something that was even more interesting—that she had met the King.

"I met him in Savannah," she said. "That's when he was in the service." The meeting apparently took place in a grocery store. "He was buying all kinds of stuff for the barracks, I guess, and I was there. I was shopping early in the morning, because I was working two jobs."

"You mean you were coming down the aisle and you saw Elvis Presley?"

"Right."

"What was he buying?"

"All kinds of stuff."

Apparently, this would have been 1958, and the military Elvis was about to ship out to Germany, where he would meet the young—extremely young—Priscilla.

"What did you say to Elvis Presley? That must have been quite a shock."

"I said, 'Hi,' and he said, 'Hi.' I didn't try to tear his clothes off, or anything like that." Miss Bonnie said the two of them carried on a conversation, although—not surprisingly—she'd long forgotten its substance. "But I know one thing," she concluded. "He was the nicest person I ever met in my life . . .

"He was good to everybody."

In fact, if you talk to a common breed of Elvis fans, you'll find that this concept—"the good Elvis," a latter-day saint who dispenses pink Cadillacs instead of eternal absolution, a St. Francis of Assisi with a guitar strap on his shoulder instead of a squirrel—is one of the most frequently cited cause for Elvis-mania, almost on a par with his groundbreaking music or his undeniable sex appeal. Miss Bonnie belonged to this sect, but I didn't think that her Elvis Fundamentalism could explain the True Meaning of Elvis.

On the TV screen behind us came the screech of a car's brakes, then a pause.

"Are you all right, Elvis?" said the TV voice. Elvis's omnipresence was starting to give me the creeps.

Elvis was certainly everywhere in the twenty-by-seventy-foot world that Miss Bonnie had created on the first floor of that corner row house in Baltimore. The following is a close-but-not-quite-complete description of what constitutes an Elvis shrine:

A corner with fourteen pictures of Elvis in various stages of life, including one in which he resembles a boyish prep-schooler, one in Army dress khakis, one in the Army with aviator goggles, one in a white jumpsuit and red scarf in which he looks like a southern-fried Tom Jones, and one from a white-linen restaurant in which Elvis is holding a pink teacup and eating a biscuit (was any second of this man's life unphotographed?!); one Tic Tac Strike shuffleboard bowling game; twelve black velvet sketches of "Elvis, 1935–1977," drawn by "Sam"; one picture of Elvis reading a newspaper; one picture of Elvis in a fur cap strumming his guitar in a rural setting; one sequined sketch of Elvis on a black backdrop, one picture (my favorite) of a long-sideburned, 1968-ish Elvis reclining on the grass in a compromising position with (no, it can't be!) Mary Tyler Moore (!), whose head is propped up by a football; so many pictures of Elvis, sideburned and unsideburned, fat and thin, that one begins to wonder whether, like Lee Harvey Oswald, there was more than one Elvis; four paintings of a cowboy-hatted John Wayne (huh?!); one poster for Elvis's movie *King Creole*, in which the King is drawn putting up his dukes; a montage of nine cover slips from Elvis 45s such as "In the Ghetto/Any Day Now"; two of Elvis's favorite recipes, for Macaroni Salad and Uncle Vester Presley's

Sunday Meat Loaf; two hardwood wall clocks that depict Elvis, one fat and one thin; one picture of Elvis in his military garb, sitting behind a jumble of microphones at a press conference; two large cloth wall hangings of Elvis, including the one with the loose hair strand that was the model for the outdoor painting, along with the famous studded white jumpsuit shot, with a Hawaiian lai around his neck; about twelve publicity shots behind the bar, of either celebrities such as George Jones and Tammy Wynette, Faron Young, Dolly Parton, Loretta Lynn, and Jerry Lee Lewis, or people I've never heard of; about fifteen yellow 45s hanging down from the ceiling, all of which seem to be "The Letter" by Bill Folsom; one candid snapshot of a 1977 Elvis who looks even bigger than his death weight of 250 pounds and which the fan who took it has inscribed "Bonnie—This is a candid photo of Elvis in a motel in Dallas TX. approximately six months before his death in 1977. He's holding a sheriff's badge in his right hand"; one calendar of Elvis album covers; one very fuzzy early snapshot of Elvis with his drummer D. J. Fontana, who has visited the bar several times; one picture of the Million Dollar Quartet—Elvis, Carl Perkins, Jerry Lee Lewis, and Johnny Cash—at Sun Records; two black-and-white snapshots of Elvis and Priscilla, including one of them kissing passionately; one pencil sketch of Elvis; one set of Elvis trading cards; one rendering by Raphael Pantalone, the creator of the wall-sized Elvis, that depicts Elvis as an Arabian sheik; six Elvis plates, including one that shows him in front of a pink Cadillac; four priceless six-inch-tall figurines of Elvis, including one of Elvis on horseback, one of Elvis in a white jumpsuit and yellow scarf, and one of Elvis in a gold jacket singing to a dog wearing a bowler hat; one highly incongruous statuette of a nude woman bent over in a compromising position; one nifty wall thermometer with a picture of Elvis that says Some Like It Cool; one bumper sticker that reads: "Elvis—Only You Can Keep His Memory Alive," and one newspaper article about the well-known pop culture and food critics Jane and Michael Stern, who for some reason chose to come to Miss Bonnie's when in Baltimore to promote a book called *The Encyclopedia of Bad Taste.*

Oh, yes, and one jukebox.

I had learned in two years of searching for America's best jukebox that the best record machines tend to be the ugliest, and Miss Bonnie's jukebox was no exception. There was no color at all, just a giant glass bubble, a four-foot-tall and four-foot-wide hulking behemoth that would have looked like R2D2 if the *Star Wars* character had been obese and sang like Elvis Presley. It was a Rowe/AMI model with 200 selections—seven for $1, of course—and it looked like a relic from the lowered-expectations jukebox days of the 1970s. There are imitators, no doubt, but I believe that this obscure dive in Baltimore, this shrine to the profane, is the location of the best Elvis Presley jukebox in America.

Or put it another way: it is almost certainly the only jukebox in America that has "Rock-a-Hula Baby"—twice. After about thirty minutes or so, as it was clear that no one was watching the slow-moving Elvis flick on TNT, Miss Bonnie finally turned on the jukebox, and soon a fuzzy version of her favorite song, "My Way"—which occupied the all-important #100 slot, naturally—came out at exactly forty-seven decibels, the legal limit in the city of Baltimore. Most of the records proved a little scratchy—as with all great jukeboxes, the local operator allows Miss Bonnie to put her own personal records on the machine—and that was the beauty of the thing, for a pristine CD jukebox would have sounded wimpy in a joint like Miss Bonnie's. Then a pause, and then Miss Bonnie's second-favorite song, #104, "The Wonder of You," with a chorus ("I guess I'll never know the reasons why I love you like I do / That's the wonder—the wonder of you.") that seemed to describe Miss Bonnie's relationship with the King. The music kept on coming—Miss Bonnie's jukebox had Elvis's first record, "That's All Right," and Elvis's last (sort of), "Moody Blue," sacred Elvis ("Cryin' in the Chapel") and profane Elvis ("Burnin' Love"), topical Elvis ("In the Ghetto") and maudlin Elvis ("Don't Cry Daddy"), Elvis doing songs other people made famous before him ("Blue Suede Shoes") and songs other people made famous there after ("Always on My Mind"). At #122/#222 was "Hound

Dog/Don't Be Cruel," along with Patsy Cline's "Crazy" widely acknowledged as one of the two most popular jukebox 45s of all time. Miss Bonnie's jukebox is 35 percent Elvis—35 out of 100—with the rest being an assortment of Elvis disciples (Johnny Cash, Roy Orbison, Jerry Lee Lewis), country (Randy Travis, "A Better Class of Losers"), pop vocalists (Dean Martin's "Houston," Natalie Cole's "Unforgettable"), and nine leftover Christmas selections on top of Elvis's "Blue Christmas."

There might be a jukebox out there on America with more Elvis songs—heck, there probably is—but it's hard to envision one with a better array of selections. On top of all that, though, Miss Bonnie's jukebox is the premier example of the genre for another reason: It embodies the singer's spirit of rebellion. This jukebox has been a key weapon in Miss Bonnie's war on the political establishment.

It all started back around 1988 or so, when the old woman who had lived without complaint next door to Miss Bonnie's passed away, and her daughter, the aforementioned Florence Chenowith, who works for a local bookbinder, took possession of her row house.

"She said she don't like Elvis," Miss Bonnie said of her next-door neighbor, and that would certainly seem to be the case, although Chenowith has been quoted to the contrary in a local newspaper.

Elvis hater or Elvis fan, Chenowith didn't like the way Miss Bonnie, like a lot of corner-tavern owners in Baltimore, kept her screen door open on a hot summer's night, and so she complained to the state liquor board. It seemed that neither the jukebox nor the TV is, by law, supposed to be louder than forty-seven decibels, which is the volume at which a normal person might watch a public-affairs show on C-SPAN. Miss Bonnie protested, but when it appeared the authorities were solidly against her, she had jukebox technicians—I guess that's what you'd call them—from the operator, Baltimore Cigarette Co., set the sound level at exactly forty-seven decibels. Still, she lost her jukebox for three tragic months, and, even worse, she lost her TV set for about two years. Things calmed down for a while, although Miss Bonnie had already had a heart attack in 1988, about when the trouble started, and later had three strokes—a fact Miss Bonnie is quick to mention repeatedly in conversation.

Then, in 1992, a new crisis emerged over Raphael Pantalone's wall painting of the King. Somebody—Chenowith was a prime suspect—complained to the zoning board in Baltimore that the fifteen-foot Elvis rendering was in essence an illegally large sign advertising Miss Bonnie's business, and would have to come down.

"The damn thing ain't bothering me," Chenowith told the *Baltimore Sun*. "I'm on the other side"—here she was referring to her actual view of the wall, not her view of the issue. "But if I had to vote on it, I'd vote for it to come down. It's degrading to the neighborhood."

At the height of the controversy, Miss Bonnie—by now a quasi-celebrity on tabloid television—declared to the media that the tavern was for sale. Yet it seemed none of her worst fears had come to pass. She had been allowed to keep the Elvis mural, and her TV and jukebox were in good working order. Still, Miss Bonnie seemed bitter—she kept steering our discussions back to the feud when I wanted to know mainly about Elvis and the jukebox.

"Now she's calling the Liquor Board again," Miss Bonnie said, conspiratorially, explaining that the authorities were once more threatening to test the noise level of the jukebox. "It boils down—somebody wants this bar. They're trying to run me out."

I looked around. It was still just me and the guy in the black-and-white flannel shirt at the bar—it was hard to imagine Mr. Bennigan or Mr. Houlihan making a huge offer. Miss Bonnie said someone had offered $30,000 recently—a good price, apparently; but she'd turned the man down, having lost her desire to sell. "Why is this going on? She's caused me to have a heart attack and three strokes."

"Somebody up high—they're using her to get to me—it's common sense," Miss Bonnie said.

It's easy to see why Miss Bonnie, fears and all, changed her

mind about selling. Having used up her lifetime husband quo-
tient, her customers and velvet hangings of the King were what
she had left. Said Miss Bonnie: "This is my living room."

And I guess that Miss Bonnie's Elvis Shrine and Literary Salon
(the latter appellation refers to an admirable series of poetry read-
ings and literacy classes which have been held there) is just like
anyone's living room at home, with a few added features: a great
jukebox, a figurine of Elvis Presley holding a teddy bear, an assortment of family members on hand to celebrate the fifty-eighth
birthday of the King.

Start with customer number one, the mysterious man in
the black flannel shirt. I had him pegged for an electrician of
some sort—he called forty-seven decibels "forty-seven *DB*," and
told me that the bar that preceded Bonnie was a dump because
it was wired for 120 volts instead of 220. But my intuition was
way off base.

"What's your name?" I asked.

The man paused for a while. "Call me Al," he said, echoing
Paul Simon. He said he was more a friend of Miss Bonnie than
a friend of Elvis.

"I like him," Al said. It was that present tense again—with
Elvis's voice talking from the TV and about 230 Elvis eyes staring
down on us, it was hard to think him a goner. "I always liked
him."

"What do you do for a living around here?"

"What do I do? This," and he pointed to a white plastic
bucket sitting on the floor, gesturing for me to take a look. I was
a little concerned—maybe this guy was a Maryland crabber, or
maybe he was a urologist bringing some work home. I undid the
cover, and my first guess was closer: the bucket was filled with
water and about 150 tropical fish—black widows, blue grommies,
scissortail, and the like, darting nervously back and forth in a
swirl.

"Oh, fish!" I said. I couldn't think of anything else to say.

It seems that Al had created a most unusual job for himself—constructing aquariums for nursing homes, hospitals, and other institutions in need of vitality, marine or otherwise. When he stopped in Miss Bonnie's for a couple of Millers, he brought his work with him.

I thought Al would be a tough act to top, but then a few minutes after four o'clock a couple more customers wandered into Miss Bonnie's Elvis Shrine—a man named John who wore a natty dark suit and a white shirt with no tie, and Deborah Williams, a thirtyish woman wearing a stylish red-and-green sweater, little or no makeup, and a bright red cap that she failed to remove during her two hours at the bar. She looked like a character from the early 1970s, like Mary Tyler Moore (coincidence?) getting ready to toss that red cap into the winter sky.

She thought to drop by Miss Bonnie's after watching the television news that morning and seeing a contest in nearby Towson, Maryland, in which Elvis impersonators competed to see who could eat the most jelly donuts—a favorite food of the King, along with peanut-butter-and-banana sandwiches and Uncle Vester's Meat Loaf. She thought Elvis's birthday might be a good time to discuss a job she wanted to do for Miss Bonnie: painting Elvis screens.

When she told me this, I thought she meant a screen like a canvas, but what she meant was window screens—she wanted to paint the King of Rock 'n' Roll on the windows in the front and side of Miss Bonnie's row house.

Deborah thought the jelly-donut-eating Elvis impersonators were pretty strange—"People who adore Elvis enough to fashion themselves after him, I think that's a strange psychology"—but she didn't think it was too strange to have Elvis staring out the windows of your house for eternity. It seems that window-screen painting is a lost art that had been popular in Baltimore earlier in the century, when homeowners attempted to distinguish their identical row houses by rendering European castles and the like on their windows. Deborah Williams wanted to keep this art alive in the 1990s, but with a difference.

"I think Elvis would be wonderful on a screen," she said,

lighting a cigarette. "He's beautiful to draw, and his popularity is indefatigable." Deborah envisioned a whole series of Elvis window screens, tracing the biography of the King in pictures—from princely pauper to bloated monarch—on the summer insect protection of Miss Bonnie's row house. She showed me one of her paintings, which was very Picassoid, a man's head that was triangular in nature.

"This is a painted gilded Mayan mask," she said, taking a drag. "It's from an ancient hallucinogenic ceremony, to be specific." I was making a mental picture of a cubist Elvis when a burly man who looked straight off the waterfront stormed in.

"Whaddaya got on the jukebox that ain't Elvis?" this burly man declared right off. I was shocked at the sacrilege, right here in the Elvis Shrine. It was like barging into the middle of a Sunday mass and demanding, "Whaddaya got to eat in this joint that ain't red wine or these wimpy little wafers?" This rude man beckoned in the direction of Miss Bonnie.

"Mom, you got Alan Jackson on there?!" he shouted, referring to the country artist whose most famous song was a plea for less rock 'n' roll from record machines, called "Don't Rock the Jukebox." I was wondering why this man was calling Miss Bonnie "Mom"—was this some obscure Baltimore term of affection?—when it dawned on me that he might indeed be one of her two sons; and he was. Dean, the son who once resembled 1977 Elvis, had slimmed down, so that he merely resembled the beer-bellied forty-two-year-old longshoreman he was, with gray stubble, a big mustache, and wire-rimmed glasses.

"I did have Alan Jackson on there," said Miss Bonnie, "but I had to take him off to get the Christmas songs on there." There were still those ten Christmas singles, like "Rockin' Around the Christmas Tree" by Brenda Lee, on the jukebox, fifteen days after the holiday. The arrival of Dean had created a critical mass in Miss Bonnie's Elvis Shrine Bar and Literary Salon, so that now all the characters—a tropical-fish entrepreneur, a screen-window artist, an Elvis-hating longshoreman, his six-times-married bar-owning mother, and a Rear Guard Baby Boomer seeking America's best jukebox—could interact freely.

The result was something like a jukebox playing oldies, folk, country, and the blues—all at once.

First, Dean was waiting for change for the jukebox, while Deborah insisted on telling the assembled audience the story of the jelly-donut-eating Elvis impersonators.

"Go over and put a dollar in the jukebox and see what you'd like," said Al, the tropical fishmonger, adding most incongruously, "You'll get married today."

"No thanks," said Dean, the former Elvis look-alike. "I'll take a jelly donut."

"Those nuns—they warned me about advising boys on playing the jukebox," said Deborah, the window-screen artist.

"Why'd they tell you that?" asked I, the seeker of jukebox knowledge.

"They said use a telephone book," Deborah said.

"What?" Al said.

"A telephone book!" Deborah said. "When you sit on a boy's lap!"

"What does that have to do with jukeboxes?" asked I.

"Nothing," said a slightly bewildered Deborah.

Al was looking across the room, shouting at Dean and the jukebox. "Why don't you play 'Silent Night'—at forty-seven decibels!"

"I need a jukebox with a country song," sang Doug Stone from inside of the jukebox. This was Dean's first selection, #168, "I Need a Jukebox with a Country Song."

Eventually, though, Dean and I stumbled into a real conversation on the True Meaning of Elvis, with Dean playing the role of devil's advocate, offering the working-man's perspective.

"I'm not nutty," Dean said. "I like him, and some of his songs. As far as being obsessed, I'm not." He looked toward his mom. "I can't get the way she is." He muttered something about the jelly-donut exhibition that morning. "It's stupid stuff. The man is dead—let him rest. They're making money off his name—that's all."

Miss Bonnie was getting upset at this blasphemy. "I've got

this shrine because I love Elvis," she said with the conviction of the Elvis Fundamentalist.

"Mom, it's a money-making racket. There's people out there making $100,000, $200,000 a year off this. Let the man rest—they're using his name as a gold mine."

Natalie Cole and her dead father were now singing "Unforgettable" from the jukebox. Dean realized maybe he was being a little hard on his mother, who, after all, was making her living with the Elvis Shrine Bar and Literary Salon.

"I love my mom and what she stands for, but there are limits to what you can do."

But Miss Bonnie was still poised to strike back. "He's the greatest," she proclaimed. "He loves kids,"—that present tense again—"and he gives away 100 Cadillacs a year. I don't know another man who did that. He made good records and good movies, and there ain't nothin' no one can say about him."

"Yeah," said Dean, "but he took it off taxes!"

I was starting to think that this Great Debate, pitting mother against son, was going to reveal for once and for all the True Meaning of Elvis, when there was an interruption—the arrival of my friend Bill, who worked as a top financial officer for a major Baltimore company and who was just as curious as I was about the Elvis Shrine. For the next three hours, Bill was an excellent companion in my search for America's best jukebox, although our interests diverged slightly. Bill wanted to know if Elvis followers thought the King was really still alive—an important question—while I wanted to know what motivated the disciples, what caused them to defy common sense and devote their lives to this simple man, this high priest of the Cadillac. In just a few hours in the capital of Jukebox America I had already met the wackiest cast of characters of my entire travels and heard a fantastic jukebox, but I felt no closer to the True Meaning of Elvis, even as the hardwood, guitar-shaped Elvis clock on the wall was ticking into the darkness.

Then, a few minutes after Bill's arrival, two True Believers of the type I had only hoped for pushed through the front door.

Every head turned, which is what always happens when an out-of-towner arrives in an outpost of Jukebox America. One was a thirty-something man with a compact frame, blue jeans, and a lot of hair—long beard, mustache, and lengthy mane, parted down the middle. His name was Pasha Veres, and I later learned he was a retired D.C. cop, tax accountant, and art student all in one, and that he grew up in the only white family on an otherwise all-black street in Washington. The other pilgrim was a woman, older yet youthful-looking, with shoulder-length platinum-blond hair, fair skin, and a slightly upturned nose. I wasn't surprised to learn that Margot McGann, lacking the windswept, waterfront countenance of a row-house Baltimorian, hailed from Austin, Texas, or that she had a job as prestigious as librarian for National Public Radio in Washington. But she was brandishing a portable camera that gave away her true purpose. Margot McGann was a gift from the Spirit in the Sky, a True Believer who was also an intellectual, an Elvis theologian who was more like Reinhold Niebuhr than the fundamentalist Miss Bonnie. I introduced myself while Patsy Cline was singing "Walkin' After Midnight."

The first thing Margot McGann did was to present me with a business card with a crudely scaled sketch of the King (his legs looked to be four feet long) that told me she was on the executive committee of something called the Elvis Country Fan Club, the "Sponsors of the annual candlelight service at Graceland."

I remarked that Baltimore seemed a strange place for an Elvis pilgrimage, which she immediately disputed because the city is "blue-collar"—right where you'd expect to find a cluster of Elvis fans. She said she knew that Maryland was a cool place—its U.S. Senator, Barbara Mikulski, used to commemorate Elvis's birthday every year in the Maryland Legislature—but she didn't know about the Elvis Shrine until she read about it, like me, in the *Washington Post*.

It seemed that Margot, like me, was a seeker of the True Meaning—but compared to her I was a bit of a piker. Of course she had been to Tupelo, and had pretty much the same reaction that I'd had ("They gussied up the place. It's too sad."). But she also used her vacation time every year to travel to Memphis, to reunite with her friends from the Elvis Country Fan Club in Austin and with other people from a universe that Margot referred to—without irony or self-consciousness—as the "Elvis world." (She used to be so afraid that her egghead friends at National Public Radio would find out about her Graceland pilgrimages that she made up elaborate fiction, answering their raised eyebrows that she happened to visit "an aunt" in Memphis every August 18. She says she finally "came out" about a year ago; her friend Pasha claims she was "outed.")

When Margot made her first reference to the "Elvis world," my eyes bulged wide open—friend Pasha later attested to this—with the delight of finding a fellow traveler from that parallel universe of Elvis seekers. But as I talked to her, it began to emerge that the True Meaning was elusive even to those on a lifetime quest. She mentioned that she'd been in Chicago once when she happened on a book lecture by Greil Marcus, the rock critic whose *Dead Elvis* is the definitive statement on post-1977 Elvismania. But even Greil Marcus couldn't explain the True Meaning. "He was asked, 'When is this going to end?' " Margot said. "He said he had figured it would decline after the tenth anniversary of his death, but it has just kept on going." That was a fact; on January 8, 1993, people were paying $44 for books of Elvis stamps that they would never send.

What did Margot think?

"It sort of represents the American dream—he invented himself," Margot said. She paused. "And he's a most handsome man." In quick succession, Margot had hit on the two most obvious meanings of Elvis, but she was quick to offer contradictions. "But if you go to Memphis, one-third of the people there are men," she said. On the subject of impersonators: "What amazes me is the international appeal. There's a Malaysian Elvis, there's a Sikh Elvis. This is true—it's not parody. It's beyond parody." In other words, Elvis embodies the American dream, but is also emulated by seekers with little concept of America; he has sex appeal, but 33 percent of his biggest fans are men.

Is he alive?

"Uh, well . . . no," said Margot, an Elvis intellectual and apparent agnostic. "Even if he faked his death, there's no way he could keep hidden for so long." Margot conceded that her view was unpopular but said, "In the Elvis world, there's a lot of room."

Then I learned something surprising about Margot, something that might explain her unromantic position on the death of Elvis. As a young adult in the 1960s, she had been a close friend of another American pop icon, Janis Joplin. The two had become pals when both were undergrads at the University of Texas in Austin. Then, a few years later, during the height of her career, Janis lived near Margot in San Francisco. "She stayed with us, before she . . . "

Margot didn't finish the sentence. She didn't have to.

How strange, that this woman could have been so close to Janis Joplin and still serve on the executive committee of the Elvis Country Fan Club. There were a few similarities between Elvis Presley and Janis Joplin—only the most obvious being that both ended up as junkies. But otherwise it's hard to think of two rock stars so unalike—the flower child and the honorary narc, the woman who sang "Oh, Lord, won't you buy me a Mercedes Benz" in bitter sarcasm and the man who would earnestly have bought her one if he had half the chance.

I asked her what people from the Elvis world thought of her friendship with Janis Joplin, but such an obvious question had never occurred to her. "I don't remember—isn't that interesting?!" she declared. "When I go back to Austin . . . ," and she paused. "Yeah, those two worlds don't intersect at all."

Except in one place, and that was Margot McGann. As darkness fell on the row houses, Margot continued to spin out more theories, theories about the unique nature of America. She noted that, as a relatively new nation, America lacked a mythology, "except for the Babe and the Blue Ox, and that was an ad for a flour company." She suggested that Elvis might be both our mythology and our royalty, that he fulfills the same role the

Windsors fulfill in Britain. Then she said a simple something that really touched me.

"I have yet to meet anyone who doesn't remember where they were when they heard Elvis died," she said.

Suddenly I was in a flashback that I have experienced dozens of times, always as clear as yesterday. It was near the end of a sweltering summer day in the suburbs of New York—August 18, 1977, to be exact. I was eighteen years old, less than a month away from college and leaving home for the first time, working at a make-work summer job at the company where my father was an executive in Manhattan; we had just arrived home together on the Penn Central train. It was about 6:30 P.M., and I went to my bedroom to change into shorts, flipping on the radio—WPLJ-FM, album-rock—like any teenager would. Their newscast—*The Source*—was on.

There was drama in the newsman's voice. "The man who sang this song is dead."

A split-second pause. I wasn't too fazed. I waited to hear the opening notes of something like Bing Crosby's "White Christmas," or maybe even somebody younger—Carl Perkins? "Blue Suede Shoes?"

"You ain't nothin' but a hound dog . . . " Elvis sang.

And fifteen and one-half years later, all grown up with a nine-week-old little girl, in this corner dive in Baltimore, I could still feel that shock in that Westchester bedroom, the way my heart missed about three beats. The King was dead. I was stunned, and that was really spooky, for I was hardly an Elvis Presley fan in 1977. My favorite band that summer was Lynyrd Skynyrd; two months later a plane crash would claim the life of lead singer Ronnie Van Zandt and two other members, yet I hardly felt a thing.

Margot McGann's offhand remark put me on the brink of the True Meaning of Elvis. I was reminded about what psychologists say about dreams, that they are a way for our inner consciousness to act out our greatest fantasies, and also our worst fears. It's funny, but when I think of Elvis and his life, the first things that come to mind are not his records or his movies but the way he did whatever he wanted, the way he could bet on a whim. After all, what red-blooded American wouldn't want to rent out a whole amusement park for a night, fly our best friends hundreds of miles in a private jet for a mere midnight snack, or—yes, Miss Bonnie—give away a new car to some lucky schlub who was nice to us? The King of Rock 'n' Roll didn't have to take a train across three states to get to work every day, and—although he was a father—probably never had to walk Lisa Marie in a 2 A.M. loop around Graceland. Isn't Elvis's life-style our greatest fantasy?

And what if you had all that and you threw it all away, popping prescription pills and gaining one hundred pounds? What if you were forty-two years old and ended up face down on that bathroom floor without any warning? Isn't that a version of anyone's worst fear?

Elvis Presley was the one person in America who acted out our own deepest consciousness on a real-life canvas that stretched from Memphis to Hollywood to Las Vegas. And, like our most vivid dreams, he hangs hazily in the front area of our daily reality, gazing down from black velvet, appearing on our jukeboxes with no warning, crashing his car on our cable-TV screen, a constant presence less like a dead man than a mass-hysteria case of déjà vu. And Miss Bonnie's Elvis Shrine and that jukebox were a center for dream therapy.

Margot McGann had helped me find my Elvis, and there was nothing more for me and my friend Bill to do except drink a beer, play shuffleboard bowling, and enjoy the greatest Elvis Presley jukebox in America. Around 8:30 P.M., we were getting ready to leave when a group of a dozen young people—straddling the legal age of twenty-one—infiltrated Miss Bonnie's. A man with a pony tail, earring, and stubble handed Miss Bonnie a license of some sort. It was from Russia.

"Who can read Russian?" Miss Bonnie shouted to the otherwise empty barroom. In deference to the arrival of these younger Elvis seekers from much farther away I stood up to leave Baltimore.

By midnight, I was back home in the green-marble reality of Lower Makefield's Condo Fields. At 4:45 A.M., I was wide awake, rocking Julia in the darkness of her room, while she knocked down a bottle of Enfamil with Iron. I was staring out into the blackness, dreaming of jelly donuts and "The Wonder of You."

Chapter 10

....

Smells Like Teen Spirit

Next I came to a place unlike anywhere else I had seen in my jukebox travels, where steel bridges and red cranes seemed to spring every which way from an endless roll of piney green hills, each roll divided with a salty tongue of cold Pacific waters, ringed by snowcapped mountains that made Jukebox America seem like a foreign nation on the other side of some rocky border pass.

This was Seattle.

If you mention this place to any true Rear Guard Baby Boomer—anyone thirty-something in the 1990s—and I guarantee that most will have the same arcane thought that I first had: The lyrics of a song, a song that my wife, Kathy, no music trivia buff by any remote stretch of the imagination, can still recite nearly a quarter-century after her prepubescent bedroom in suburban Broomall, Pennsylvania, was plastered with posters of Bobby Sherman. The song is the theme to *Here Come the Brides*, and it speaks of blue skies and green hills, a city "like a beautiful child, growing up free and wild."

But after *Here Come the Brides*—that hour-long drama about a schooner full of hot young babes of the nineteenth century shipped out to Puget Sound to meet loggers who just happened to look like Bobby Sherman and David Soul—was canceled by ABC in 1970, and after that theme song sung by Sherman faded out, we didn't think all that much about Seattle. It was a faraway place filled with laid-off aerospace workers, losing baseball teams, and rain.

Then, suddenly—I can pinpoint the month, it was January 1992—Seattle was in our face.

We were in the same place that you will find most Rear Guard Baby Boomers at 11:55 P.M. on a Saturday night—propped up in bed, struggling against sleep to watch *Saturday Night Live*. A man appeared on our TV screen with matted, unwashed blond hair and at least three days' growth—like some crude mountain logger from *Here Come the Brides* who lost all the girls to Bobby Sherman. His name was Kurt Cobain. Then some electric guitars played a dense sludge.

"I feel stupid and contagious," Kurt Cobain sang. "Here we are now—entertain us."

"Who are these people?" Kathy said. "They're awful."

"They're Nirvana," I said. "Believe it or not, this is the most popular band in America right now."

"Oh." Kathy stared at Kurt Cobain for about three seconds. "Could you turn it down a little? I think I'm going to go to sleep."

That Monday, the *New York Times* had a story—on the business page, no less—about Nirvana and their radio hit song, "Smells Like Teen Spirit." Kathy read the story and mentioned it to me when I got home. "The *Times* says Nirvana does this good song that's catchy and melodic. How come they didn't sing it on TV?"

"That was it."

"Oh."

Nirvana, of course, is from Seattle—and within a couple of weeks so were about half the other albums in *Billboard*'s Top 10, the ones that weren't rap or Garth Brooks. They had names like Pearl Jam, Alice in Chains, and Mother Love Bone. What really bugged me was not that these groups were so popular but that—having just turned thirty-three, a married homeowning commuter living in an exurban wasteland with no college radio station—I just didn't know them or their sound. For the first time since I joined the chorus of "Henry VIII" by Herman's Hermits on the bus to first grade, I was out of the pop-music loop.

While all this was happening, I was grappling with a different problem. My search for America's best jukebox hadn't struck pay dirt any farther west than Louisiana. This wasn't an accident. It's true that a bar in San Francisco had the first coin-operated jukebox in 1889, in a pre-earthquake cowtown that's a dim memory today. But most major jukebox developments—Rock-Ola and Wurlitzer, the Mississippi juke joints, Frank, Patsy, Elvis—took place east of the Rockies. However, I still had this nagging feeling that the interminable neon buzz—the sense that I was missing something—wouldn't be fully extinguished unless I doused myself in the ice-cold waters of the Pacific Ocean. Or at least Puget Sound.

The popularity of the new music that people were calling "grunge" was only part of the reason for choosing Seattle. The Pacific Northwest had a proud rock 'n' roll heritage, particularly in the early and mid-1960s. The two best-known Northwest bands—the Kingsmen, whose mumbled 1963 interpretation of "Louie, Louie" still inspires heated barroom arguments three decades later, and Paul Revere and the Raiders of TV's *Where the Action Is*—hailed from Portland, Oregon, to the south but made frequent stops on the banks of the Puget Sound and left their mark on today's grungers. More significant—if less well remembered—were Seattle's own bands of that period, the Sonics and the Wailers. With names inspired by the city's two main exports—airplanes and a bad pun on fish—and with a hard-driving wall of sound and pile-driver beat, the Sonics and the Wailers were a little too edgy for uptight record executives in New York and L.A., on the other side of those snowcapped mountains. But their rebellious riffs carried the seeds of 1990s grunge—and you could dance to them. The Sonics' best song,

"Psycho," was manic where Nirvana's take on the subject, "Lithium," was merely depressive. And in the 1960s, you would have found the Sonics in the same places where one always found the best American regional music—on independent-label 45s and on jukeboxes.

The idea of hearing the Sonics' minor hit, "The Witch," on a jukebox seemed worth spending $375 for an round-trip airplane ticket. More important, I thought that Seattle jukeboxes would be my secret key that might unlock the secret of grunge music and its popularity that seemed so alien to us Rear Guard Baby Boomers. Two days, I thought, and I would be back in the pop-music loop.

So on Memorial Day weekend 1993, I found myself on a Continental flight from Philadelphia to Seattle by way of Denver. When the suburban housewife seated next to me was not trying to sell me on the merits of the recently deposed George Bush, I was able to look out the window and take in the sweep of Jukebox America. Around 10:30 A.M., I saw the Sears Tower and tried to imagine Tony and Rosa Mangiullo, sweeping up their bar from Friday night's blues show. Then, a few guys in ten-gallon hats watching the French Open tennis from the cocktail lounge in Stapleton, then an hour of mountain flying with no humans or jukeboxes in site. Between Spokane and Tacoma, I anxiously held my new Sony Walkman up against the airplane window and listened to AM radio from someplace called the Tri-Cities and a static-filled "I Fought the Law" by the Bobby Fuller Four.

Then, at about 3:30 PDT, I was in a place called Jukebox City.

Jukebox City is a 27,000-square-foot antique warehouse in the shadow of the Kingdome, just south of downtown Seattle. The place is run amok with neon, glowing pink or green in different corners as if the place were radioactive. There are Elton John's Captain Fantastic pinball game, neon Art Deco wall clocks, and 1930s ads for Quaker State, Kellogg's Pep, and

AAA Root Beer; a larger-than-life blowup of Buddy Holly stares down in disbelief. But mainly there are jukeboxes, including several off the main floor in various stages of disrepair or undress, like R2D2 visiting a health spa. In the far left corner was the main display area, starting with the archetypal jukebox, the 1948 Wurlitzer 1015, the Bubbler, in good working order for a mere $11,950—about what I paid for my Honda. I spent more time studying a bland pale-blue Wurlitzer Americana that appeared to be from the late 1960s—it was $500 "as is," a fantasy within reach.

There I met Harold Hagen, a legend in Seattle and a nationally known expert who writes for a magazine called *Always Jukin'*, a techie column dense with references to "electrical selector plungers" and "tray pickups."

In person, Harold was the kid from the Audio-Visual Club in the eighth grade, all grown up. Tall and thin like a loose wire, with gray strands on his head, Harold was wearing a blue-flannel shirt, a strictly accidental concession to grunge fashion. It was protected, in fact, by a plastic pocket cover. When I met him he was surrounded by a half-dozen half-naked jukeboxes, parts strewn around like last night's clothing.

"So what do you think of this new music from Seattle?" I asked him.

"I haven't had much exposure," Harold said. Then he told me who he did like—Jerry Lee Lewis, Fats Domino, and Little Richard. Then we picked up a book about jukeboxes, and he showed me the two that he has at home—a classic Seeburg 100-R from 1954 and an AMI Continental from 1961 that has a bubble top like an old washing machine and that was featured in the movie *Ghost*. That was the essence of Jukebox City, a hardware store for music lovers.

Later during my stay in Seattle, I drove onto an elevated expressway—it reminded me of my beloved Chicago Skyway—past massive unloading cranes and tall stacks of containers containing, no doubt, the latest stereo components from Japan. On the other side of this rainbow, at the foot of a quiet residential hillside—was a place called the Luna Park Cafe, a fairly new restaurant owned by John Bennett, the antique-jukebox impresario of Seattle. I ordered something called "Luna eggs"—basically scrambled eggs laced with green onions, mushrooms, tomato, and cheddar cheese, served with hash browns for $4.95.

Until 1988, the building had housed a dive bar that the little history on the menu called "the infamous Pat and Roy's tavern." Now this former dive—located down the street from the vacant site of a 1906 amusement park called Luna Park, which had attractions like The Original Human Ostrich—was all gussied up, with a Clorox-clean white facade and a bright red Coca-Cola sign from the 1950s. The inside looked like Jukebox City with a coat of white paint; there were classic 1930s roadhouse ads like Call for Philip Morris. The focal point, of course, was the jukebox—an antique 1958 Seeburg that said Music for Everyone in bright red letters across the top and had chrome fins like the Batmobile on the bottom. It started playing "My Girl Lollipop" by the Chordettes. John Bennett's music machine was heavy on girl groups from the early 1960s but also had some inspired choices, like "Ne Ne Na Na Na Na Nu Nu" by Dickie Do and the Don'ts.

I started picking through my $4.95 eggs, and I noticed that in the middle of this city famed for its ethnic diversity, from Native Americans to the newest Fujianese immigrants, everyone there on a Sunday morning was even Waspier than me. There were fathers in blue denim or rugby shirts from the Gap's latest spring line and their adorable children with hair that ran the gamut from platinum blond to strawberry blond, bumming quarters from Dad for the jukebox or for a Batman ride from the 1960s that was in the front of the cafe.

The blondest of the blond, a three- or four-year-old girl, was sitting in a trance looking behind the bar, where there was a 1959 Philco black-and-white TV, the kind that is all picture tube. Raspberry jam was smeared on her face, but she did not move.

Barney was on TV. The little blond girl started waving her hand in the air.

"Can I get you something?" the waitress asked.

The girl didn't look up. "No," her father said. "She was just following *Barney*."

Before I came to Seattle, everyone told me about Jukebox City and the Luna Park Cafe—essential stops, I was told, for a man searching for America's best music machine. So I saw them, and I had mixed feelings. I had a lot of admiration for what John Bennett, Harold Hagen, and the others were doing—keeping the 45 and even the 78 record alive for a generation being raised on *Barney*, repairing lift levels and plungers, the mysteries of antiquity. But they were reprogramming them for suburbanites and exurbanites, people who shopped from the Land's End catalogue, paid $4.95 for a plate of fresh eggs, and who liked stale music with the Ramada Inn conformity of VH-1. I felt conflicted, perhaps, because these people were . . . they were me, dressed just like the others in a silk shirt and some blue jeans from Structure. The reason I paid so much attention to these blond, blue-eyed girls was because I now had one of my own, Julia, at home—and I missed her a lot. But after two years on the jukebox trail, there was still a part of me that also wanted something else.

That part of me wanted the jukebox to blast the Sonics, not the Chordettes. And it didn't want the Luna Park Cafe, it wanted "the infamous Pat and Roy's tavern" back.

I walked out to the surrealist effect of Ross Perot demagoguing on that fuzzy Philco tube, another contradiction of time and space, a man who wanted to return America to the black-and-white world of 1959, a *Barney* for the grown-ups of exurbia.

Luckily for me, there is one mystic in Seattle who understands the yin and the yang of Jukebox America, who not only knew the hardware but the software, the classic Rock-Ola and Seeburg models and the Sonics and the Screaming Trees—and I had stumbled onto him. His name is Charles Cross, and he is the editor of *The Rocket*, a monthly magazine that chronicled the rise of grunge and other local music.

I called him on the phone once, from the press dungeon underneath New York City Hall, and he sounded normal enough—although when I came to the door of his modest house in an evergreen Seattle neighborhood, I half expected a shock of grunge-dried hair like Kurt Cobain's. That was a silly thought, for Charles Cross was a clean-shaven thirty-six-year-old with tortoise-shell glasses and a two-martini lunch haircut. Unlike the grungers in their lumberjack boots and layers of flannel, Charles was dressed sensibly for an unseasonably warm Memorial Day weekend in Washington State, with shorts and a T-shirt that said Nuke the CD.

Charles Cross is quite successful for a man of his age and of his profession, journalism. He edits not only the *The Rocket* but a national magazine for Bruce Springsteen fanatics called *Backstreets*, and he has authored two books, glossy picture tomes about Springsteen and about Led Zeppelin. And his home is furnished with priceless collections and with objets d'art—in an off-beat way.

The centerpiece of his smallish living room is a Seeburg model 100-C music machine from 1954—a type that is popular with music lovers who collect jukeboxes because it's the earliest antique model that offers 100 selections.

"When I bought this from a guy in Montana, it had all records from 1964—the year the Beatles came out," he said. "You should always keep one song from the original," he added, pointing out "Please Please Me" by the Beatles. Most of the rest was the way that I would program a jukebox of my own were I so lucky—classic oldies alternating with newer, equally cool selections like REM's "Radio Free Europe."

Soon Charles Cross and I were engaged in rapid-fire conversation, for we had a lot in common. He was taking a break from his own cross-country tour of America, to all fifty states in search of the best anecdotes for a travel book about Elvis Presley. After that, he said, he wants to write a history of the jukebox. He was fully in touch with the problems of the shrinking Jukebox America—particularly the problem with "the hole." While some record labels—especially small, independent ones—are still selling 45s to American consumers, most now come with the same small center hole that 33⅓ LPs use, not the traditional larger 45

RPM center hole that older jukeboxes are designed for. Charles used to buy 45s from England—but soon small holes took over the UK as well.

"So what will you do?" I asked.

"Holland," he proclaimed. "Just last month I discovered that Holland is still using the big holes."

Then he took me on a 78 RPM–paced tour of his house, starting with a ten-foot-long coat closet that is lined with thousands and thousands of CDs—it reminded me of the Robert Klein comedy routine from the 1970s about "every record ever recorded," from "Tri-state's Best Unsigned Artists" to R & B great Arthur Alexander to Buckwheat Zydeco to hundreds of Springsteen bootlegs to—well, everything. Then we went down to his basement, where he wanted to show me a rare pinball machine—Gottlieb's "Punk," pulled from the market because it played songs like the Sex Pistols' "God Save the Queen" without the permission of the artists. The machine was covered with a dozen heavy winter coats.

"This is what happens when you don't have a coat closet," he said.

Then we sat down and talked about Seattle. Like most residents, Charles was not born there. He was raised in Virginia and briefly sampled New York City and the Parsons School of Design before deciding the city was "too weird." Just like those logging pioneers of the early 1870s portrayed by Bobby Sherman and David Soul, Charles Cross headed west to Seattle—in the early 1970s.

But the dramatization that inspired Charles Cross was not *Here Come the Brides*, but a popular movie of the period, *Cinderella Liberty*, a seedy sailor flick set in Seattle.

"The whole downtown strip, Pike's Market, was total sailors' bars, filled with merchant marines, with pinball and pool tables," he said. "That's what I fell in love with. In some way, it was the lost Seattle. It was literally unchanged from the '50s." There was a genuine sense of loss in Charles's voice. While Silicon Valley, L.A., and San Diego to the south were filling up with red-tiled strip shopping centers and suburban interchange office parks, a major slowdown by the area's major employer, the aerospace industry, kept Seattle in a time warp. "The '60s did not affect the city visually. That was the time of the Boeing depression. But it was still a great place to live. You could move here and live reasonably."

It was in that lost Seattle—about a decade before Charles Cross arrived in town—that a rock 'n' roll band called the Sonics first broke the sound barrier. Although the band has been frequently cited by better-known rockers—from Johnny Rotten of the Sex Pistols to Bruce Springsteen—as an influence on their music, their story is mostly forgotten and their records hard to find. Charles Cross tracked down most of the band in 1985 for a story for *The Rocket* that was entitled, simply: "The Northwest's Greatest Band Will Never Die."

It was around 1963 or so when a group of high school musicians started hacking around in the garage of their drummer's house, in a working-class section of Tacoma, the small city about twenty minutes south of Seattle. The primal noise was somewhat similar to the *Dr. Strangelove*–era bombers that flew from nearby McCord Air Force base, and the drummer's dad suggested they go by the name Sonics.

"We were really primitive," guitarist Larry Parypa told Charles Cross. "Nobody in the group was very good musically, but I don't think being good would necessarily have been an asset. It had balls."

The band strained to the outer limits of its capabilities. Like the Wailers, who started a year or two before them, the Sonics started playing mostly instrumentals. But the band shifted more into vocals when the enigmatic Gerry Rosalie joined the group, and soon they were renting St. Mary's Parish Hall for $15 a night and throwing parties. The bass player from the Wailers, Buck Ormsby, had started a small local label called Etiquette Records, with the idea of recording both the Wailers and other local bands, and he soon signed up the Sonics. Their first single, in 1964, was a dance tune called "The Witch," with a cover version of Little Richard's "Keep a Knockin' " on the B-side.

Like its Pacific Northwest ancestor, "Louie, Louie," the lyrics to "The Witch" were controversial.

"We even had a couple of kids come down to the basement and try to work out a dance for it," new drummer Bob Bennett (the first one with the garage and the band-naming father had been booted out) told Charles Cross. "But that didn't seem to work so we changed some of the words. They all ended up sounding like swear words—witch rhymed with bitch and all. Our biggest problem was not that we had dirty lyrics but that they all rhymed with dirty words."

It took some time, but the big Top 40 station of the Pacific Northwest, Seattle's KJR and its pioneering disc jockey Pat O'Day, finally added "The Witch" to its playlist. But the station wouldn't play the song before 3 P.M., when housewifes might be listening.

According to Charles Cross, the band's highest point came in 1964, in an emptied joint called the Red Carpet Teen Nightclub in Tacoma. They had just finished a late gig and had to go into the studio that morning to record a new B-side for "The Witch." It took them all of fifteen minutes to come up with "Psycho."

Twenty-nine years later, in his living room, it was hard for Charles to contain his excitement as he put on a CD, a Sonics retrospective called "Full Force," for his visitor.

"Here's 'Psycho'—their greatest song," he said, emerging from his CD-lined coat closet. Simultaneously with that pronouncment, lead singer Gerry Rosalie was belting out an incredible "Whaaaaaaaaaaaa!!," like the band had switched on its electric guitars while standing in a giant puddle.

"Oh, baby!" Rosalie sang. "You drive me crazy!" The band behind him was playing a riff that made "Louie, Louie" sound like the latest Antonio Carlos Jobim record.

"This is 1964!" Charles said. "Those chords—people are playing them right now."

The Sonics are the critical link—the glue that unites the lost Seattle of *Cinderella Liberty*, and Boeing assembly-line workers with the new Seattle of Kurt Cobain, flannel shirts, and art-school dropouts. Said Charles Cross: "I've always argued that the grunge sound today is the Second Wave," although he's quick to add that he's not sure how well Nirvana or Pearl Jam knows the Sonics songbook. Instead, the Sonics were a major influence on a generation of Seattle bands in the early 1980s— like Green River and the Young Fresh Fellows, groups that made some noise on college radio but never had the national success of their descendents. Like the Sonics before them, these groups grew up in that mountain-ringed, culturally isolated Seattle that allowed musicians to develop their own sound with a minimum of outside interference—the same Seattle that nurtured Kurt Cobain.

There are some similarities between the Seattle of the Sonics and the Seattle of the Screaming Trees. The most interesting, to me, is the continued popularity of the 45. Go to any of a half-dozen small independent record stores on Capitol Hill or near the University of Washington campus, and you'll find a bin of brand-new 45s, many recorded by Puget Sound bands. This is hardly the Second Coming of Jukebox America, however, for the rules have changed dramatically. These new Seattle 45s—many have those dreaded small holes—are a means to an end; a way for a few hundred local intelligentsia to buy their vinyl release and then talk it up at trendy bars like the Mecca Cafe, creating a "buzz" that will allow the group to come to the attention of the likes of David Geffen. In the Sonics' day, their 45s like "The Witch" backed by "Psycho" were the end product, the raison d'être for being a rock 'n' roller. Ultimately, if their single release was an AM-radio hit in several large and diverse cities across America—Pittsburgh, San Jose, Cleveland, and Orlando—it was because their 45 caught the ear of station program directors who had the nerve back then to select songs with their own ears, not from a consultant in L.A. or MTV.

In the Seattle of 1993, I was able to find just one jukebox that had "The Witch"—or any Sonics song at all—and it needed some special attention from Harold Hagen, for like many of the shrines of Jukebox America it was on the fritz. It was another classic antique—a Rock-Ola Rocket model, from about 1950, with three plays for twenty-five cents and green Coca-Cola style glass in its shell—and Charles Cross had purchased it several years ago for the front of *The Rocket* Magazine office, near downtown in the ultra-hip section called Denny Regrade. Just like Charles Cross's home jukebox, the selections were on target, including the Wailers' version of "Louie, Louie," newer local heroes like the bluesman Robert Cray, even "Merry Christmas Baby" by Bruce Springsteen.

"It hasn't worked since the office Christmas party," Charles said. He turned on a switch on the side, and the pale green neon of the base flickered dimly. "It takes a while to warm up." I stared at the soft green light and realized that my chances of hearing the Sonics on a 45 in Seattle were fading too.

In Charles's office, behind his desk, is a framed letter from Gerry Rosalie, the lead singer of the Sonics, written after he read the 1985 article on the band. Near the end, he wrote: "Currently I am working on writing new music."

"Did he ever?" I asked.

"No."

Still, after my first five hours or so in Seattle I was beginning to think that the only way to find a great jukebox here was to knock on the doors of cool people and check out the Rock-Ola, the Seeburg, or the $11,995 Wurlitzer Bubbler in their living room. On the way from Charles Cross's house to his downtown office, we stopped at moosehead-and-dartboard-ish corner bars with names like Latona Tavern and La Boheme and even a diner called the Twin Teepees, finding in every case no more music than in a mausoleum.

When I dropped Charles back at his house, he drew me a map to a restaurant called Frangior's that served Cajun food and which, in his opinion, had Seattle's best working commercial jukebox. It was located almost across the street from the Kingdome, where the Mariners were playing the Detroit Tigers that night.

I found a parking place and walked up to the entrance of

the storefront restaurant. It was 8:30 P.M. on a Saturday night, and I was ready for a heaping plate of jambalaya. Frangior's was a funky joint with bright orange walls, a picture of Malcolm X, Dixie and Mardi Gras beer cans, and a lunch counter with pecan pie piled high. From the outside I could easily see the jukebox—a pale blue Wurlitzer Americana, that affordable working-class jukebox I had seen in earlier Jukebox City. It was chock-full of classic R & B and jazz—Fats Waller, Bobby "Blue" Bland, "Rock Me Baby" by B. B. King, and Billy Eckstine. A handwritten sign said: THE NEEDLE FOR THIS JUKEBOX IS A TEMPORARY ONE AND CAUSES THE REC-ORD TO SKIP—PLAY SONGS AT YOUR OWN RISK.

This great American jukebox was just three feet away from me, separated only by the glass of the front door—and a sign that said, Closed.

I pounded on the glass for two or three minutes while a couple of staffers who were cleaning up tried to wave me off, pointing to the sign in the door and then assuming that I was crazy, or illiterate, or both. Finally a woman, a young Asian, came to the door.

"This other sign says that you're open until nine o'clock on Saturday," I said.

"We ran out of food."

It was time, once again, to regroup. Frangior's had a great jukebox, but—except for "Foxy Lady" by unlikely Seattle native Jimi Hendrix—it really belonged somewhere like the side of those railroad tracks in Greenville, Mississippi—not two blocks from the Puget Sound. These jukeboxes—Frangior's and the Luna Park Cafe's and a sterile engineering grad-student hangout in the University District called the Big Time Brewery and Ale-house that on a pure song-selection basis (Bob Wills and the Texas Playboys, "Good Girls Don't" by the Knack, the Ohio Players, Creedence, even an obscure indie band from Hoboken called the Cucumbers) had maybe the best working jukebox in Seattle—seemed to simply fall from the sky. They told me less about Seattle than a *Here Come the Brides* rerun.

I had been traveling and jukebox-spotting for about twenty

hours now with no shower, and I think my hair was starting to look like Kurt Cobain's. It was time to go grunge.

About 10:30 P.M., I arrived at the Crocodile Cafe, which no less an authority on Generation X culture than *Details* magazine called the top alternative music spot in Seattle. A nearly block-long entertainment mall for twenty-somethings that opened in 1991, it was fronted by a brightly lit restaurant festooned in beads and plastic crocodiles where Saturday-night dates were swilling microbrew and sky-high mounds of french fries. I wandered past an array of backward baseball caps to the high-ceiling cocktail lounge, where knowledgeable sources—more than one—assured me I would find the world's best grunge jukebox.

It turned out there was a hole in their knowledge. The music—which was hard to hear over the chatter of the packed throng—appeared to be coming from what surely looked like a CD player behind the bar, and when I asked about the famed jukebox, the bartender gave me a dirty look. There was no jukebox.

But here I was, in the grungiest spot in the world, so I decided to pay $6 to see the live entertainment, which for that night included bands such as the Cherry Poppin' Daddies, Groovezilla, Bob's Your Uncle, and Trip Reality. I was ushered into a large open room, mostly dark except for some Day-Glo playing-card symbols and other bizarre psychedelia on the back wall. I went to the back and leaned against the wall. Just in front of me, a twentyish young dude in a flannel shirt, a sweater wrapped around his waist, knee-length denim shorts and black shoes—I couldn't tell if he was really on the cutting edge of fashion or just a geek whose time had come—was rotating to the music. Next to him, a guy in jeans and a white shirt was fumbling to add on an extra layer of flannel.

Meanwhile, it was about ninety-seven degrees inside the club, and all this flannel was making me sweat.

I looked to the stage, where a big goofy guy in a baseball-cap beanie—he might have been a twenty-something play on

Harold Hagen if I didn't know better—was kneeling on the edge of the stage and singing, while another guy in striped Bermuda shorts with a goatee was prancing around shouting "Go, go, go, go." Then I realized the beanie man was not really singing but rapping, that the music was not really grunge but a strange cross between psychedelic and rap—the Spin Doctors meet Dr. Dre.

The acid guitars and the "Go-go-go-go" guy came to a stop. "This next one's called 'Generation X,'" the beanie man proclaimed, and launched into another rap. I looked around the room again. The women looked perfectly normal, like young club-hoppers you might find on Philadelphia's Delaware Avenue or Chicago's North Halsted on a Saturday night. The men looked like the cast of *Revenge of the Nerds IV*.

On the way out, I asked the doorman the name of the band.

"Silly Rabbit."

By 11:30, I was in my hotel bed.

At about 6:15 A.M., I popped back up again, sleepless in Seattle. I called home, three hours ahead.

"You'll never guess what Julia did today!" Kathy said.

I tried to guess, anyway. She was only seven months old, so I ruled out walking, talking, and borrowing the car keys. "Hmmmm," I said. "She rolled over from her back to her tummy."

"Yes! You should have seen her. She was so cute." Kathy was in high spirits, but I felt like a heel, like Harry Chapin in "Cat's in the Cradle"—though one assumes that the narrator of that song is at least engaged in a respectable business venture.

I, on the other hand, was back on the grunge trail later that day. The first of my major stops was to be a bar/diner called the Mecca Cafe, but before that I stopped next door at a highly touted independent record store called Park Avenue Records. The owner is a jukebox collector who keeps a classic twenty-record Rock-Ola from the 1950s in his store, stocked with solid gold like "Move It on Over" by Hank Williams and "Lucille" by Little Richard. It was mute, of course, and the CD player was instead blasting some song that cried "Baby's on a mission" over and over. Still, about 80 percent of the store's space was given over to vinyl records—there was even a heading for the Sonics, sold out, of course. Then there were three boxes of independent-label 45s. Many of these were Seattle bands—there was "Sleepy-house" by Veronica Lake on Cher Doll Records (with a small hole), "Stuck on You/Hollywood" by Gorilla, "Just What It's Like, Uhhh," by the Deflowers, and "I Don't Want to Live" by the Derelicts.

Flipping through the box was a guy, about twenty-five, with a wispy red goatee, torn shorts, black shoes with white socks, and green surgical garb. He was also wearing a backpack, with a bicycle crash helmet strapped tightly on his head. He wouldn't tell me his name, but he was buying a 45 of "These Monsters Are for Real" by Heavens to Betsy.

"I heard about it from friends," he said. The young man didn't have much interesting to say, but I scribbled down the name of the record. He walked away, only to return about sixty seconds later with a troubled expression.

"You're not going to use the people's name?" he asked, referring to the band.

I told him I might. After all, releasing a record is not usually the best way to keep a low profile.

"I'm not sure if they'd like that," he said.

The surge of publicity that came with Nirvana's popularity in 1992 had made young Seattle a little tense, a little suspicious of outsiders, maybe even paranoid in some cases. The world had discovered them—the *New York Times* even ran a big feature on grunge in its new "Sunday Style" section. In fact, anyone who was remotely cool in Seattle didn't even call the music "grunge" anymore—a fact I tried to respect by calling it "formerly-called-grunge music."

I soon ran into more distrust, a few minutes later, next door at the Mecca Cafe, a hot spot that became even more hot to some and less hot to others because Madonna had stopped there a few months earlier. Most of the square-footage is a diner that looks little upgraded from when it opened in 1930, while the bar is a tiny wood-paneled space to the side only slightly larger than Charles Cross's coat-turned-CD closet. On the wall behind the bar were hundreds, if not thousands, of tiny square drink coasters, each with a drawing from the customers. One was a crude drawing of a fish that said "Drink Drink Drink Drink I Wanna Drink Drink Drink Drink Drink Drink"; another said "Mecca Death," and the best was entitled "Madonna Cow," a bovine creature with a large conical bra covering her udders.

I sat down at the bar next to a man with long and thick dark hair, two silver earrings in his left ear, and a long leather jacket—he looked like grunge royalty. I learned that he was the guitar player in a local band, and then I saw him getting up to leave, squeezing past my stool in the cramped barroom.

"Excuse me, I'm searching for the best jukebox in America," I proclaimed, as if I were asking him the correct time. "What do you think of the jukebox here at the Mecca Cafe?"

He threw me a look: Another geeky writer from the East Coast, seeking to discover the secret of grunge. "This is the second best jukebox in Seattle," he proclaimed in a postgame interview tone. "The best jukebox is the Frontier Room. I gotta run."

So what was the second-best "formerly-called-grunge" jukebox in Seattle like? Pretty good, for a generation that was mostly born after *Here Come the Brides* premiered in 1968 and that remembers vinyl records the way that we remember Watergate. It was a Rowe/AMI CD box—a make that by 1993 had a virtual monopoly on the bar jukebox business in postmodern Seattle, for CDs and music were synonymous to Generation X—with choices like "Raw Power" by Iggy and the Stooges, the best of Clarence Carter, standards like big-band, Patsy, Frank, REM's greatest hits—and a healthy smattering of local staples like Nirvana, Pearl Jam, and the *Singles* soundtrack.

I wandered next door into the diner and met the owner, a ruggedly good looking man in his fifties with a salt-and-pepper beard and brawny sailor's arms, who looked more like a character from *Cinderella Liberty* than from *Singles*. His wife of the last three years, a fortyish blonde with big hoop earrings, was sitting on a diner stool. He told me the history of the Mecca Cafe, how his father opened it in 1930, the depths of both the Depression and Prohibition, and how after the 1934 Repeal his old man had prospered by selling beer for a nickel when everyone else charged a dime. The father moved seventy-five kegs a day.

But times changed. About three years ago, when the owner remarried, the Mecca Cafe had one of the most unprofitable bars in Seattle. There was a jukebox that played 45s, but the older bartender didn't like the music—he kept the TV tuned to soap operas and tended bar for two or three regulars. He'd even unplug the jukebox if no one was looking. Then the younger bride came along with some ideas for boosting business—one of which was simply to force the old man to keep the jukebox on constantly.

"He couldn't take the change," the owner said. The old man retired, and the Mecca Cafe recruited some young, plugged-in bartenders who reprogrammed the jukebox and told all their twenty-something friends about the new hangout. And that was all there was to it: *Barfly* to *Singles* in three easy steps. The owner of the Mecca Cafe was the polar opposite of Charles Cross, unsentimental about the lost Seattle—because the lost Seattle just wasn't profitable. He had a similar attitude about replacing the 45 RPM jukebox with the CD model about a year ago. "It was a piece of junk—it would always break down at eleven o'clock at night," he said. "There was no dollar-bill changer. This new machine is functional. It even broadcasts when the music shuts down."

The owner kept talking and talking, describing in great detail his problems with the restaurant workers' union in Seattle and how the union boss, a reputed organized-crime figure, was found murdered during the labor unrest—the owner, who told me he didn't do it, was even mentioned in the newspaper as a possible suspect. He then invited me to return that night for a special soul food menu. He explained that a member of his non-union kitchen staff, an African American woman, had volunteered to cook southern-style once a week, and was working hard.

"It gives you a whole different attitude towards black people," he said.

Time to leave for the Frontier Room.

The Frontier Room was perched on the cutting edge of the Seattle scene, so nouveau that my slightly-behind-the-times contacts hadn't even known to mention it before I came to town. It was located on 1st Avenue North, just north of downtown in Denny Regrade. A steady drizzle was blowing in from the Puget Sound when I arrived just after 8 P.M. At first I thought I must have wandered through the wrong door: just a decrepit lunch counter with a couple of old-timers sipping coffee and smoking Marlboros. But I kept walking through a series of dark passageways, past cases of beer and the hot water heater, until I stumbled into a dark, smoky cubbyhole with no windows and little oxygen—Seattle's coolest bar.

There were about twenty people in the bar. Looking out at several tables, I saw the fronts of baseball caps and the backs of flannel shirts staring back at me—a typical Seattle scene. The jukebox—that omnipresent Rowe/AMI CD machine—was over in the back. A thirtyish African American guy in a San Diego Padres baseball cap was taking his time on the selections before he found the only two contemporary R & B selections, Silk and Mary J. Blige. Then I flipped through the selections, another eclectic mix: Reba McIntyre and Billie Holiday, the Sex Pistols and the soundtrack to *Twin Peaks: Walk Fire with Me*, Sinatra and *Disco Years: Lost in Music, Volume IV*. I put in a dollar, played some selections that included "Diggin' Up Bones" by Randy Travis, partly because I missed Kathy and that was a song that we'd fell in love with on our honeymoon somewhere between Taos and Santa Fe—and partly just to gauge the reaction.

I pulled the last remaining bar stool in the corner. Throughout my jukebox travels, I had found it relatively easy to overcome my natural shyness with strangers, but in these grunge clubs it seemed harder for some reason. So I watched as a parade of young people—they said they were twenty-something, but each one looked to be ten-something—came up to the bar. Every single one was blond—some strawberry, some streaked, like those innocent children I had seen frolicking in the Luna Park Cafe, all grown and ready for action—and they presented various forms of identification, none of them a Washington State driver's license, to the bartender, a stout, tough-looking middle-aged woman.

The first young girl ordered a Cape Cod. Then a young long-haired dude in a windbreaker and shorts presented an ID that looked like it was printed up in Times Square.

"Where is this from?"

"Utah."

"Utah—I can't take it."

The long-haired guy became boorish and confrontational. "I have to do what I'm told to do," said the bartender. But then she served the next young woman, whose ID was from Michigan. The next one presented an ID that was folded, stapled, and mutilated.

"I'll have a gin and tonic, and one for my friend in the back room."

"Does he have an ID?"

"Yes, he does."

"Okay."

I felt very out of place, more at a loss than that night that Kathy and I had watched Nirvana on *Saturday Night Live*. The Frontier Room smelled like Teen Spirit. There was, however, one guy sitting across the bar who looked to be the same age as me—he had an oval, clean-shaven face, wire-rimmed glasses, and was wearing a baseball cap for a ship called the USS *Saratoga*, wearing it forwards. But he was engaged in an animated conversation with two women, one on either side of him, and just before I was about to walk over to start a conversation he started demonstrating a pair of handcuffs. A few minutes later I went over anyway.

"You look like someone I went to college with," I said. He did, in fact, resemble someone I vaguely remembered from fifteen years ago, but mainly I couldn't think of anything else.

The man's name was Kelly Graber, and he had attended Washington State, about 2,800 miles away from me. He later was ordained by an outfit called the Universal Life Church, and got a job in Seattle with the *Saratoga*, the last wood-hulled commercial passenger ship in America, where he was both crew member and chaplain, performing an occasional wedding on the deck.

"We come here because we're friends with the regular bartender. This is her," he said, gesturing to the woman with long black curly hair who was seated on his right. (It was her night off.) It was a strange friendship, the handcuff-wielding ship chaplain and this bartender, whose patter over the next half-hour or so was partly about gross body secretions and partly about her nontraditional sex life. The woman on Kelly's left was his girlfriend, a woman with brown curly hair and a soft gray sweater who headed a drug program at an area hospital and seemed far too sweet for a windowless bar on a Sunday night.

It was a strange half-hour. I kept trying to steer the conversation toward my interests, Seattle and jukeboxes, with minimal success—although the middle-aged working bartender overheard me and tossed in her own opinion when I mentioned Randy Travis.

"Ooh, I'm going to marry him someday," she said. About two minutes later, "Diggin' Up Bones" finally came up. The bartender said, "Uggh, who played that?"

"I thought you were going to marry Randy Travis?"

"Well, whoever picked that one picked a shitty one."

Meanwhile, the off-duty bartender kept talking about human discharges. My plane to Philadelphia was leaving at 6 A.M. the next morning, just nine hours away, and I thought my jukebox travels were winding down to an anticlimax—when finally I got Kelly to focus on the jukebox question. "Here's what you should do," he said. "Go to 24th Street in a neighborhood called Ballard, to a place called Tor's. It's a fisherman's bar. Some of these fishermen are loaded. The guy sitting next to you could look like a regular slob but he's worth a million dollars."

"Tor's?" I asked. "How is that spelled?"

"T-H-O-R-S."

"Oh. Thor's."

"No. Tor's. T-H-O-R-S."

The terrain he suggested—the Ballard neighborhood, about fifteen minutes north of downtown—was not unfamiliar. Earlier that Sunday, slightly bummed out about the sterility of the Luna Park Cafe where I had just eaten those $4.95 eggs, I went in search of a greasy spoon that was near the bottom of a tip sheet Charles Cross had written out for me. The place was called Hattie's Hat, and when I finally found it after eleven wrong turns I was sure this was a big mistake—the outdoor sign looked like a poster for a bad Lulu movie from the 1960s, in dated shades of red and gold, depicting a woman's hat with a daisy sticking up.

Nevertheless, I wandered inside and for about twenty minutes was enraptured by its quirky charm, signaled by a massive mural behind the lunch counter that tried—somewhat unsuccessfully—to depict the history of the Pacific Northwest, with crudely drawn settlers plopped down in a glacierlike setting. Behind the lunch counter an older woman who looked like she had been working there since Repeal was transfixed by the Indianapolis 500 on TV, slowly flipping a stack of hash browns every minute or two without moving her eyes from the set.

Even an uninspired chat with the man at the counter next to me, a trash collector who was a native of Alberta, Canada, didn't stop me from patting myself on the back for finding an offbeat outpost of Jukebox America. But then things weren't quite right, starting with the jukebox, a modern Rowe/AMI part-45, part-CD job that was a little too heavy on Michael Bolton, Vanessa Williams, and the Judds. Behind a partition there was a bar—Aunt Harriet's Room—with dimly lit photos of Rodin's *The Kiss* at each end of the bar and a rude bartender who wouldn't let me photograph the mural. The bar was filling up with the kind of people who go to a dark barroom at 11 A.M. on the Sunday of Memorial Day weekend. A weather-beaten man in a red Boeing cap sat down next to me—my heart rose, a true Seattlean!—and ordered a Bloody Mary.

"I don't usually do this on a Sunday morning," he told me. "I'm here because of my best friend. He just found out the other day that he has cancer."

I was touched for about three minutes, until the conversation degenerated to his ideas about Boeing's plan to lay off 20,000 people—it didn't bother him—and various women he knew or had known, none of whom seemed to be his wife. I had to leave for about fifteen minutes to buy film, and when I returned he was drinking clear booze and trading sexual boasts with a slovenly architect friend. Bored, I looked down the bar and saw a passed-out woman's feet protruding from the last booth.

Still, during my fifteen-minute interlude I had driven around the neighborhood and fallen in love with Ballard, the quintessential American fishing town, with streets lined with gray and beige warehouses like North Coast Seafood Processors or Ballard Inflatable Boats, where the storefronts advertise Fresh Copper River Salmon, or Johnsen's Scandinavian Ford or Swedish pancakes with Real Ligonberries, $3.95, where side streets give way to sunglared vistas of trawlers, red cranes, and ice blue waters. I wasn't sure this was the "lost Seattle" that Charles Cross had spoken so eloquently about the day before, but it seemed as close as I would find in 1993.

It seemed real.

Now, eight hours and thirty minutes before I blasted off from Seattle, I was driving toward the Ballard Bridge, looking for an archeological layer of Jukebox America that hadn't been buried under flannel shirts and heavy boots, looking for salvation from a ship chaplain, the Right Rev. Kelly Graber. I turned onto 24th, a deserted shopping street except for clusters of cars every few blocks, in front of fishermen's bars. Then I saw a window filled with neon beer signs. The facade said TOR'S.

It took a second for my eyes to adjust to the bright lights—a sure sign of untrendiness, hundreds of watts brighter than the Frontier Room. It was a big square room, with 75 percent of the space allocated for a pool table and darts. I would love to report that the jukebox blasted out "The Witch" when I entered the room, but the reality was "Creque Alley," by the Mamas and the Papas, a song from 1967, the particular time warp that Tor's seemed locked into.

But things change. The jukebox at Tor's, like a lot of neighborhood taverns across America, was now that dreaded Rowe/AMI CD player. While I half-expected some guy named Tor in a Viking hat behind the bar, it turned out that the owner/bartender was a woman named Anna Christianson, blond, attractive and strong-looking, a woman who had worked for a fish processor for a couple of years before deciding just three months before my visit that she'd rather work sixty-five hours a week on her feet.

"So the reason I came here is because I heard you have a great jukebox," I said.

"It's getting better," Anna said. "I brought a few CDs from home." I asked her which ones, and this Rear Guard Baby Boomer, Hard Work Division, thought for a second before naming Steely Dan. I wondered what was wrong with the jukebox before she took over, and she cited one CD—the greatest hits of Johnny "Battle of New Orleans" Horton—that's too popular with the old-time fishermen to remove.

"I would have a revolt if I got rid of him," Anna said.

It turned out there had been a Tor—he had owned the joint for about forty years until he retired a few years ago, selling it to the man who sold it to Anna. Normally, about a third of the customers are fishermen, but there were none tonight, because the salmon were running off the coast of Alaska in late May. Instead, there were working-class people—an old-timer dreading his next shift driving a taxi, a young pool-cue-wielding Native American with long straight jet-black hair parted down the middle, a bunch of thirtyish white guys in beards sitting close to pitchers of draft. I talked to several of them—and encountered none of the suspicion and distrust that seemed so prevalent in the grunge bars.

"I'm thinking about changing the name to Babe's," Anna said.

"Why Babe's?"

"That's what we call everyone in here. Everyone's a 'Babe.' "

I ordered a Redhook Ale, brewed in Seattle, and struck up a conversation with the guy next to me, who wore blue jeans and a rugby shirt, had a long pointy beard, and was named Bob. We talked about Ballard—Bob and Anna feared the yuppies were moving in—and the Frontier Room—"everybody there's out to prove something"—and Hattie's Hat—"stay away from there, that's an alcoholic's bar."

A few seconds after my new friend warned me about Hattie's Hat, he drained the last drops of beer from the large pitcher he had been working on, solo, and ordered another. "Are you sure you want that," said Anna, and she rolled her eyes. It was a tough call for an emerging businesswoman—she finally pulled down the tap lever. As she did, "Do It Again" by Steely Dan came on the jukebox.

A few minutes later, I put down the weight of my jukebox notebook and tried to pretend for about forty-five minutes that I was a regular at soon-to-be-formerly-Tor's-possibly-Babe's. I put a dollar in the CD jukebox and played "No Retreat, No Surrender" by Bruce Springsteen, my song for the good people of Ballard. I finished my beer, and picked up a pool cue, taking about fifteen minutes to beat a woman in a floral-print dress and about ninety seconds to lose to the neighborhood pool shark. By then, I had forgotten all about the Frontier Room, backward baseball caps, the Mecca Cafe, "Luna eggs," and Jukebox City— I was no closer to understanding grunge than that dark midnight that Kurt Cobain—soon to be departed—appeared on my TV screen. I hadn't heard the Sonics on a working jukebox, either, but I saw their simplistic garage-band work ethic alive in Ballard. In a fit of madness, I declared the jukebox at Tor's—with its CDs of Steely Dan, Pure Prairie League, and Johnny Horton—the best jukebox in Seattle.

My hotel wakeup call was less than five hours away. I had

a date with a beautiful, blue-eyed blond babe—a babe named Julia. But before I fell asleep, I kept thinking about ligonberries, Boeing aircraft, the opening scream from the Sonics' "Psycho," *Cinderella Liberty*, merchant marines, and the theme song from *Here Come the Brides*—about Charles Cross and his lost Seattle, a beautiful child, growing up free and wild.

Chapter 11

....

Nowhere to Run

"So, where is the best jukebox in America?" This was the lowest moment in all my jukebox travels. I was sitting in a place called Traffic Jam & Snug, which was supposed to be one of the hippest restaurants in Detroit. It was a large brick fortress that looked like a nursing home from the outside. In the back room of this Michigan institution—it has its own dairy and brew pub on the premises—there were stained-glass windows and wagon wheels and hanging buckets, reminding me of the Houlihan's back near Lower Makefield, with a little less funk. The food was good, but the menu was laced with items like ratatouille and lentil burgers—in other words, the restaurant screamed 1970s, the decade of "Disco Duck," Fleetwood Mac, and the beginning of the death of the jukebox in America. Now my dinner companions—my New York friend Adam, back on the jukebox trail, two Detroit journalists, and a grad student in feminist studies—had asked me a question I wanted to avoid.

"Well, there was this one in this juke joint in the middle of nowhere in Mississippi that was really incredible—except that it didn't work," I said. I looked at my audience of four, slightly interested but more puzzled. I prattled on about my best experiences— about Little Blue's, about Patsy Cline's barroom-brawling pals, about partying in Mamou, Louisiana, at 10 A.M. on a Saturday, and about an Italian presenting Maxwell Street blues on the Latino side of Chicago. But it was a tale long on character and short on denouement, and it was still missing the Juke of the Covenant.

And Detroit was my final jukebox journey, which was probably for the best. For one thing, Kathy's incredible display of patience was wearing thin: about the time our flight took off from Newark she came down with a sinus infection, Julia got cranky, and laundry and baby bottles began piling up, all while I was off to go bar-hopping 800 miles away. Money was tight, and each jukebox jaunt was more costly than the one before. Yet for every place in Jukebox America that I didn't visit, I imagined an unlimited frontier of music machines, a panoramic west-Texas desert with jumping mariachi joints behind every cactus. The neon highway-motel Vacancy sign in my soul had been tinkered with, but it was still buzzing.

Except now it was like 4:30 A.M., and just a couple of rigs were left on that lonely road.

Little did I know that my Friday night meal at Traffic Jam & Snug—it seemed to last for forty days—was merely a temptation by the Spirit in the Sky to test whether I had the resolve to press forward. I did, but the next twenty-four hours were less reminiscent of the Bible than straight out of Dickens—call it "A Jukebox Carol"—as I was visited by the ghosts of Jukeboxes Past, Present, and Future and then come to see where everything came together, where a gin-joint-reformed Scrooge was trying to save the Tiny Tim of a city called Detroit.

The Motor City would surpass my greatest expectations.

And my expectations had been running high, for Detroit was where Jukebox America once had its finest hour. In 1959, a Ford assembly-line worker, failed professional boxer, and somewhat successful songwriter named Berry Gordy Jr. started his own record label in a small house on West Grand Boulevard in Detroit. Along with thousands of other African Americans, his father—Berry Gordy Sr., or "Pops"—had moved north to Detroit in the Great Migration and opened an establishment named the Booker T. Washington Grocery Store. Music historians say Berry Gordy Jr., one of eight children, quit high school to get rich boxing like his idol, Detroit's own Joe Louis, but he found it hard to make much money as a featherweight. And a life on the assembly line had little appeal. Berry Gordy Jr. was upwardly mobile in an America where such dreams still seemed within grasp, and with his venture, which eventually became Motown Records, he took on the pop music world with the can-do spirit of a Henry Ford.

"At his job in the Ford plant," African American studies professor Gerald Early wrote in the *New Republic* in 1991, "as Nelson George and others have pointed out, he was made aware of how production can be efficiently organized and automated for the highest quality. At Motown in the '60s, producers could write songs and songwriters could produce, but artists, both singers and session musicians, were not permitted to do either; and with this type of control Motown could put out a highly consistent product."

The result was history—an uninterrupted decade-long run of the greatest jukebox 45s ever. It started in 1960 with Barrett Strong's "Money (That's What I Want)," peaked from 1964 to 1966—the heyday of the Supremes, the Temptations, and the Four Tops, among others—and died about the time the Jackson 5's "I'll Be There" faded out, near the end of 1970. Almost all the Motown stars grew up right there in the shadow of Detroit's smokestacks (the Jackson 5, of course, came from that other industrial outpost of Jukebox America, Gary, Indiana), grasping for that next rung on the ladder, from sweaty southern fields to steamy auto plants to show business.

Unlike other great forms of American music—jazz, the blues, country—the music of Motown has been imitated by more recent groups like Simply Red or Boyz II Men, but never quite replicated. Some of Motown's strength was the talent that Gordy assembled on West Grand Boulevard—the songwriting team of Holland-Dozier-Holland or bassist James Jamerson, for example—but much of the secret lay in the concept, a vision that unfortunately seemed possible only in the optimistic Great Society days of the 1960s.

In the 1950s, African Americans weren't shut out of the pop-music charts, but many of their best songs were appropriated and made into even bigger hits by whites from Pat Boone ("Ain't That a Shame") to Elvis Presley ("Hound Dog"). In the 1970s, blacks took funk to their side of the FM dial, whites took heavy metal to theirs, and the rift has never healed. But in the 1960s, Motown billed itself The Sound of Young America, and that meant all young Americans, from the prep schools of New England to the projects of West Detroit. Seamlessly fusing the grit of rhythm 'n' blues with the sheen of white pop, Berry Gordy created equal-opportunity records that reflected Detroit, where blacks were paid the same high wages as whites on the assembly line.

The reign of Motown was the era of the color-blind jukebox.

But Gordy's American Dream was just that—a dream—for too many people in Detroit. Denied the rising expectations of the booming Vietnam War–era economy, blacks in Detroit erupted in a riot in July 1967 after police raided an illegal drinking club. When the fires—there were more than 1,600—finally burned out, forty-four people were dead. It was the worst American riot of modern times before the Los Angeles uprising of 1992. Middle-class whites moved out in droves—the city's population today is less than one-half what it was in 1950. Motown's records took on a harder edge, from the Supremes' "Love Child" to Edwin Starr's "War." Then, in 1972, Berry Gordy Jr. did the unthinkable. He left Detroit for Hollywood, saying he wanted to produce movies. Just like Gordy, Detroit's car makers were also drunk with success, producing antiquated gas-guzzlers and failing to shift gears when the Arab oil embargo struck in 1973. Thousands of jobs were lost, and today only two auto plants are left in Detroit. For many of the one million souls still left in the city there is little hope, either of a recording contract or modest factory job. The week I arrived, the whole city was on edge because two white police officers who had beaten to death an unarmed man named Malice Green were about to stand trial. In 1993, the hottest debate in the city was a suggestion to close down dozens of inner-city blocks that were more than 70 percent vacant—and fence them in.

Meanwhile, a colleague of mine, *New York Newsday* columnist Dennis Duggan, told the story of a man who recently ran into Berry Gordy Jr. at a lavish party in La-La Land, lounging by a swimming pool.

"How's Detroit?" the man asked.

"Detroit?" said Berry Gordy Jr. "Where's that?"

As Adam and I drove into the city from Detroit Metro Airport on the flat landscape of I-94, there is still a facade of normality. There is a Goodyear tote board that brags about American car production (year-to-date in June 1993 was 520,486); a few seconds later appeared a massive Uniroyal tire, at least fifty feet wide. We even saw wispy smoke coming from one of the stacks at the Ford Motor plant in Dearborn.

Then there was a sign for the city limits of Detroit, and we exited onto West Grand Boulevard. It was a wide street lined with the sturdy brick prairie-style homes one sees throughout the Midwest, but many of them were boarded up, and some were burnt out. That is a common sight in Detroit, as was the Gothic Roman Catholic church building inscribed as "St. Matthew's Church" but bearing a wooden sign in front for the Enon Tabernacle Missionary Baptist Church (Where Everyone Is Someone and Christ Is All; Rev C. L. Moore, Founder and Pastor). Then came the boarded-up and graffiti-covered Rio Grande Motel, and across from that the James H. Cole Home for Funerals, with a garish rendering of a cross and hands clasped over a Bible. Next to the home for funerals, embalmed since the year 1972, is 2648 West Grand Boulevard, "Hitsville USA"—the former Motown headquarters, now the Motown Museum.

What is striking about the Motown building is its simplicity: it is just a squat, square urban house (Gordy paid $800 for it in 1959), painted in now-fading shades of white and royal blue, with a large "Hitsville, U.S.A." still scrawled in a dated blue script above a first-story picture window. I had seen the Motown Museum once before, in 1989, not long after it had opened—a good thing, for on this day the museum was closed for major renovations. I remember at that time I was unimpressed by the exhibits—knickknacks like album covers for *The Supremes A Go-Go* and a Michael Jackson flower-power costume from 1974—but awed by the centerpiece of the museum, Studio A. There you can stand at the engineer's control panel, which looks like the cockpit of a Boeing 727, and look out at the modest hardwood-floored room where "I Can't Help Myself," "Baby Love," "Tears of a Clown," and every other great Motown song was recorded.

When Adam and I walked in on a Friday afternoon, the only music was the pounding of work crews—wires were hanging from the ceiling, and fresh coats of blue paint the color of a Motown 45 label covered the walls. The new curator, Dr. Rowena Stewart, a former curator of the African-American Museum in Philadelphia who had just arrived in town, took us to her office in the house next door.

A historian rather than a music expert, Stewart was beginning to examine Motown with the slow diligence of an archaeological dig. She argued that Gordy managed to take all the major components of African American music—gospel, blues, and jazz—and combine them into something that didn't quite sound like any of them. "He wanted it to be American music," she said. "He wanted everybody to have ownership of this music. It's so funny—people come in and say, 'Gee, that was my song.'"

It was clear from visiting the museum and talking to the staff that Berry Gordy Jr., was a man well in step with his times, somehow uniting the seemingly diverse threads of the Baby Boom, pop music, and the car culture that created the sleek, youthful 1965 Mustang. In Studio A, Gordy installed a device that played back the master tapes of recording sessions through a tinny, mono speaker, to see if a song had the right sound for AM Top 40 car radio. And Gordy also supported the Movement of his times, civil rights. His was the first record label to issue a speech by Dr. Martin Luther King on LP—quite appropriate, for Motown was the music of integration, not the aggressive black nationalistic music that would come in the 1970s. In 1963, Martha and the Vandellas sang: "Summer's here, and the time is right for dancin' in the streets." By 1969, black-wannabees the Rolling Stones sang: "Summer's here, and the time is right for fightin' in the streets." In 1972, Gordy left town.

"He was smart—he knew when to leave," said Stewart, who draws her paycheck from the Gordy fortune.

It was time for us to leave, too. That small faded white building next to the home for funerals, the Motown Museum, is the only trace left of the greatest music ever made in America. There is no equivalent of Chicago's blues bars or Mississippi's juke joints—no "Motown club" with an all-Motown jukebox, where the Four Tops or Martha Reeves appears every Friday. While blues and jazz are rooted in the red American soil, like a stand of Delta cotton, Motown music was as light and puffy as the smokestack emissions from the Ford assembly line, destined to disperse into a million irretrievable molecules.

While Berry Gordy left Detroit, a retired bus driver named James Jenkins stayed behind.

The early part of James Jenkins's story is similar to many Detroit residents. He was born in the South—South Carolina—and had a decent standard of living (his family owned the first Victrola in the neighborhood) before his father died in 1928. His family moved to Asheville, North Carolina, but the Great Depression hit; on June 3, 1936, Jenkins arrived on a Michigan Central train in Detroit with just $4 in his pocket. His plan was to attend college, but the state had quotas for blacks, so he ended up on the Ford assembly line earning $6 a day until there was labor trouble in 1941. For the next thirty-two years, Jenkins drove a city bus and hovered on the fringes of the city's jazz scene, booking small shows.

On May 24, 1974, Jenkins was driving down I-94 to Ann Arbor when an announcer cut into the music and said that Duke Ellington had died.

"I thought, 'Where is the memorabilia, where is the history?' We got all kinds of little Halls of Fame—the sports, the guild, everybody else—but nobody is building a great memorial to these people who gave us so much—we danced our souls out, we bought the records, we bought the sheet music, we paid the admission, you understand . . . The country was built on music."

It was right then and there that this Detroit bus driver decided to take his meager life savings and devote the rest of his life to building a museum—the only one quite like it in the world.

Now James Jenkins is seventy-seven years old. His Graystone International Jazz Museum is located in a modest downtown storefront, formerly a Kay's Drug, at 1521 Broadway, somewhat obscured by the People Mover, a futuristic elevated train that Mayor Coleman Young Jr. built in the 1970s, allowing tourists to travel from the walled compound known as the Renaissance Center to a few heavily policed spots like the Greektown restaurant district without having to walk on a city street. The People Mover doesn't stop at 1521 Broadway, and when Adam and I pulled up on a steel gray Saturday morning, with an icy wind blasting off the Great Lakes, there were no cars, either, and we parked right in front.

Jenkins met us in the doorway—bespectacled, looking about a decade or two younger than his real age, and nattily attired in a white-pressed cotton shirt and matching pants, cream-colored sports coat, red handkerchief, and straw hat. His talking—which was almost nonstop for the next eight hours— was high-pitched, singsong, and fast, like those hard-bop records that supplanted Duke Ellington in the '50s.

"Aren't there any other jazz museums?" I asked. "What about Chicago, or New Orleans?"

"Listen—I went to Chicago and looked for the jazz museum," he said with a laugh. "They got a room there at the University of Chicago on the South Side, and I went there, and I was inquiring, and nobody never heard of it, and nobody knew nothing about it. Finally, somebody told me, 'Oh, yeah, go up to the fourth floor,' and, see somebody, they were goin' to come up there and unlock a room. They got four or five 78s in a bin. And

I can't tell you what I saw—and how much big money they get-tin.' "

His Graystone Museum started small, too, in a section of the Amalgamated Transit Union hall on West Grand Boulevard, just a block from the Motown headquarters. The museum has moved twice to larger quarters, but after nineteen years James Jenkins's collection was still fairly modest. Much of the drug-store-sized exhibit consists of an impressive array of pictures—mostly dozens of portraits of jazz greats that trace the history of jazz from Ma Rainey to Milt Jackson. Interspersed are classic album covers—"One O'clock Jump" by Count Basie on 78—and the occasional instrument, like J. C. Heard's drum set. The highlight is a collection of artifacts—the microphone stand, a seat, the fountainhead—from the Graystone Ballroom, the historic jazz house that featured black bands in the 1930s and was demolished in 1980 despite pleas from Jenkins and others.

The jukebox located near the entrance was a testament to the difficulty of assembling a world-class museum. The first time Jenkins and I spoke on the telephone had been eleven months earlier, and his voice perked up when I explained that I was looking for jukeboxes.

"You find me a jukebox," he said. "I need a Seeburg from the early '30s. The first time I saw one was in 1928. Fats Waller had just recorded 'Feet's Too Big'—I think it was the late '20s or early '30s."

But the jukebox that James Jenkins ended up with was a chrome-heavy Wurlitzer model that said Hi-fidelity Music and appeared to be from the early-to-mid 1960s. It had last been played around 1974—one could tell from the selections still listed—"Public Enemy No. 1, Part 1" by James Brown, "Jive Turkey, Part 1" by the Ohio Players, and "You're The First, The Last, My Everything" by Barry White.

There was no jazz on the jukebox at the Graystone International Jazz Museum.

That jukebox set the tone for a three-hour tour that Jenkins gave us that afternoon—a tour of sites of historic jazz clubs, like the Graystone Ballroom, that for the most part have been torn down or shuttered tight. These after-hours joints, dance halls, gin joints, and whorehouses live on largely in the mind of James Jenkins, who painted a picture of heavyweight champ Joe Louis or small-time gangsters throwing down $20 bills at the Flame Show Bar, or long-forgotten bands like the McKinney Cotton Pickers (their name chosen by the Graystone's white management) toiling until the wee hours of the morning.

"Here was Sonny Wilson's Forest Club—he owned it. I was a bartender there in '42. Sonny Wilson ran the Joe Louis Chicken Shack. The old Purple Gang—gangsters, the underworld—hung out there. This was where Joe Louis and Wallace Beery were having dinner, and I got their autograph." While James Jenkins kept up his nonstop soliloquy, we were pulled over in the service road of I-375, the Chrysler Expressway. "What this freeway did is tore things up," Jenkins said. He kept talking about boxers, gangsters, booze, and jazz, but every time I looked to where he was gesturing there was merely a tractor-trailer rolling by.

The highlight of Jenkins's tour was a place on the city's near east side called Paradise Valley, an uptown party district that reigned from the 1930s through the 1950s. There had been jazz joints like El Cino, Melody Club, B&C Club, Rhythm Club, the Band Box, Club 666, Russell House, and Henry's Swing Club, with after-hours joints and houses of ill-repute sandwiched in between. Two of the clubs, the Plantation and the Chocolate Bar, were what was known then as "black-and-tan" clubs, where the performers were African Americans but the audience tended to be chic slumming whites, just like at the famed Cotton Club in Harlem. Today, they've paved Paradise Valley and put up a parking lot, a massive one surrounded by a rusty barbed wire fence. On the other side of the street is a hulking brown warehouse for Hudson's, a department store that closed downtown and moved out to suburban malls. The clubs died out slowly, many in the 1950s when the west side of Detroit opened up to African Americans. These facts did not stop Jenkins from launching into another excited, mile-a-minute rap.

"Over on this corner was the Turf Bar—all the swingers and the pimps and everything hung out there. The Turf Bar was the big sports bar, and on this corner here was the B&C, and they changed the name to the El Sino, and the big bands played there, big nightclub, and down here was the Victory Club upstairs." While James Jenkins talked, the stiff Great Lakes wind howled. There wasn't another soul in sight.

There was only one club left in Paradise Valley, a place called the 606 Horseshoe Lounge, and while James Jenkins was pointing every which way a squat, solidly built man in olive-colored jeans, a matching denim windbreaker, and a matching hat emerged. He was Joe Watson, the grandson of a prominent black politician and real-estate broker with an office right there in Paradise Valley. The minute he emerged, James Jenkins started badgering him for old photos of Paradise Valley that could serve as the basis for a mural he wanted to commission.

"That building there," Joe Watson pointed, "was the Turf Club originally."

"No, the Turf Club was over on that corner," Jenkins countered. "That was a restaurant."

"The Turf Club was here."

"No, no! The Turf Club was here."

"No, that was the El Sino. No, not the El Sino—the El Sino was there, then the restaurant, Chinese food shop, barber shop."

"Wait a minute. Wait a minute. Wait a minute. Wait a minute," shouted Jenkins. "The barber shop was over here with the B&C—and on that corner was the Turf Club."

"Well, that was *way* back."

"That's I'm talking about. That was 1935."

"Well, that was four, no three years before I was born."

And so it went for about ten minutes, the two men standing on weedy street corners, gesturing wildly into the stiff wind, sometimes pointing in the same direction and sometimes in different directions, remembering boxers promoting fights from the back of pickup trucks and sidewalks packed with people. Then a third man came out from a doorway down the street and joined the obscure discussion. He said he was a massage therapist, and his name was Pour Lamoor, a bastardization of the French.

Adam, Jenkins, and I walked into the 606 Horseshoe Lounge. I wasn't sure what I expected—maybe a man in a boxing shorts and a couple of pink ladies—but the last bar in Paradise Valley was a fairly normal joint, with a low ceiling and a long bar with lunch counter stools. There was a Seeburg jukebox from the mid-1980s that was stocked with a mix of contemporary black music like Maze and "Freak Me" by Silk, mixed in with old warhorses like Marvin Gaye and Dinah Washington. On one wall was a sign for a "rent party" that night while on another wall was a clipping from a local black newspaper that said "Millions for Greektown, Zero for Paradise Valley," reflecting bitterness over the funneling of community development funds toward the mostly white club area in the 1960s and '70s.

The owner, a short man with glasses and a goatee, grasping a mixed drink, came out to meet us.

"How did you survive when all the other places didn't?" I asked.

He thought for a minute. "By hanging on a thread. As history has it, we developed a clientele a long time ago, and as they diminished, so does the business."

Then we walked back into the stiff wind and the parking lot void of Paradise lost. Later that day, we said goodbye to James Jenkins, the Ghost of Jukeboxes Past.

The Motown Museum and James Jenkins gave me a firm historical footing to search for the jukeboxes that still remain in Detroit—and there are hundreds of them. But many of the best jukeboxes are not located in the city proper but in an entirely different place, an area called Metro. Metro is like modern Rome to downtown's crumbling Forum, the twentieth-century city that sprouted around the ruins, a monument to Henry Ford, with a couple million residents—mostly white—shuttling by car from home to office park to the mall, none of which, or course, are too close to Detroit. Many Metro residents have no more connection to Detroit than they do to Cleveland or Birmingham, except through athletic teams like the Pistons, who perform in shopping-mall safety twenty-five miles from Detroit's ground zero.

It was in Royal Oak, the so-called Greenwich Village of Metro, twelve miles out, that Adam and I arrived at 1:45 A.M. on a Saturday morning at a place called Gusoline Alley, which a newspaper called *Metro Times* has declared the area's best jukebox for the last two years. A heavy wooden door was locked tight, fifteen minutes before closing, and only by explaining the urgency of my quest did the bouncer, a burly tattooed biker of a man, agree to let us in the door.

Once inside, we could barely move. It was a long wood-paneled bar, lined with simple beige booths and plastered with hubcaps, antique signs for Gulfpride—World's Finest Motor Oil, and other floating debris of the automobile era. Every inch was filled with young bodies—a costume party for wannabes from an untrendy town, a few faux bikers in leather coats, a few backward baseball caps.

"So what do you think?" I asked Adam.

"Very young rowdy crowd. A meat market."

Luckily, the best jukebox in Metro was located in the near corner. It was the monopolistic Rowe/AMI CD model, but lest I sound dismissive let me quickly add this: if my search had a special "CD Jukebox" category—and it doesn't—then Gusoline Alley would win the trophy for the best CD jukebox in America.

It wasn't just the cool juxtaposition of radically different recordings—Patsy Cline next to the Pixies, for example—although that was part of it. And it wasn't just the playlist that encompassed snippets of every type of worthwhile jukebox music—John Coltrane, Ornette Coleman, Howlin' Wolf, Screamin' Jay Hawkins, Elvis Costello, Joe Jackson, the Replacements, Dinosaur Jr., the Sex Pistols, the Beastie Boys, the *Sun Records Story*—even, yes, Motown's *16 #1 Hits from the Late '60s*—although that was another part of it. It was that Gusoline Alley had something I had never seen on a CD jukebox—and that I rarely saw on 45 jukeboxes anymore: local Detroit / Metro bands on small, independent labels, bands with names like The Dusk, The Alternative, the Birthday Party, and Tad. Most of the local bands had crudely drawn labels for their CDs, but one CD didn't even have cover art, just a white slip of paper that said: Discipline/Title: Push and Profit (pre-release)/Strung Out Records.

Adam, a fan of many of the 1980s and '90s CDs on the jukebox, was in something of a high-technology trance, guzzling a beer and babbling something about "the whole album concept." I took a more levelheaded view, but I wanted to meet the maestro behind the machine, a bartender named Patrick Tierney. Shortly after 2 A.M., while the burly tattoo man was shoehorning lust-laden Generation Xers out the front door, Patrick emerged from the back, wearing black jeans and a plain white T-shirt, a cigarette dangling from his lips. His jet-black hair was slicked back and he wore long sideburns—he looked more than a little bit like the King himself, in a fuzzy black-velvet-rendering kind of way.

I asked him why Gusoline Alley (the owner, of course, is named Gus) decided to go with CDs for presenting its funky mix of alternative music, rather than 45s.

"We had a 45 jukebox until . . . less than three months ago," he said, taking a drag on his cigarette. "But 45s were becoming difficult to get ahold of. Newer music was difficult to get on 45. A lot were coming out with the smaller holes. And people seem to like it"—the CD jukebox—"more. I think the selections are up to date. It pretty much plays nonstop. It's still four songs for a buck, and we stock our own CDs."

With great pride he pointed out the final dozen or so CDs—almost all were local Metro bands, and a few of the band members were regulars at Gusoline Alley. Fingering his cigarette, he talked about one of his favorite CDs, from a band called Goober and the Peas—which that week's *Metro Times* had featured on the cover, describing them as "Hank Williams meets the Velvet Underground and they all go for a ride in a big pink Cadillac." The band was currently off touring the West in an RV called "Mallard" after issuing its CD, *The Complete Works*, on an indie label.

"They come in here and spend money," Patrick said. "Why not play their songs?"

Now Patrick Tierney was on a roll, talking about his jukebox philosophy to two fellow travelers, about how he wanted to challenge his customers, expand their musical tastes.

"I don't want to sound pretentious, but I see this as a way to play a lot of music that you won't hear on the radio . . . Even if you're only into Nirvana and all new music, you'll hear something good—Miles Davis, Hank Williams, John Lee Hooker."

Adam piped up. "So would you say your jukebox has attitude?"

"I like to think it does."

Patrick Tierney was the Ghost of Jukeboxes Present, the man who took the evil specter of CD jukeboxes and tried to infuse them with a human soul. There was only one thing that bothered me about the jukebox at Gusoline Alley, and that was—with the possible exception of a stray Marvin Gaye song—there was no overlap with the jukebox at the 606 Horseshoe Lounge. Patrick Tierney was challenging the leather-jacketed Xers of Metro to think about Ornette Coleman—but not about Detroit.

But the biggest surprise in Detroit/Metro was the visitor with no human face at all—the Ghost of Jukeboxes Future. His name was the Grim Reaper, the death of jukeboxes foretold.

Our first morning in Detroit, the Replacements' "Kiss Me on the Bus" still ringing in my ears from Gusoline Alley just about five hours earlier, I flipped through the *Metro Times* with Goober and the Peas on the cover and came across an ad for a place called The Music Menu—A CD Cafe. It was located in Greektown, and for the "menu" of music it listed "B. Marley, Miles Davis, Iggy Pop, Billie Holliday [sic], REM, James Brown, Pixies, KD Lang." It sounded like a less-hip Gusoline Alley, but I filed the information away in my brain.

Later that day, Adam and I had an hour to kill between James Jenkins and meeting his friends again, this time at a Polish restaurant in Hamtramck, and we made a wrong turn right into the two blocks of Greektown. We parked the car, strolled past about eight Greek restaurants, and found ourself at the door to The Music Menu. We walked in and Van Morrison was blasting from a giant sound system. I looked for the CD jukebox but saw nothing, just a few Generation Xers throwing darts and milling around a cavernous black bar/restaurant, with black Formica and upholstered booths straight from *The Jetsons*. Embedded in each Formica table was a silver-plated disc, an imitation of a CD.

"Too bad it looks like a bathroom," Adam said.

We sat down to order something to drink. I looked across the blackness toward the bar, and noticed shelves of compact discs, hundreds of them, and figured out that this was the deal, that it was simply a joint where the bartender played a lot of CDs.

I figured wrong.

A minute later a waitress, a perky young blonde, plopped three items down on our Formica slab. "Here's your food menu," she said, "and here's your music menu."

The food menu was pretty basic, except for the corny names like "B. B. King Wings," "R and Bean Dip," and "Cheese Styx" ("unlike the defunct '70s pop band, these actually have taste"). The music menu was something else entirely, a thirty-three-page compendium of hundreds of CDs—I was too tired and too depressed at this development to get an exact count—that started with Adam and the Ants and went all the way (shakily, under my ideas about alphabetization) to Buckwheat Zydeco.

The third thing the waitress handed us was a small slip of paper upon which we could write the songs we wanted to hear. It would cost twenty-five cents a song, although there were also timed rates that—unlike a jukebox—take into account the wildly varying lengths of songs, so you could buy a fifteen- to twenty-minute stretch for $2. The idea—which I wanted no part of—was to hand the slip over to the waitress when she took your food order. The bill would come later.

You didn't even need change.

"This is amazing—they have eight Springsteen albums!" Adam gushed. I threw him a dirty "Et tu, Brute," look he didn't seem to notice as he rattled off favorite albums of ours like *Party Mix* by the B-52s that were on the menu.

I suddenly thought of James Jenkins and his bargain-basement jukebox, listing the Ohio Players and Barry White when he wanted Duke Ellington and Billie Holiday. Sure enough, this vast music menu had not one but two CDs by Duke Ellington, a live concert and *The Duke Meets the Count*, recorded with Count Basie.

This was music for a generation that was raised on fifty-seven channels on the television and *Wayne's World* as often as desired on the VCR—entertainment on demand. In theory, the music menu—with literally thousands of possible selections—takes the concept of a jukebox to its next logical technological destination, but I failed to see the improvement. I'm not advocating a return to the Wurlitzer 1015 "Bubbler," which played 24 78s; but somewhere in there—maybe the 1950 Seeburg with its 100 sides—was an optimal number for choice, with discretion. In limits, there are challenges. Consider the jeopardy: who would pay twenty-five cents to hear a song by Goober and the Peas when he could play his favorite obscure album cut by the Cure, the same album he plays over and over again on his home CD player? In theory, of course, someone *else* will play Goober and the Peas while you're there. But with a jukebox, one can always learn a new song by checking the "Selection Playing" digits on the machine. Here, there is no machine—no chrome tail fins, no green or red neon. There are only sound waves—and a giant void.

If I had seen The Music Menu—A CD Cafe right after my Detroit low-point, that 1970s dinner at the Traffic Jam and Snug, I would have been devastated. I would have concluded that all my jukebox searching was in vain, that America's best jukebox had met its rusting end in a junkyard somewhere, that the last great juke joints only existed in the minds of elderly men like James Jenkins.

But between those two low non-jukebox moments, something truly incredible had happened—we visited a place called Honest? John's Bar and No Grill.

*   *   *

Honest? John's Bar and No Grill is located at 416 Field, in a strange section of Detroit, a kind of no-man's land that runs east the length of Jefferson Avenue along the Detroit River, the narrow waterway that separates Michigan from Ontario. On the right side of the street, every few blocks or so, is a series of spanking new riverfront condominiums with names like Harbortown—walled fortresses with large gates and uniformed security men watching the entrance. But if one were to turn left and go in just a block or so, he would see the worst that Detroit has to offer—entire blocks that have returned almost to the natural prairie state of the Midwest, with a burned-out or boarded-up house or two scattered about like stray Monopoly pieces.

Right in the middle of this demilitarized zone sits Honest? John's Bar and No Grill, a modest one-story brick structure that, in neon, says simply "Honest," "?," and "John's" in its three windows.

There is a spacious free parking lot across the street, and the second our car pulled up we were engulfed in a sudden thundershower off the lakes. We scurried under an awning and there, partly protected and partly getting wet, was John—not Honest? John, although the moniker would be appropriate—but John Thompson, the co-owner and guiding force behind one of the wackiest bars I'd ever seen.

John Thompson struck me as a boxer who'd taken one blow too many. His face was rugged, even punched out, his skin was pale—not unusual for a bar-and-no-grill co-owner who surely rarely sees the light of day—and his words were fast and badly slurred, despite the fact that he gave up heavy drinking a few years ago. His voice reminded me of a white Muhammad Ali, and for the next hour or so he danced around the tiny tavern, firing verbal jabs like it was a sparring ring.

"So I'm here looking for the best jukebox in America," I proclaimed for about the 100th time in the last two years.

"Well, every week we take the best mover off—just to piss off the regulars."

Then my jukebox search took something of a detour, because before I could inspect it, John Thompson had launched a verbal flurry, mostly about his two favorite topics—his bar, and himself.

He handed me a card that showed about thirty-five men in front of the bar, mooning the camera. "This is for 'Grin and Bare It So the Churches Can Share It,' " he said.

"Huh?"

"So the churches can share it—you know, in the summer they got no money."

I was realizing the mooning was some charity event for local churches, but John Thompson kept on talking. "We raised $105,000 in the last year and a half by doing everything—by 133 turkeys we delivered last Thanksgiving, by jumping into the Detroit River we earned $60,000, in September we'll have a homemade raft race." He said the raft race was named for Gabriel Richard, a Roman Catholic missionary and a founding father of Detroit in the late eighteenth century. "He was into crossdressing, so some of us will cross-dress for the event." He later told me that once Honest? John's and a neighborhood church raised money on Easter Sunday by barbecuing 500 pounds of rabbit.

It turned out that John Thompson used the bar and its customers heavily to promote a charitable campaign that was called Honest? John's Shakedown Society. The society's motto is: It's a long way to your car.

"It should have been, Give it up now or give it up in the lot," John said.

Before I knew it, John Thompson was dragging me and one of my companions, a *Wall Street Journal* reporter named Doug, into his cramped office in the back. I wondered if he was planning to shake us down, but instead he pulled a large calendar from the middle of a big stack.

"We have a big senior citizen business during the day," he said. "We lost a senior not too long ago, about a year ago. So we put up money to have a calendar made up and do a burial funded by the Shakedown Society. They raised $7,000."

"And that paid for the burial?" I asked.

"We sold these and put it into a special fund—for when they kick."

He started flipping through the pages. The black-and-white photography was both jarring and touching. There were shadowy shots, a pale and wrinkled white man in a fedora, an African American man with a placid and knowing expression, relaxed in a polo shirt and love beads. The images were sharp and uncompromised—no soft lighting or blurry focus. A few—grannies on motorcycles, for example—were silly, but most managed to give these elderly Detroiters the dignity they were more than due after a hard life, on the line or even on the streets.

"She'll probably go in the next couple of weeks," said John, pointing at a gray-haired woman. He flipped the page. "He'll probably go by the end of the summer."

"They're real sick, huh," I said with an air of concern.

"Well, they're old—eighty-three and eighty-seven."

He pointed out an elderly African American and said that he and his co-owner—a surgeon named Carl Christenson—took over as trustees of his grandson's college fund when a local factory cheated him out of his retirement money. Then he pointed at two elderly women with faces like cookie-baking grandmas from a TV ad.

"A couple of old ladies here used to work the streets," he said. "They worked the bars around the old Uniroyal plant."

For all his charity, John Thompson had a hard-nosed view of the world. His story—which would probably take a month of rugged investigative reporting to confirm—is that he grew up white in a predominantly black part of Detroit, fell into a pattern of teen delinquency, and was rescued, at least partly, by a local minister. As a young man in the 1970s, Thompson—a somewhat-recovered alcoholic, a slurry Sam Malone—got involved in the bar business, but then left around 1985 after a murder in a joint he was running. He stayed out for five years, when he and his M.D. partner took over Honest? John's—which had been founded in 1954 by the real Honest? John but was faltering under a second owner. He vowed that things would be different this time around.

"I have a strict rule here," he told me. "Nobody uses the word *nigger*, no druggies inside the bar, if you piss off the women you're out the door, and if you're an asshole you're out the door."

It wasn't exactly the Ten Commandments, but it seemed to be working. It looked like the clientele at Honest? John's Bar and No Grill was as diverse as the patrons at Gusoline Alley were homogenous—there were whites, ranging from our own button-down *Wall Street Journal* reporter to a pool player with a scraggly beard and bulging Charlie Manson eyes who looked like he wandered to town from a survivalist camp, and there were blacks, both "buppies" like a local TV news reporter and some guys with baseball hats fresh off the assembly line.

How does John Thompson accomplish this in the war zone of Detroit?

"This is a classic story," he said. "A woman moved in next to me. I have a big fence, big security, I'm very security minded. She had one of those little Maltese dogs, and the dog got let out—the dog got lost. She came over here, and I thought she had been raped there was so much pain in her face. So I brought her back—and I found out the dog had been stolen. Now there are dope houses in the neighborhood that I take care of—because there are kids in dope houses. Christmas they get toys, turkeys at Thanksgiving, hams at Easter. So I go over to the dope houses, knock on the door. A half-hour later, the dog's on the front door—washed, in a box."

In two and a half years, Thompson said, there hasn't been an incident in his parking lot. "They know we're not a bunch of white people just down here trying to get rich."

"How does it go with the clientele—in terms of integration?" I asked awkwardly.

"They get along."

"What's the breakdown of black and white people?"

"Sometimes it's eighty-twenty, sometimes it's fifty-fifty—every night is different. Gays, straights, you know—and then you've got sports fans."

On one level, John Thompson was clearly the reformed scrooge of my Dickensian jukebox tale of Detroit—dispensing toys and turkeys to the Tiny Tims of crack houses, a man who understood the power of redemption. But on another level I saw something else, something I had come all the way to Detroit in search of but which I had abandoned any hope of finding amid the boarded-up mansions and the despair.

I found the spirit of Berry Gordy Jr.—in the body of a white tavern owner.

It sounds strange, but to me the similarities were striking. Both men were entrepreneurs with a gift for self-promotion. And both men clearly had a dark side—one well-placed Detroit source told me that John can still display a ruthless side that undercuts his charity work. Yet when all was said and done, both Berry Gordy Jr. and John Thompson worked in their offbeat ways to bring people together—Thompson with his charity work and his one-of-a-kind bar, Gordy, of course, with his music. Both men looked out at the stark landscape of Detroit—mansions and poor houses, weeds and condo towers—and somehow saw not the things that made us all different, but the things that made us all alike.

And John Thompson had gone one better, for he never gave up on the Dream. That was even reflected, believe it or not, in the jukebox at Honest? John's Bar and No Grill, a jukebox I finally got to check out when John Thompson's tongue eventually wearied.

Like almost all the other good music jukeboxes I had seen across America, it was nothing pretty to look at—just an old Rock-Ola model from the mid-1980s, as square and as dull as a central Michigan landscape. John Thompson told me—suddenly remembering about forty-five minutes into his patter that the jukebox was the reason I was here—that he could replace it anytime with a CD jukebox, but he didn't want to. For one thing, he had about 2,600 45s at home, enough to ensure a steady rotation and to replace any song that got too popular. But the big issue was cost, for Honest? John's 45 RPM jukebox played a whopping eleven songs for a dollar, one of the best bargains I'd seen in Jukebox America.

"Sure, I could go to the CD jukebox tomorrow," John said. "If you buy one, they cost about five grand, and people want anywhere from fifty cents a tune to three for a dollar. I have no restaurant—it's a bar-and-no-grill. The least we can give you is cheap music."

The selection of 45s was as wacky and as varied as his customers. It started with the #100 selection, the incongrous "You Could Have Been a Lady" by forgotten pop-metal-rockers April Wine, then segued right into Louis Armstrong, then went into a mix that was heavy on classic R & B—"People Get Ready" by the Impressions along with a lot of homegrown Detroit stuff like "It's a Shame" by the Spinners, "My Girl" by the Temptations, and "Can I Get a Witness" by Marvin Gaye. Then there was blue-eyed soul from Squeeze ("Tempted") and Elton John; there were groups that weighed in with several songs, like the great '70s funksters the Ohio Players and, most important, Prince, whose ambiguity—both in matters of sexuality and of race—seemed somehow most appropriate for the polyglot of customers of Honest? John's Bar and No Grill.

I duly noted Honest? John's as one of the best jukeboxes in America, and stepped away. The clock had just struck twelve—we were walkin' after midnight. Adam's Detroit friends were tired and wanted to go home. I turned around, and Al Green, slow and sexy, came on to the jukebox. A tall man, an African American in a yellow baseball cap, led a short white woman—she couldn't have been more than four-and-a-half feet tall—out into an open space in front of the jukebox. The woman wrapped her arms around the man's hulking waist, and they swayed slowly, unevenly, to the record. Then another couple—again, the man was black and the woman was white—joined them in front of the jukebox.

Outside, Metro/Detroit was a racial powderkeg, a fuse that threatened to explode with the Malice Green case. They were two separate cities—one black and one white—staring each other down across a silly and invisible line. But from the jukebox inside the sanctuary of Honest? John's came only slow, soothing rhythms and simple harmonies—a beautiful ballet in living black-and-white. That moment crystallized everything I had come to learn about Jukebox America during my two years of road trips. When I left the townhouse conformity of Lower Makefield, Pennsylvania, I was looking for nothing more than a good time, and some good music. But now I knew that there were still jukeboxes in America that offered that—and something more. There was Tony Mangiullo, bringing his Italian brand of black blues to a Latino neighborhood, and Jesse Richardson, uniting the real-estate cheeses and the hard-drinking brawlers of Winchester, Virginia, with his Patsy Cline jukebox. There was the bug-bitten night that Ezell Landrum, Mississippi Delta factory man, and I bragged on our families while Elmore James blasted through that static-ridden jerry-rigged jukebox. These were moments that were only possible in the place I called Jukebox America—they aren't happening in exurbia, where every townhouse will soon have its own channel on cable TV and its own factory outlet at the mall. There were two common threads to America's greatest jukeboxes—music, and bringing people together.

Then Al Green faded away, and the moment was gone. But I knew that—at least for those three minutes—I had finally found what I was looking for: America's best jukebox.

It would have been fitting to end my entire junket right there, to head straight for Detroit Metro Airport and never look back. But there was a whole day left and—quite by surprise—there would be a fitting postscript to the journey.

It happened in Hamtramck, a nifty one-square-mile city that is the spiritual cousin to Hoboken, New Jersey, with its postage-stamp size, authentic Polish restaurants and delis, and lively concentration of cool bars. The idea was to hit a place called Lili's, the hard-fought jukebox rival of Gusoline Alley in all the magazine polls. When we got there at 8:30 on a Saturday night, the jukebox—again, incredibly, one of the best in America—was turned off and even blocked off by technicians setting up the stage for a lineup of bands that included Johnny Allen's Kielbasa Kings. Lili—a red-haired fiftyish gypsy woman with a thick eastern European accent, a self-proclaimed Iggy Pop fan—wouldn't even let us in the door; the show was sold out.

This seeming setback was in fact the latest show of good fortune from the Spirit in the Sky. Lili's son suggested we instead try the Norwalk Tavern, a nearby shot-and-beer dive that recently had been "discovered" by young hipsters. We walked in, underneath a red-and-blue neon Norwalk Tavern sign straight out of the 1950s, a little before 9 P.M. We were a Banana Republic army of well-off thirty-somethings. There were about ten old geezers at the bar—gray men in auto-parts caps and faded windbreakers—and their suspicious heads turned in unison when we walked in.

My friends wanted to leave, and when I ducked outside to a pay phone to call Kathy—this was the brief window of opportunity between Julia's bedtime and hers—they wanted to kill me. I took a different view: the old-timers were harmless, and the jukebox, a Rock-Ola Sybaris from the video-game era of the early 1980s, was pretty fine. There were some neat oldies like "Pleasant Valley Sunday" and "Radar Love," nine polka selections including "The Cluckee Song" by John Lipinski and Polka Pleasure—and there was "The Blob" by the Five Blobs. Still, it wasn't quite as thrilling as it would have been before seeing America's best jukebox. At least not until I looked up at the bar.

There were two thirty-ish women at the bar, and they were flipping through a square box of 45 RPM records, heatedly arguing about the relative merits of "Cool Jerk" by the Capitols. They were about to restock the jukebox at the Norwalk Tavern. It's a process that goes on hundreds of times every day in Jukebox America, but never while I was present—until now. The catalyst was a man named Paul Lichota, who runs a local record store and is a long-time customer who stops by every few weeks to change the selections—with a major vote from the regular customers. This was Jukebox America at its best, democracy in action.

Eddie, the Norwalk's geriatric bartender, was open to whatever the customers wanted. "He likes a mix," Paul said. "He's an old guy, so I put in acid stuff from the '60s—he never heard them during the '60s."

Within minutes, the electorate had chosen six "new" 45s— "Cool Jerk," "My Guy" by Mary Wells, "I Can't Explain" by the Who, "Maggie May" by Rod Stewart, "Satisfaction" by the Rolling Stones, and "Sloop John B/Wouldn't It Be Nice" by the Beach Boys. So Paul Lichota whipped out his screwdriver and within seconds had worked the jukebox's top off. To Adam, the ever-working journalist, the naked inner workings of the jukebox seemed like something really exciting, a big story.

"This is just like the Pentagon Papers," he said as we stared at curved pieces of steel and the simple turntable.

But now came the moment of truth—five older selections would have to be put to sleep.

A woman in red shrieked. "He's taking out 'Tempted.' Oh my God."

"Aren't you upset about taking 'Tempted' out?" Adam asked.

"Nah, I got the tape at home," Paul said.

Then Paul Lichota, the Terminator, came to a Van Halen selection whose time had come. Meanwhile, he was disbursing title strips to various patrons to mark the new 45s. I demurred— only because my handwriting skills remained back in the second grade.

Now Adam was annoyed with me. "Come on," he said. "This is your big chance."

"Okay, okay." In my infantile scratch, I wrote out "SLOOP JOHN B" and "WOULDN'T IT BE NICE" and handed it down to Paul, who duly slid it under the glass, selection #103/ #203. I had only been in Detroit for about thirty-one hours, and I had accomplished more than I had ever dreamed of. It didn't seem possible to solve Detroit's overwhelming economic and racial problems. I hadn't lured Berry Gordy Jr. back to Detroit. I couldn't revive the glory days of Motown or even Paradise

Valley—in fact, a story in that Sunday's paper announced that the Little Caesar's pizza mogul wanted to obliterate what was left of the historic black district to build a baseball stadium. Instead I had accomplished what was possible: I had made my own semi-permanent, illegible mark on Jukebox America.

Chapter 12

....

Let's Stay Together

The road phase of my search for America's best jukebox ended in a manner similar to the way it all began: crossing a big river into New Jersey.

But now it was almost two years after that hot October afternoon when I had nervously walked off a PATH train and into Hoboken, New Jersey, looking for a Sinatra jukebox that didn't even exist. And even longer—856 days and nights, to be exact—had passed since that snowy night when the Spirit in the Sky and His chosen prophet, Nancy Sinatra, sent me into the wilderness of Jukebox America to search for that vanishing frontier.

So much had changed since that cold February night. Now New Jersey, Nancy Sinatra's native state, no longer represented the beginning of the American frontier, the open lands to the west. Now I was approaching the Garden State *from* the west, from my home in Lower Makefield, crossing Philadelphia's Ben Franklin Bridge into the backwaters of Camden, New Jersey. It was just after noon on July 3, 1993, and the Delaware Valley was already smothered in a wool blanket of humidity—the twin spires of Philadelphia's Liberty Place were shadows in the haze of my rearview mirror.

Kathy—who had missed out on almost all the jukebox adventures, from the scenic swamps of Louisiana to the snowcapped peaks of the Pacific Northwest—was finally right where she belonged, right by my side. But this hardly seemed a reward, for we were cruising a scenic vista called Admiral Wilson Boulevard in Camden, a pleasuredome for sexually and alcoholically repressed residents of the Quaker State back across the river.

It was an ugly American strip highway, except that instead of a CVS there was a giant supermarket called The Booze Shop, and in the place of an Arby's there was a lounge advertising "couch dancing."

In the midst of all this sin, a voice of innocence spoke from the backseat of our brand-new Honda Civic with four doors.

"Da da."

I was entering a whole new phase of my life: Jukebox parenting.

Detroit was supposed to be the end.

I had no doubts about what I saw that rain-swept midnight in Motown, the slow dance of humanity—man and woman, black and white, entwined by the universal soul of Al Green, united by America's greatest jukebox. That was supposed to be the cure, the switch that turned off the neon buzz in my soul—the final sign from the Spirit in the Sky. But while I had followed every other mysterious sign—even when Nancy Sinatra was the messenger—this was one I wanted to ignore.

Let it be.

Every kid—even an egghead raised in the comforts of suburban Westchester County—knows the rules of the backyard basketball hoops, that you don't go inside until you make that twenty-foot jumper as the buzzer sounds to end the imaginary seventh game of the NBA Finals. Detroit was that last-second swish—yet I wanted the ball back.

No matter how many Rock-Olas, Wurlitzers, and Seeburgs I saw—and now I had seen my version of America's best jukebox, along with a half-dozen worthy runners-up—I couldn't shake the notion, as bitter cold as the snowflakes that fell on me in New York City all the way back in 1991, that a world without jukeboxes was the equivalent of a hospice. I imagined myself in black and white, the next weathered face on John Thompson's calendar back in Detroit, next in line to—as he so eloquently put it—"kick."

Now I had been all over the country, from the windswept streets of Hoboken to the blue skies and green hills of Seattle, and yet after all this time I hadn't moved past the fourth stage of jukebox withdrawal: bargaining. I wanted to make one final trip . . .

To a truck stop.

"Why do you want to go to a truck stop?" This was my wife, Kathy, the voice of reason speaking, and she had something of a point. When I was a mere ten-something—this was the 1970s, the era of C. W. McCall's "Convoy" and the CB-radio fad—I saw hundreds of truck stops on our yearly junket from Westchester to Peoria, all from the safety of our Ford LTD station wagon. Truck stops were things to be avoided: they had greasy food, unshowered truckers, questionable hygiene standards, and gift shops selling baseball caps with dirty slogans.

Then in 1987, during a long and largely unsuccessful newspaper reporting project about the solid-waste business, a photographer and I hitched a ride with a trucker hauling a load of municipal trash from Oyster Bay, New York, to Oakland, Ohio. The first night, we all stopped at a Union 76 truck stop outside of Stroudsburg, Pennsylvania, and our trucker dropped about two dollars worth of quarters in the jukebox there. Over the next couple of days, we stopped at a couple of other truck stops, and they all had great jukeboxes, stocked with the sad and solitary songs of George Jones and Merle Haggard—the soundtrack for America's loneliest job.

I recalled that raw, all-American jaunt five years later, when

I saw a story about a small, independent record label called Diesel Only Records, an extraordinary business venture run by a most unusual man, a journalist-cum-musician named Jeremy Tepper.

Jeremy Tepper is the nexus where the shadowy worlds of jukeboxes and truck stops meet. Fresh out of New York University, Tepper went to work as a reporter for *Modern Truckstop News* (the proof that in America there is a trade magazine for everything). From there he became an editor at the trade magazine *Vending Times*, which covers the industry servicing vending machines, video games, pinball machines—and jukeboxes. On nights and weekends, Jeremy Tepper performed as guitarist and occasional singer with a rock 'n' roll band the World Famous Blue Jays.

It was the late 1980s, and the Jays were on the cutting edge of an unusual and—to be honest—not exactly lucrative trend on the starving art-school-grad overrun streets of New York's East Village. These were true rock 'n' roll rebels—they rejected the REM-based postmodern nihilism of most New York City bands in favor of something way-out: the bourbon-soaked sounds of country music and rockabilly. These bands worshipped a Holy Duality—Hank Williams Sr. and His Only Misbegotten Son, Hank Jr.

They called it "rig rock"—too hard for country-music radio, too weird for rock stations, but just right for eighteen-wheelers. Then in 1989 Jeremy Tepper—this truck stop/jukebox/music expert, surely the only such person on the planet—had a brilliant idea: Why not record these offbeat New York City "rig rock" bands on 45s and market them for the jukeboxes at hundreds of truck stops across the country? Everyone else in the record business was cutting back on 45s because nobody bought them anymore—except the operators of 160,000 or so 45 RPM jukeboxes across America. They bought an estimated 36 million 45s in 1990 out of just 40 million sold. To fill this growing gap came Diesel Only Records.

In its first three years, Diesel Only released twenty-five records on 45—all produced for about $1,000 apiece at Coyote Studios in the Williamsburg section of Brooklyn, a neighborhood evenly divided between Latinos, Orthodox Jews, and twenty-something slackers. I learned about them in the fall of 1992 when I read that Tepper had released an album, a compilation of Diesel Only's best singles called *Rig Rock Jukebox*. Needless to say, I was swept away by the concept and bought it the next afternoon on cassette so I could listen to it immediately on my Walkman. It quickly became my favorite record. The best songs included the pounding guitars of "Why I Drink" by Go to Blazes, the boozy girl country of Courtney and Western, and "Do It for Hank" (Jr., that is) by the World Famous Blue Jays. Over time, my favorite became "Baltimore" by the Five Chinese Brothers, the ultimate ode to Generation Y angst.

> The older we get the more we stay the same
> Chasing after something that doesn't even have a name
> We'll always trade what we've got for what we had before
> Everybody's a fool for something, I'm a fool for
> Baltimore.

This was music that validated the entire point of my jukebox quest; it was far better than anything that you could hear on the sorry state of American radio in the 1990s, far better than anything on compact disc before these 45s were compiled. These were national anthems for the struggling state of Jukebox America.

I called Tepper on the phone and explained the nature of my quest. He told me he had just launched his own magazine called *Street Beat*, a coin-op trade mag heavily weighted toward jukeboxes, and was coming to Bucks County, Pennsylvania, the next week to interview executives at a company that makes electronic dart boards and trivia games.

When I met him in person, Jeremy Tepper seemed larger than life. Tall, jowly, and of some heft, with a radio DJ voice, long sideburns and hair tossed upward, he looked more like a trailer-park rockabilly singer from Tennessee than a New York magazine editor. He knew more about jukeboxes than anyone I had met so far in my adventure—about how the whole jukebox record distribution business worked, about how records like Clarence Carter's "Strokin'" became hits on jukeboxes without getting radio play—and he knew that 45 RPM records were the dinosaurs of the record industry, but in their extinction he saw an opportunity.

"It's like when Top 40 radio started—this is uncharted territory," he said. "We're making it up as we go along, and that's what I love about my life, you know. There's a historic moment where this industry is converting from vinyl to CD—it hasn't happened since the '50s, when it went from 78s. We're making history—and I just want to play it out. I'm not going to go take another job next year and leave this all behind."

It all sounded to good to be true—and the problem was, a part of it was.

That's because the next logical step, of course, was to visit a truck stop and hear a Diesel Only 45. That sounded like an easy task—truck stops, after all, were the mythology of Diesel Only, the hook that got Jeremy Tepper favorable write-ups in the *Village Voice*, the *New York Daily News*, and *Spin* magazine. But it was hard for Jeremy Tepper to tell me what specific truck stops carried his records, because Diesel Only Records was merely the first link in a four-link chain—he sold the records to "one-stop" record distributors, who sold them to jukebox operations who serviced the actual truck stop jukeboxes. He ultimately suggested two truck stops—one in Nogales, Arizona, and one in Youngstown, Ohio—but neither fit into my immediate travel plans.

What I wanted, in the waning days of my jukebox adventure, was something close to home. Remember again, I was in that bargaining stage—not just with the Spirit in the Sky but with my family, whom I had abandoned too many times in the last two years. Jeremy Tepper did suggest one truck stop in my newly adopted state, Diamond Jay's on I-80 in west-central Pennsylvania—a favorite road-trip stop for the World Famous Blue Jays, for both the "Jays" connection and its state-of-the-art pinball machines. The band was so enamored of Diamond Jay's that it shot the cover slip for its "Good Morning, Mr. Trucker"

45 in the parking lot there. That made it a good candidate to have the record.

And it turned out, when I called the general manager of Diamond Jay's, that this truck stop had a lot going for it. It had just been named the second-best in America in a poll of long-haul truckers, and it had a cool-sounding 45 RPM jukebox chock-full of country records—except that "Good Morning, Mr. Trucker" was not among them.

It got worse.

I called the Union 76 station near Stroudsburg, the jukebox that I remembered so vividly from the long-haul trash trucker, and got the manager on the line.

"I have a question about your jukebox—" I began.

"Our jukebox?" the man said. "We don't have a jukebox anymore. We took it out two years ago."

I was flabbergasted. "Why would you do that?"

"The noise, the complaints."

"What kind of complaints?"

"You know, complaints about it being too loud, some don't like this song, some don't like that song."

It got even worse. The woman who answered the phone at the Truckstops of America in Columbia, New Jersey, recoiled from my question as if I were an obscene caller—she honestly sounded like she didn't know what exactly a jukebox was. Another woman got on the line. "Our jukebox? Let me check." She came back on in ten seconds. "What am I saying? We don't have one, haven't for about five years."

Ditto the Milton Truck Stop in east-central Pennsylvania, which had once boasted the World Famous Blue Jays on its juke-box—a jukebox which, like the others, exists today on some scrap heap.

The bottom line is that there were no truck stops in my future. That should not diminish the achievement of Diesel Only Records, which was releasing probably the best, freshest music in America in the early 1990s. But a central part of their legend—the part about the truck stops—seemed to be a myth. There were, of course, dozens of jukeboxes that played Diesel Only

45s—but many were located in too-cool dives like Nightingale's and the Great Jones Cafe in New York, where most of the eighteen-wheel wannabes don't even have driver's licenses. In a final irony, the way many a barfly was now getting to hear Diesel Only recordings was through the *Rig Rock Jukebox* disc—from a CD jukebox.

But the problem ran even deeper. Ultimately, five of the six truck stops I called had no jukebox at all. Just a few years back, truck stops had been the beating heart of Jukebox America—a gathering place for a certain type of frontier American, hard-working, nomadic, and independent. Now that heart wasn't getting the oxygen it needed. Jukebox America was dying before my very eyes.

Uncaring relatives would have pulled the plug.

Except for one thing. I knew that the family of Jukebox America—all the bar owners, the vinyl record producers, the old-time jukebox distributors, the nostalgia freaks, the millions of Americans who still love and appreciate really good music—wouldn't let that happen, at least not without the fight of a lifetime.

I have no false illusions. The 45 RPM jukebox is doomed. It won't disappear off the planet, of course; Victrolas and 78s are still around—there was a Victrola stocked with 78s sitting smack in the living room of my Lower Makefield townhouse. But we didn't play it, either, because we had a fairly modern turntable and cassette player fifteen feet away. Victrolas are merely high-priced antiques, and that's all 45 RPM jukeboxes will become—probably by the year 2000, possibly sooner.

In the year 2525, if man is still alive, if woman can survive, they surely won't have CD jukeboxes, either. I'm no technology expert—I just recently figured out how to record a TV program when we're not home—but I predict the day when every bar and diner is wired by AT&T to a central computer somewhere in the swamps of Jersey that will offer every recording ever made, five bucks a play.

The story of Jeremy Tepper is an important one, and—although it wasn't exactly what I wanted to hear—it seemed to encapsulate everything I had discovered about Jukebox America during my search. Jeremy Tepper had a great idea, but he was no Horatio Alger story, no Bill Gates of Microsoft. Diesel Only Records was not making him rich and probably never would—it was merely making beautiful music. That's because there are no big winners in Jukebox America—but there are no losers, either. Its citizens are dreamers, people who like money, but love people, good music, their families, or their corner of the world too much to amass a fortune. They were Mike Milo waving good-bye to Frank Sinatra at that 1947 parade, Miss Bonnie meeting Elvis in the peanut-butter aisle of a Georgia supermarket.

They were Jukebox Heroes.

They believed in something—a lost cause, which is the only cause worth fighting for. They were most surely unsung heroes—indeed, not a single soul I met in all my travels across Jukebox America, with the quickly forgettable exception of Charlie Dick, was well known outside of his or her neighborhood. And yet, collectively and anonymously, they gave this nation more music than Patsy Cline, more brotherhood than Frank Sinatra (a lot more), and more fun than even the King.

And so I used my next-to-last jukebox quarters to make phone calls, to see what was happening on the front lines of our losing battle, the Jukebox Resistance.

Some were down, but not out.

I called Agatha Upchurch at the 924 Club in Banner, Illinois, and discovered what I expected—that almost nothing had changed in the palace of my boyhood jukebox memories. The Singing Bartender had drawn some customers in his few appearances, but then he and his Winnebago hit that long, lonesome trail back to Texas. Aggie Upchurch seemed both befuddled as to who I was and morose about the future of the 924 Club. "It's pretty slow," she said. When I asked her why, she gave me the same answer as eleven months before. "The new laws they put in"—those "new" drunk driving laws from a decade ago. "People just don't get out like they used to."

I called Lavonda Hunt—Miss Bonnie—down in Baltimore at her Elvis Shrine Bar, and she sounded so miserable she made

Aggie Upchurch sound like a regular picnic. Now several of the neighbors were petitioning against her bar, and the city liquor board threatened to close her for six months if she couldn't keep her front door shut. Was business good, at least? "It's real bad—I don't think it's ever been like this, ever since we went to court. But I'm going to hang on. I don't want to lose this place."

But Miss Bonnie didn't hang on. About three months after we spoke, I was sitting at my computer terminal in my Manhattan office, waiting for call-backs and basically bored. So I ran a quick computer search to see if any stories with the word "jukebox" had appeared in the newspaper in recent weeks. What came up gave me a chill. The paper had run a one-paragraph obituary on Lavonda Hunt of Baltimore, mentioning her one-of-a-kind bar and her Elvis jukebox. I felt not only sad but more than a little guilty for viewing her as something of a hypochondriac. Miss Bonnie had died of a heart attack, just like the earlier one she'd blamed on her enemies.

I wanted to call Little Blue down in Longwood, Mississippi, but that was impossible because he had no phone. But I did reach Perry Payton, the undertaker/blues impresario, at his Flowing Fountain nightspot on Nelson Street in Greenville. He told me that—as he'd heard it—Little Blue never did make the move to the larger joint in Freedom Village, but was still presenting the blues every Sunday from that magical rice paddy in the middle of nowhere. He also told me the Blue Note, the dilapidated joint across the street where we'd seen T-Model perform, had closed that winter—"His wife got sick so he gave it up."

The others were fighting back harder than ever.

I called Jesse Richardson in Winchester, Virginia, and discovered that he wasn't at home—where retired people are supposed to be—but was still helping out at Frye Amusements, the jukebox distributor where he'd worked for thirty-eight years. "If you worked all your life, it's hard to quit," he said. He said the Patsy Cline Memorial Committee was studying the idea of a museum in the house where Mrs. Hensley, Patsy's mother, still lived. I asked him what happened to his wonderful Patsy Cline jukebox. "We moved it to an antique mall." Why there? "They"—the

Memorial Committee members—"use it to try and pick up a few bucks here and there."

I called Fred's Lounge in Mamou, Louisiana, on a Saturday morning, and was delighted to hear a roaring accordion riff almost drowning out the voice on the other end. Sue Vasseur, Fred Tate's former wife, came to the phone and said that she and Tate's other survivors had weighed two or three offers to buy Fred's—and turned them all down. "Nobody talks about selling it anymore," she said. "The family has gotten used to the routine of working every Saturday." How's business? "We're packed," she said. It was 9:45 A.M.

I called Tor's in Seattle, and Anna Christianson answered the phone, with Elvis and "Suspicious Minds" playing loudly in the background. Her campaign to bring the Ballard fisherman's bar into the 1990s was continuing unabated—she had added Peter Gabriel, Melissa Etheridge, and Seal to the CD jukebox, and she said she had definitely decided to change the name to "Babe's" sometime in 1994. But what about Johnny Horton? "He's staying—he's there for good."

Leo DiTerlizzi was still where he belonged—ambling slowly behind the bar at his Grandevous in Hoboken. Now seventy-eight, he had every intention of pouring gin when his joint celebrated its fifty-fifth birthday in the summer of 1994. More important, his kinfolk, who helped him manage Leo's, had amassed a collection of about a dozen Sinatra compact discs and successfully placed them inside the record machine, making the world's greatest Frank Sinatra jukebox that much greater.

David Rockola died in January 1993—just a couple of months after his son Donald had mostly closed down the operation in Addison and sold the company named to a man in northern California named Glen Streeter who owned a firm called Antique Applications that had been making nostalgia jukeboxes. I was pleased to learn that Streeter did retain a few employees from the Rock-Ola Manufacturing Corp.—including Frank Shultz, the one man there who seemed to understand jukeboxes.

But the brightest neon light in all of Jukebox America had to be Tony Mangiullo.

I called Tony in Chicago and he launched into a lengthy monologue about the still up-in-the-air fight to save Maxwell Street—as a place not just for blues musicians but for African Americans to shop cheaply and start small businesses—and about a Piano Festival he'd recently hosted for Chicago's best keyboard men. He said Iceman Robinson's band had dissolved—no surprise there—but that he was still performing.

There was something else that Tony didn't volunteer—I learned of it quite by accident about two months later—which was clearly weighing on his mind that summer night. On the eve of Memorial Day weekend and the Chicago Blues festival, a waitress and her boyfriend were busted by undercover cops for selling cocaine inside the confines of Rosa's. The liquor authorities shut down the blues bar for seven days and threatened to yank his license for good. I read what Tony told the *Chicago Tribune*—that he had no knowledge of the woman's activities and that if she was peddling drugs then he was glad she got caught—and I believed him.

The episode had clearly influenced his response when—in June—I had naively asked him about business and whether he planned to stay in that Hispanic enclave on the West Side.

"For me to stay here—it kind of represents a challenge, because I always have to have talented music to keep people interested. I have to always be the best to bring people over here. You really have to be tough—it's a challenge. But culturally, to me, I would not be so satisfied to have a club where all I have is white people or black people or just Hispanics. I believe part of my achievement is to create an environment where everybody's welcome—from different classes, different economic classes, to make my place a social event."

I couldn't have said it any better than this bluesman born in Milan, Italy.

*   *   *

It was their fight to save the 45 RPM record, the friendly neighborhood tavern, and the jukebox that drew me to these Jukebox Heroes; but from them I had learned something different, something unexpected—a lesson so many Generation Y people were resisting. The lesson was buried somewhere in all the choices they ultimately made—from Mike Milo settling down to the life of a merchant in Hoboken to the Mississippi bluesman Blind Jebby, missing his chance to be in a movie to care for his dying wife.

I learned about roots.

Ultimately, things are a lot like a well-stocked Seeburg 100-A jukebox, with dozens of great choices—but with limits. For me, life's selections had proven every bit as musical as "Tears of a Clown" or "Radio Free Europe." I had a beautiful, loving wife, a comfortable home, loyal friends—and now a healthy, rambunctious baby girl. Despite all of this, there will still be nights when I sing "Twinkle Twinkle Little Star" to Julia while thinking about Iceman Robinson picking on his blues guitar, afternoons when I daydream about a Bud tall-boy at Little Blue's Cafe as I scrub our shower tiles. But every time I traveled to some remote outpost of Jukebox America, my thoughts clung more and more to what I was leaving behind. Just like Ezell Landrum, the once-rowdy Mississippi juke-jointer, said over and over, "I love my family."

I am still haunted by the night that Julia rolled over for the very first time—while I was trapped in a Seattle grunge bar watching an acid-rap band called Silly Rabbit.

There was no doubt that my generation, the Rear Guard Baby Boomers, had missed a lot—the 1960s, revolution, free love, the 1950s, *The Honeymooners*, Patsy Cline and the "Sound of Young America." But there was a real danger in all that generational angst, a danger of missing what really mattered. Now it was the time for getting over that, to love the ones we're with.

And so I entered the final stage of moving to a township

with no jukebox: acceptance. It was a new and wonderful feeling, to have that neon road sign in my soul burning No Vacancy, to have that awful buzz under control. I still don't have a full handle on my greatest fear, my one-way ticket on that Mystery Train ride to wherever Elvis now resides, but even that worry managed to fade as a daily concern.

Even better, I was learning how to cope with a place possibly more frightening than Elvis's resting place, that living exurban Hell, Lower Makefield. For within a half-hour or so driving distance of the massive Condo Fields, within the limits of my new life, there *were* jukeboxes—not the four-star competitors of Jukebox America, nothing with quite the uniqueness of a Little Blue's or a Rosa's or an Honest? John's, but worthy outposts, juke joints that were continuing to fight the good fight into the 1990s.

Just two weeks after Julia was born, Kathy and I—crazed from 336 hours of virtual sleep deprivation—implored her father and his wife Marilyn to babysit. We thought about checking into a local Red Roof Inn, but instead we drove to downtown Philadelphia and the 16th Street Bar and Grill, a homey bar with orange-rust walls, Mediterranean food, and the city's best jukebox, with funky artist's renderings on the title strips for each 45. We played Frank's "Witchcraft" and Aretha's "I Never Loved a Man" and Lulu's "To Sir with Love" until our Philadelphia freedom ran out.

In that same year, we had discovered a place in a rural outpost of Bucks County, thirty minutes the other direction from Philadelphia, a place called The Pineville Tavern that dates back to 1742. By day, this rustic hunting lodge of a bar was a hangout for Schaefer-drinking farmers and construction workers, while at night came the Invasion of the Condo Snatchers, who played rock 'n' roll on the workmanlike jukebox of this colonial tavern and gradually, tentatively, learned to mingle with the natives, parking their Beamers smack next to the Chevy pickups with their gun racks.

I hope these places—the juke joints of my new greater

Philadelphia–New York exurban area—can survive the onslaught of compact discs, canned music, the "new laws" on drunk driving, fast food, and whatever else is killing the great jukeboxes of America in the 1990s. I don't want to suggest that bars don't have their dark side—some provided an all-too-comfortable home for the regrettable minority of alcoholics I met across Jukebox America, and the "new laws" that Aggie Upchurch and Jesse Richardson reviled were a badly needed response to the scourge of drunk driving. But for most, the corner tavern and the neighborhood juke joint were merely places to meet their fellow Americans, from down the block or sometimes from the other side of the tracks.

In marked contrast, the Houlihans and Bennigans that are taking their place are large and airy—designed to prevent spontaneous social contact, not promote it—and their canned music is undemocratic. They are empty without jukeboxes, the musical voting booths that give each citizen a voice, be it Patsy's or Frank's or even Dale Evans's.

This was my new fear. If our newest generation, Julia's generation, grows up in a segregated, cable-TV America where people from unlike backgrounds and social classes do not meet—where the white bricklayer cannot play pool with the black TV reporter, where the Latino secretary can't join the Italian club owner to hear the African American blues guitarist—then I fear seriously for their future.

Julia won't be able to step inside some of the juke joints that I visited until she turns twenty-one—that will be the year 2013. Most of them will be gone, and all of them will be irreplaceable. But as a parent I can teach her the values of Jukebox America—about neighborhood, roots, music, and fighting for all the worthwhile lost causes. Julia had just turned eight months old—not too early to start.

That's why I decided to end my search with a beginning: Julia's first jukebox.

*   *   *

This might be a slight exaggeration, but it seemed like our New Jersey jukebox expedition required twice as much preparation as it had taken to travel 3,000 miles to Seattle. We repacked Julia's diaper bag, prepared bottles of formula and apple juice, and tossed about a half-dozen rattles and a red chewable horse named Flicka into a canvas bag. We left fifty minutes later than I planned.

We reached our destination—a prefab "Memphis barbecue" joint called Red Hot and Blue on Route 70, near the Camden–Cherry Hill border—by about 12:30 P.M.

"Finally," I thought.

"C'mon, Peanut, let's get our lunch," Kathy said.

"Waah," Julia said. That was her way of saying her fanny hurt, because just the day before she had come down with a case of diaper rash. So we hung out in the sunbaked parking lot for another five minutes, while Kathy changed Julia's diaper and I surveyed the terrain.

Red Hot and Blue was oddly appropriate for the new phase in my life—a half-breed, one of the world's only exurban juke joints. It had two potential strikes against it: the restaurant-bar is actually an outpost of a chain based in Virginia, and it's connected to a Holiday Inn. However, back in the good old days— before they killed their wonderfully garish green-and-neon arrowed signs in the late 1970s—Holiday Inns were hotels for Jukebox America. And Red Hot and Blue was in a good spot, almost smack on the borderline between the despair of arson-plagued Camden and the reflective-glass office parks of Cherry Hill. The inside was immaculate—normally a cardinal sin for juke joints—so the management tried to counteract that with dozens of pictures of authentic barbecue pits, smoky roadside shacks from Memphis and elsewhere across the South, and with a flip slogan: The best barbecue in a place that isn't condemned.

The draw, of course, is the jukebox—a jukebox *Philadelphia* magazine rated the region's best in 1992. From a distance it looked just like a Wurlitzer Bubbler from the 1940s, but on closer inspection it was a replica, a brand-new Rowe/AMI model.

The music was authentic, though—a Brunswick stew of Memphis soul and Delta blues, flavored with a dollop of Elvis Presley. Selection #100 was "Memphis" by Chuck Berry, then four B. B. King songs, then classic singles like "Evil" by Howlin' Wolf, "Down the Road I Go" by Albert King, and "Hobo Blues" by John Lee Hooker. The only sour note was the CD-inspired price: four for $1.

So I put in my buck, and started Julia out with a proclamation from the King: "Suspicious Minds." Sitting in her stroller, facing us in the booth, Julia was spinning around her red rattle, faster and faster, as Elvis and his gospel-tinged backups hit the chorus.

"She likes Elvis!" Kathy declared.

Julia was fast learning the restorative power of the blues, for I'm sure that to her eight-month-old mind, nobody knew the trouble she'd seen—specifically colic, a bad diaper rash, and teething. Then played "Polk Salad Annie" and "Respect Yourself," to which Julia—now sitting on Kathy's lap, joyfully pounded the rattle on her thigh the way Veronica in the Archies played her tambourine. I grabbed my camera, and Julia quickly stuck the rattle in her mouth. Enough kid play, I thought—time for the moment of truth.

We arose from our booth and approached the Red Hot and Blue altar. I threw down another dollar-offering and then lowered Julia down to the shrine of the selections. She grabbed at the numbers but wasn't quite strong enough to push the buttons down, so I pressed where she pointed.

1-9-9.

The jukebox dispensed its sacrament, as a 45 RPM record—with a big hole, of course—slid out from its mysterious inner workings. The suspense was killing me.

"What is it?" Kathy asked.

I tried to read while spinning my head around at 45 RPM. It was "The Breakdown, Part 1" by Rufus Thomas. The voice of the Memphis soul man emerged from the speakers, a funky early 1970s dance riff. "Children, break on down . . ."

Julia and I danced to her selection, her first public choice, while the Memphis horn section riffed away. Kathy snapped some pictures, and about a dozen diners—an all-American gumbo of whites, Indians, blacks, families and couples—looked on as if we were all quite insane.

I still couldn't bring things to an end, though. For a second I was a little frustrated, because I wanted a little deeper meaning to Julia's first jukebox selection. Then I remembered that my very first jukebox selections had been a meaningless jumble, from the Jackson 5 to "Spinnin' Wheel" and "Yummy Yummy Yummy." Julia's choice didn't have to make sense—as long as it was her own.

Still, I thought I should be a parent and start teaching her something about good music. So I played her a string of songs like "Mystery Train" and "Sweet Soul Music" by Arthur Conley—songs that probably won't fare well in the transition from 45s to CDs. Julia, with some bemusement, danced with me under the pale blue neon glow of the barbecue joint's wall sign—two pigs dressed like the Blues Brothers.

"Why can't I play some songs?" Kathy said. "I never get to play any."

So Kathy put in her dollar and played a mix of soul standards, like "Grits Ain't Gravy," with Elvis Presley, "Can't Help Falling in Love." Julia gave me a deep look like it was our dance at her wedding, three decades or so hence. Then she grabbed my 'Florida Marlins cap and flung it to the ground.

In the midst of the mayhem, Kathy played the song I had heard on the jukebox at Honest? John's in Detroit, the jukebox that I had decided was the best in America, that Al Green song that magically united the Motor City for three minutes—a song for all families, my new family, the family of Jukebox America. The song was "Let's Stay Together"—"loving you whether, whether times are good or bad, happy or sad."

The words and the music seemed to drift slowly in the July haze, moving west toward the heartland, out past the apple orchards of Winchester, Virginia, the rice fields of Longwood, Mississippi, and even past the fishing docks of Seattle. Tomorrow was July 4—another day for Jukebox America, but a special day for all its citizens, people who still care about brotherhood, sisterhood, and freedom of choice. It was Independence Day.